BENSHI,
JAPANESE SILENT FILM NARRATORS,
AND THEIR FORGOTTEN NARRATIVE ART
OF *SETSUMEI*

BENSHI, JAPANESE SILENT FILM NARRATORS, AND THEIR FORGOTTEN NARRATIVE ART OF *SETSUMEI*

A History of Japanese Silent Film Narration

Jeffrey A. Dym

Japanese Studies
Volume 19

The Edwin Mellen Press
Lewiston•Queenston•Lampeter

Library of Congress Cataloging-in-Publication Data

Dym, Jeffrey A.
   Benshi, Japanese silent film narrators, and their forgotten narrative art of setsumei : a history of Japanese silent film narration / Jeffrey A. Dym.
   p. cm. -- (Japanese studies ; v. 19)
   Includes bibliographical references and index.
   ISBN-0-7734-6648-7 (hc)
   1. Silent films--Japan--History and criticism. 2. Narration for silent films--Japan. I. Title. II. Japanese studies (Lewiston, N.Y.) ; v. 19.

PN1995.75.D96 2003
791.43'0952--dc21

ı oↄ৪৪ ৷ɜɜı T

2003054061

This is volume 19 in the continuing series
Japanese Studies
Volume 19 ISBN 0-7734-6648-7
JaS Series ISBN 0-88946-157-0

A CIP catalog record for this book is available from the British Library.

Front cover photograph courtesy of Matsuda Pictures

The Edwin Mellen Press
Box 450
Lewiston, New York
USA 14092-0450

The Edwin Mellen Press
Box 67
Queenston, Ontario
CANADA L0S 1L0

The Edwin Mellen Press, Ltd.
Lampeter, Ceredigion, Wales
UNITED KINGDOM SA48 8LT

Printed in the United States of America

TO MY PARENTS

TABLE OF CONTENTS

FOREWORD

One of Japan's finest artistic achievements in the modern age has been the cinema. During the Golden Age of Japanese cinema in the years following the Second World War, Japan dazzled the world with such films as *Rashōmon*, *Ugetsu*, and *Gate of Hell*. All of these were period pieces (*jidai-geki*), drawing on Japanese history and legends and displaying the wonderful aesthetic sensibilities of the Japanese as adapted to a modern medium of art.

Japan had just suffered devastating defeat in war, but its arts and culture were for the first time exerting a profound influence on the tastes of people the world over. Not only the cinema but also Japanese residential architecture (exemplified by the Katsura Detached Palace in Kyoto), ceramics, wood block prints, traditional costuming, and even the classical tea ceremony were, in addition to other arts and crafts, attracting worldwide attention. This was most clearly observable, perhaps, in the increasing vogue for exhibitions of things Japanese in museums and other formal venues; but it was also evident in how more and more people were incorporating what we may call features of Japanese culture into their daily lives. Americans probably led the way in the enthusiasm for Japanese culture by virtue of the close ties established between Japan and the United States during the postwar Occupation and maintained through alliance in the ensuing Cold War.

Of all the arts, the cinema played a special role in the postwar period in almost literally introducing the Japanese for the first time to other peoples, especially Westerners, and in humanizing them. Japan and the Western allies had fought a long, brutal, and cruel war in the Pacific, during which there was all too little understanding of the enemy on either side. In the United States, which played the largest role in the fight against Japan and later dominated the seven-year Occupation of that country, ignorance about Japan and the Japanese on the part of not just the American people but also—and most importantly—their leaders was of a magnitude difficult to imagine today. Only a handful of Americans had made any serious study of Japan before Pearl Harbor. Ignorance fueled racial prejudice and, as John Dower has documented in *War Without Mercy*, led Americans to view the Japanese as sub-humans and even vermin.

In postwar movies, especially the "home dramas" (*shomin-geki*), Americans and other Westerners could see that the Japanese were very much human and that they shared the same feelings as people everywhere. Many of the home dramas—for example, the films of Ozu Yasujirō (*Tokyo Story*, *Early Spring*)—were masterpieces in the portrayal of human relations, particularly within the intimate context of family life. The home drama became, indeed, a special realm of distinction for Japanese directors. In part this was because they were able to draw on centuries-old traditions of domestic plays of the puppet and *kabuki* theaters.

Thanks to the scholarship of the past half-century, we now have a substantial literature in English dealing with the Japanese film and its history. But there is at least one major subject of that history that, until now, has been largely—indeed, almost totally—ignored by scholars both in Japan and elsewhere: the story of the *benshi*, or narrators, who provided the dialogs and commentaries for films of the silent era from the early years of the twentieth century until the 1920s. Filmmakers in America and Europe also experimented with narrators of various kinds, but they never became important elements of the American or European cinemas. By contrast, the *benshi* not only became leading participants in the presentation of silent films in Japan, some achieved a status in public popularity comparable to the movie stars of later times.

Jeffrey Dym has now undertaken a major study of the almost forgotten *benshi*, the "Poets of the Dark," and I think the first reaction of the reader of his study is likely to be astonishment that the *benshi* have been "forgotten" for so long. For their story provides not only fascinating insight into the early years of the Japanese cinema, but also fills a large gap in the long history of theater in Japan. Much about the early cinema in Japan, as in the West and elsewhere, was thoroughly new and modern. But the influence of theaters past was also important. Japan, for example, had a long tradition of theatrical chanting, the most significant of which, perhaps, was that of the puppet theater of the Tokugawa period. The serious student of Japanese cinema can hardly overlook the historical role of the *benshi* both as a link between traditional and modern theater and as a cultural phenomenon of Japan's early twentieth century.

Jeffrey Dym has created a rich portrait of the *benshi*, placing them firmly in their place in Japan's cinematic tradition. He has also written a larger account of the cultural history of the late Meiji and Taisho periods. This manuscript is a fine and much welcome contribution to the scholarship of this time, a time that until now has been largely examined by scholars in terms of political, social, and military developments. The publication of this work will surely greatly increase appreciation of Japanese culture in the early twentieth century.

H. Paul Varley
University of Hawaii

ACKNOWLEDGEMENTS

Although this work is authored by only one person, it is really the fruition of numerous people aiding, comforting, and guiding the author all along the way. To everyone who has helped me, I offer my deepest thanks. There are several people to whom I am especially grateful.

First, I wish to thank Dr. Sharon A. Minichiello for all of her kindness and guidance. Her years of aid and advice have incalculably benefited me and I am eternally grateful. Dr. Harry J. Lamley and Dr. Takie S. Lebra taught me much in the classroom and provided invaluable comments along the way. Dr. Margot A. Henriksen offered keen insights into the world of film and cultural studies. I am especially grateful to Dr. H. Paul Varley, for reading the final version of this work and writing the Foreword. Doug Rice, Don Harrold, and Dr. Bruce Reynolds also deserve special thanks for reading and commenting on the final manuscript.

Portions of chapter 2 are based on an article that I wrote entitled "*Benshi* and the Introduction of Motion Pictures to Japan" which was originally published in *Monumenta Nipponica* 55:4 (Winter 2000), pp. 509-539. I would like to thank the editors for their advice and permission to reproduce the work here.

Many people in Japan also generously offered their time and knowledge. Professor Iwamoto Kenji facilitated my study at Waseda University, while Imaoka Kentarō and Kodama Ryūichi proved to be invaluable consultants for my ideas. To Wakao Kayo, Satō Chihiro, and especially Hirose Jun I will always be indebted. To the librarians and archivist throughout Japan who helped me locate sources, many thanks. I am especially grateful to Yasui Yoshio, Matsudo Yutaka, Matsudo Makato, Asahina Kuniaki, Higashi Harumi for their kindness. I also want to thank Shin Chul, Inoue Yōichi, Waka Kōji, and Sawato Midori for sitting down with me to discuss their vocation and art. Thanks to these modern-day *benshi* the art of *setsumei* lives on in performance form. For sharing his collection and bountiful knowledge about the world of Japanese cinema with me my profound appreciation goes to Makino Mamoru. He was more than a mentor.

I also want to thank my parents for all of their support and my daughters Zoe and Nina for brightening my days with their smiles and laughter. My most heartfelt thanks belong to Eiko, my wife and best friend. Her support, encouragement, and companionship over the years sustained me through the process of research and writing this work, and has made my life immeasurably better.

1

SETTING THE STAGE

Once There Were *Benshi* Who Performed *Setsumei*

Tucked away in a far corner of Asakusa's Sensōji Temple, in a place where few of the millions of people who visit this popular Tokyo tourist destination ever venture, stand several granite slabs that form an eight by twelve-foot curved wall. Fifty-five names are carved into the right half of this memorial.[1] On a bronze placard situated to the left of these names is the following inscription:

> Around the middle of the Meiji era, motion pictures first entered our country. Simultaneously, *benshi* who gave *setsumei* were born. Many talented masters appeared in succession, and their popularity surpassed that of movie stars. Although they added to the splendor of our nation's cultural development, they vanished after talkies appeared at the beginning of the Shōwa period. Lined up here are the names of the famous *benshi* of years past. This is to commemorate them.

These men called *benshi*, who added to the splendor of Japan's cultural development, not only vanished from cinema after talkies appeared, but they and their narrative art of *setsumei* also almost vanished from people's memories. Despite the fact that these talented entertainers contributed to the grandeur of Japan's cultural heritage by creating the unique narrative art of *setsumei*, few Japanese born in the postwar period can name a *benshi* or accurately describe what they did.

Who were these purveyors of culture called *benshi*? They were, in short, "silent film narrators." During Japan's silent film era (1896–1939), a *benshi* (or a group of *benshi*) would situate himself in the shadows next to the screen and from there supply a vocal narration called *setsumei*, to enhance the moving images. The *benshi*'s primary job was to guide spectators through a film by helping them understand the action on the screen. In addition to conveying narrative meaning, *benshi* had to impart emotion to the movie. He had to provide *setsumei* that would shift the audience from laughter and love to anger and tears. The *Benshi* accomplished these tasks by using mimetic voices to supply dialogue for the characters, creating vocal sound effects, bringing intertitles alive through dramatic and interpretive readings, and inserting interesting poetic commentary. Moreover, he had to execute all this dozens of times a week, in an entertaining yet unobtrusive fashion, using beautiful Japanese, always while developing new material for the next film.

Both *benshi* and *setsumei* were an integral and potent component to silent movie performances in Japan. As intermediaries between a film and an audience, *benshi* had a strong influence on how spectators viewed a movie. This authority increased as the *benshi* perfected the art of *setsumei*. In 1910, one writer viewed *benshi* and their *setsumei* as a side dish that made the main dish of the film more delicious.[2] Over the ensuing years, they came to occupy a more prominent position. In the 1920s, this prominence compelled one writer to assert that the *benshi*, along with the screenwriter and the director, constituted the three main creative ingredients of cinema.[3] By the early 1920s, *benshi*'s *setsumei* was no longer a side dish but rather an essential ingredient that audiences could not do without.

A variety of people influenced films on the production side, but the *benshi* assumed complete authority over the content, once the film was projected onto a screen. *Benshi* possessed a great deal of freedom when performing *setsumei*, and, although the majority of *benshi* remained true to the film, a few digressed to the point that they completely changed the narrative meaning of the story. Some *benshi* wielded so much power that they could turn comedy into drama and drama into comedy, at will. A second-rate *benshi* could destroy a good movie; a first-rate *benshi* could turn a lesser movie into a highly entertaining production. The same film seen with different *benshi* could generate contrary impressions. Similarly, since every performance was unique, the same film seen with the same *benshi*, but on a different day, could produce different sentiments. Consequently, the audience's reaction to a particular motion picture often depended on the skill and the mood of the *benshi*.

Setsumei not only helped spectators to understand a movie, it also allowed them to hear the voices from within the movie and to become one with the film. Movie *setsumei* was "seeing" with one's ears, and the more skilled the *benshi* was, the more the audience felt they were a part of the world being projected onto the screen. In other words, *benshi* helped transport spectators into the diegetic world of the film.

Benshi, which literally means "orator" or "speaker," was not the only word used to signify silent film narrators. Throughout the silent era, several other appellations were employed, among them *kōjōkatari* (narrator of statements), *kōjōii* (speaker of statements), *kōjōya* (master of statements), *kowairoya* (impersonator), *serifushi* (deliverer of dialogue), *katsuben* (motion picture orator), *kaisetsusha* (commentator), and *setsumeisha* (explainer). The word used to denote *benshi* varied, depending on the time and the region. One problem with all of these words, including *benshi*, is that they do not accurately define the role of the *benshi*. A *benshi* was more than an explainer or commentator; he was more than a master of statements or a deliverer of dialogue. English labels, such as narrator, lecturer, spieler, barker, and commentator, also fall short of clearly defining the *benshi*. Even though *benshi* is a term not without its problems, I use it throughout this work because it is the word most readily associated with silent film narrators in Japan today.[4]

The narrative art that the *benshi* created also has a variety of appellations. I use the term *setsumei*, which literally means "explanation," to denote silent film narration, because that is the word most frequently encountered in the contemporary sources of the late silent era. To avoid confusion, I use *setsumei* as an all-encompassing term for any kind of narration that accompanied a film.

In pre-World War II Japan, if you asked someone about *setsumei* in the context of cinema, they would probably know that you were talking about movie explanation performed by *benshi*. Today, however, if you ask someone about *setsumei*, it is highly likely that they would not know what you were referring to, in part because *setsumei* is such a common word. Unlike other narrative arts in Japan, such as *gidayū, rakugo, naniwabushi, manzai,* and *kōdan*, for which there is a single-word signifier that refers solely to the narrative art, "motion picture explanation" lacks a distinct signifier. Moreover, *setsumei* is rarely mentioned in discussions of Japanese narrative arts. Despite this fact, throughout this work, I argue that *setsumei* deserves the same recognition as other narrative arts in Japan. When narrative art is defined as the skillful production of a beautifully orated story, executed by one who seeks to gratify the aesthetic emotions of an audience through the perfection of his craft, then *benshi* clearly are narrative artists, and *setsumei* clearly is a narrative art that belongs in Japan's narrative pantheon.

Benshi in Other Countries

Starting late in the second decade of the twentieh century, the notion that *benshi*—silent film narrators—existed only in Japan began circulating in trade journals, among cinephiles, and in scholarly monographs. In 1919, one writer praised Japan's "invention" of *benshi* in this way: "Soon after motion pictures were introduced into Japan, *benshi* were born. *Benshi* do not exist in foreign countries. After we Japanese learned how to make bread, we created An-pan—a combination Japanese–Western confection. Similarly, after motion pictures were imported, we invented *katsuben*. In other words, this is the second great invention by us Japanese."[5] Over the years, the impression that *benshi* only existed in Japan came to be held as a truism and spread from Japan to the rest of the world. For years, scholars around the world viewed the existence of *benshi* as a Japanese anomaly. Recent scholarship, however, has revealed that silent film lecturers existed in almost every country.

The aural supplement to motion pictures found in America came in a variety of forms. One style involved one to eight people situating themselves behind the screen and adding dialogue and sound effects for the moving images, thus giving the audience the impression that the sound was emanating from the screen. Another popular approach was for a lecturer to use motion pictures as a visual enhancement for a lecture on a specific topic. Predominant traveling exhibitors—those men who trekked around the country showing movies in different towns and cities—employed "lecturers" and "impersonators." Some of these exhibitions had fanciful names, such as Adolph Zucker's Humanovo.[6] Concerning the Humanovo, which was a mimetic form of talking picture, the *Cincinnati Commercial Tribune* reported, "Under his magic spell the picture is no longer a picture, for it becomes real life."[7]

The peak years of these "talking pictures" in America were 1908–1912. One reason for this was a desire for respectability. Throughout 1907 and 1908, a dispute raged in New York City over showing movies on Sundays. Members of the clergy and other righteous souls worried about the propriety of people attending movies, nickelodeons in particular, on the Christian sabbath. The moral battle came to a head on December 24, 1908, when Mayor George Brinton McClellan ordered all nickelodeons closed on Sundays. The only movies allowed were those "illustrating lectures of an instructive or educational character."[8] Consequently, many theaters hired a lecturer, so that they could stay open on Sundays. The ban was short-lived, as the motion picture industry, theater managers, and fans mounted a strong attack against the blue law. Nevertheless, for the next few years several theaters continued to employ lecturers to give their programs an air of respectability.

6

Between 1908 and 1915, narrators also performed throughout Europe, in places ranging from Spain to the Netherlands, France to Poland.[9] In addition to acquiring respectability, another reason why lecturers became more prevalent in America and Europe at this time was because movies were becoming longer and stories more complex. Most early films were short and based on easily recognizable themes. Starting around 1908, filmmakers began creating more complex narratives. The only problem was how to narrate these tales: visually or aurally.

In a series of articles published in *Moving Picture World* between 1908 and 1912, W. Stephen Bush, a lecturer himself, championed the cause of motion picture lecturers. Bush believed that over 30 percent of the movies shown were difficult to understand on their own, and that spectators needed lecturers to help them follow a film. Moreover, he argued, narrators enhanced the dramatic experience of a movie.[10] Anonymous editorials also supported lecturers, with statements such as, "There should be a competent 'narrator' in every first-class moving picture theater and there will be."[11]

Despite the popularity of shows by certain traveling lecturers and the advocacy for narrators by men such as Bush, narrators vanished from virtually all American and European venues by 1915. One of the primary reasons for their disappearance was the new cinematic methods that filmmakers developed and employed to visually tell longer, more elaborate narratives.[12] As film scholars Tom Gunning, Miriam Hansen, Charles Musser, and others have shown, between 1908 and 1912, filmmakers devised framing, editing, acting, mise en scène, and other techniques, which allowed them to set forth longer narratives without the aid of a live human voice. Producers did not like exhibitors using lecturers to narrate their films, because it meant that control of how the audience understood the film was at the site of exhibition rather than the place of production. One of the underlying motives for devising these cinematic techniques, therefore, was a desire by producers to maintain complete control over their product by ridding cinema of lecturers. They wanted to create a self-sufficient narrative. The result of this "visual narrator system" was that, in America and Europe, motion pictures became an essentially visual medium in which the aural component—henceforth only music—was always considered subordinate and insignificant.[13] By contrast, in Japan, the aural component of *benshi* was invariably a principal ingredient, and it was the *benshi*, much to the dismay of some producers, who had the final say over how audiences understood the product.

Although narrators existed in America and Europe, they only performed at some of the larger theaters or with traveling exhibitions. They never worked in more than a small percentage of the theaters. During the initial 15 or so years of cinema in America, most people saw movies at tiny nickelodeons, which, given their meager profit margin, could not afford to hire narrators. Moreover, many of these "lecturers" were just that: lecturers. They were men who lectured and used film as a supplement to their talk. They viewed themselves as respectable educators, not as entertainers.[14] The first *benshi* also provided a *setsumei* that was very lecture-like, but virtually all *benshi* considered themselves to be entertainers first and foremost.

What all the evidence—about silent film lecturers, narrators, commentators, and impersonators in America and Europe—reveals is just how unusual such audio appendages were outside Japan. Although a handful of men continued to lecture with motion pictures throughout the silent era, and beyond, in America and Europe, they were an aberration that had little impact on the cinema history of their respective nations. Yes, one can find lecturers if one looks hard enough, but they were never a central component in the cinematic experience, they rarely prospered, and they were the exception rather than norm. With the advent of the visual narrator system, live oral narration essentially disappeared from national cinemas around the globe, as did memory of their existence.[15] In the West, lecturers probably participated in less than 1 percent of all silent era exhibitions; in Japan, *benshi* were always a part of the "silent" cinematic experience.[16] In Japan, *benshi* were a powerful and influential institution; outside Japan, they were a fringe curiosity. In Japan, *benshi*, *setsumei*, and film formed an inseparable unit;

outside Japan, the film itself was all that was important. Hence, the often-stated assertion that *benshi* only existed in Japan does, in many ways, contain merit.

By "outside Japan," I mean outside the Japanese wartime empire and Japanese overseas communities.[17] *Benshi* worked in the Japanese colonies of Korea and Taiwan, as well as in the puppet state of Manchukuo. They were also active in cities with a high concentration of Japanese emigrants, such as Honolulu, Los Angeles, and San Francisco. In all of these places, indigenous, transplanted, and visiting *benshi* from the home islands performed *setsumei*.

In the Japanese colonies, *benshi* emerged shortly after Japan began exerting its influence over the territories. In Korea, for example, the first time the word *benshi* appeared in print was in 1907, two years after Korea became a protectorate of Japan. Exactly how many *benshi* there were in Korea is unclear, but their numbers appear to have been rather limited, and only about 15 achieved fame. Native Korean *benshi* performed in either Japanese or Korean; visiting and expatriate *benshi* performed solely in Japanese.[18]

In addition to the Japanese colonial empire, *benshi* were active in cities with a large population of Japanese emigrants. In Hawaii, *benshi* began performing in 1908 and flourished throughout the silent era. As in Japan, large banners, with the *benshi*'s name printed on them, waved in the Honolulu trade winds, outside the theaters that catered to the Japanese. As was the case in Japanese colonies, some *benshi* were emigrants, and others were hired from Japan. The Los Angeles Fujikan theater frequently contracted popular *benshi* from Japan. These *benshi* usually provided *setsumei* for Japanese movies. In fact, most of the motion pictures that Japan exported abroad during the silent film era were meant for overseas Japanese.[19]

Why Japan?

Throughout the silent era, one of the fundamental tasks of the *benshi* was to explain the foreign exotica contained in occidental movies. This was one of the reasons why the first exhibitors attached *benshi* to the initial exhibitions of motion pictures in Japan, almost all of which, for at least the first few years, included only foreign-made films. Since there were many particulars about Western customs, manners, history, traditions, and culture that Japanese audiences did not understand, exhibitors reasoned that a person was needed to clarify them for the audience. That person was the *benshi*. Although the *benshi* often discussed unrelated matters, along with the foreign elements in a movie, they also served an important role in helping Japanese fans appreciate foreign films at a higher level. The very first *benshi* also discussed the invention and mechanics of motion pictures, thus informing spectators about this latest import from the West. Without *benshi*, the public might have viewed motion pictures simply as a curious novelty. With *benshi* supplying authoritative and educational commentary, however, cinema gained respectability. *Benshi* were also needed—moreso later on than at the very beginning—to translate the foreign language intertitles contained within the films. In short, one of the reasons why *benshi* were a central part of Japanese cinema from the very beginning, and why Japanese audiences welcomed and accepted them, was because *benshi* were needed to explain the foreign exotica and language contained within the Western films, as well as describing the working of the movie projectors themselves. According to one silent era Japanese film critic, if the Japanese had invented cinema, they would not have needed *benshi* for the foreign exotica, and, consequently, would not have needed *benshi* at all.[20]

Still, even if the Japanese had invented motion pictures, *benshi* might have been a part of cinema in Japan from the very beginning, because Japan has a long and illustrious tradition of commingled performances, that is, performances in which two (or more) separate but equal forms of narrative information, usually one visual, the other aural, coalesce into one presentation. The aural element, provided by a narrator or commentator, was often physically separate from the visual element, but spectators experienced an aesthetic harmony, because two separate sources of information were united into a whole that was greater than the sum of the two parts.

One of the oldest manifestations of commingled presentation is *etoki* (mandala preaching, picture explanation). *Etoki* was usually performed by a priest who displayed pictures or mandala of a specific religious doctrine or historical tale to an audience, then expounded upon the doctrine or events depicted, pointing at the picture to visually reinforce what he was saying. Some performers improvised; others worked from a memorized text or read from a book. According to the medieval Japanese literature specialist Barbara Ruch, in *etoki*, "painting, story, chanter, and even the sounding of musical instruments (often pure sound rather than music) combined to create a total audio-visual experience rare, if not unique, in the premodern history of world literature."[21] One could say the same of *benshi* and silent films in the history of world cinema.

In *kabuki*, *nō*, and especially *bunraku* puppet theater, an individual chanter (or a group of chanters) carries all or part of the vocal narration of a performance. In *kabuki* and *nō*, the characters themselves and the chanter(s) usually share the vocal burden; in *bunraku*, the vocal element is performed solely by the *jōruri* chanter(s); and in most *bunraku* plays, a solo chanter provides the voices for everyone in the drama. Thus, when a narrator appears in traditional Japanese theater, he is removed from, yet corresponds with, the characters. What emerges is a divided but total spectacle.[22] Some of the reasons for this structure lie in the origins of the particular theatrical form. *Bunraku*, for example, in the seventeenth century, emerged from the mixing of two independent art forms: puppetry and *jōruri* storytelling. *Jōruri* texts became the basis for many *bunraku* plays, and are a significant part of those *kabuki* plays adapted from *bunraku*.

Jōruri and *setsumei* are similar, in that they are both forms of commingled theater that require a coordinated effort between the audio and visual components. In *jōruri*, however, the oral component is primary, and the visual one is a supplement. The puppets follow the chanter's lead. It is said that the true *bunraku* aficionado comes to listen, rather than to watch. *Setsumei*, on the other hand, was subordinate to the moving pictures. It had to follow the lead of the film. Although secondary to the film, *setsumei* was still a cardinal element of the show.

The most immediate precursors to *benshi* were the narrators for *gentō*, Japanese magic lantern shows.[23] *Gentō* was a popular form of entertainment throughout Japan at the end of the Tokugawa period (1600–1868) and the beginning of the Meiji era (1868–1912). The Dutch introduced magic lanterns into Japan in the 1770s, roughly 100 years after they emerged in Europe.[24] Over the ensuing years, *gentō* evolved into a theatrical form of presentation in which one or more projectionists manipulated from 1 to 10 projectors. Several projectors might cast nonchanging scenic images onto the screen throughout the show; other projectors cast changing images of the characters of the story. Some projectors were stationary, but others were manipulated by the projectionist to instill the slides with a sense of movement that resembled live performers. Added to the visual element of the slides was an audio narrative provided either by one of the projectionists or by a separate narrator. The oral narration, which was frequently accompanied by a shamisen, further infused the slides with life. Advertisements for *gentō* projectors and slides continued to appear as late as 1916, nearly 20 years after the introduction of motion pictures into Japan, attesting to the continued popularity of this form of entertainment.[25]

Oral narration accompanying a visual art was thus part of a long tradition: It was not fabricated specifically for motion pictures. When exhibitors attached *benshi* to movies, audiences readily accepted them, because they were accustomed to commingled theater. *Benshi* did not emerge "because, psychologically, the Japanese like to have things explained to them."[26] Rather, the adding of *benshi* to motion pictures furnished Japanese audiences with a native form of presentation—a visual entertainment to which a vocal component was added. Silent movies without a *benshi* would have been too alien.

Although *benshi* and movies are part of Japan's commingled performance tradition, commingled narrative arts only partially influenced the art of *setsumei*. As I show later, *setsumei* is the amalgamation of various narrative traditions. Both commingled narrative arts, such as *jōruri* and *nagauta*, and those vocal arts that individuals performed without any pictorial aids, such as *naniwabushi, ra-*

kugo, and *kōdan*, influenced the tone and cadence of *setsumei*. The main reason for placing *benshi* and *setsumei* in the commingled tradition is to show that Japanese had a proclivity toward commingled performances. They saw nothing unusual about adding a *benshi* to cinema and thus welcomed the union of a detached voice and moving pictures. For Japanese audiences, there was nothing incongruous about it. Moreover, by situating the motion picture experience within Japan's vocal narrative tradition, *benshi* transformed film from a Western-based dramatic form into a readily acceptable Japanese form.

From the first motion picture exhibitions, *benshi* established a central position in Japan's silent cinematic experience that proved impossible to break. In the West, narrators were a part of only an infinitesimal percentage of shows and thus, except for a handful of traveling exhibitions, were easily effaced. In Japan, on the other hand, *benshi* were always a part of the show. Audiences became so accustomed and attached to *benshi*, so used to watching the film with their eyes while listening to the *setsumei* with their ears, that they found it difficult to enjoy a film without them. *Benshi* were such a powerful attraction that efforts by filmmakers and reformers to rid Japanese cinema of this "anachronism" proved ineffectual. In short, one of the most important reasons why *benshi* existed in Japan was because they became a fixture of silent cinema early on. Theaters that tried to show movies without them were unable to compete.

Thus, once the Japanese began producing their own films, no one questioned the appearance of *benshi* next to the screen, even though the films did not contain any foreign exotica that needed explaining. This resulted, in part, from the continuation of commingled exhibition practices inaugurated with foreign films and, in part, because many of the first Japanese movies were based on theater productions. Many films were basically filmed plays—movies made by setting a camera in front of a stage and recording the drama as it was staged. Since the characters in the theatrical production had a detached voice added to them, it seemed only natural to append a voice to them when they were projected onto a screen.

Benshi also provided *setsumei* for Japanese films, to help audiences follow the action, which tended to be difficult to understand on its own. Generally, Japanese silent movie storylines were more fragmentary and less self sufficient than their Western counterparts. Thus, audiences relied on *benshi* to explain the time frame in which scenes took place, to clarify the relationship between the characters, and to point out when the scenes changed to a new location (something that was not always apparent). *Benshi* did not clarify everything, and often their *setsumei* diverged from the film text; nevertheless, like the chorus in an ancient Greek drama, they generally advanced, as well as explained, the action unfolding before the audience's eyes.

Along with theatrical and cinematic reasons, there were also economic factors that help explain why *benshi* flourished in Japan and nowhere else in the world. For one thing, Japanese movie theaters tended to be larger than their Western counterparts. In 1922, years after the boom of small nickelodeons, 64% of theaters in the United States still seated fewer than 500. By contrast, the average capacity of cinema houses in Japan in 1918 was over 1,000 seats.[27] On the basis of theater size alone, scholars have postulated that it was economically infeasible to sustain lecturers in the United States.[28]

What one must also factor into this line of reasoning is the makeup of the American audience. Immigrants constituted a large portion of the first audiences in America, and, unless each theater catered solely to one group of people, supplying English (Italian, Yiddish, or any other language) narration to guide spectators through a movie would be wasted on a large segment of the audience. This linguistic barrier, perhaps more than theater size, explains why narrators did not catch on in America.[29]

In a corollary to the theater size argument, some researchers assert that one of the reasons Japanese had large-capacity theaters was because of the added cost of *benshi*.[30] *Benshi* were an added expense, but just how much of a net expense they were is open to debate. One contemporary writer declared that one half of a theater's operating costs were for *benshi* and musicians.[31] This probably seemed true to outside observers who focused only on the large salaries that *benshi* received. Upon closer inspection, however, a *benshi*'s salary appears to have constituted only a small percentage of a theater's total expenditures. In 1926, just before Tokyo's newly renovated Musashinokan—one of Japan's finest theaters—opened, the theater's management revealed its expected monthly expenditures (in yen).

Print advertising	5,300
Posters, programs	3,000
Signs	1,000
Thirty musicians	4,000
Eight *benshi*	2,000
Five projectionists	600
Thirty ushers and other personnel	1,200
Twelve greeters (*Omotekata*)	720
Managers	2,500
Electricity, water, gas	1,500
Entertainment tax	2,500
Film rental	20,000
Miscellaneous expenses, entertaining clients, and insurance	5,680
Total	50,000[32]

These figures indicate that *benshi* salaries accounted for only 2,000 yen out of 50,000 yen budget. In other words, *benshi* salaries constituted 4% of monthly expenditures. Given that this budget does not include mortgage or rent, which must have been a large expenditure, it seems safe to assert that *benshi* salaries accounted for less than 4% of total operating costs.

At different points throughout the silent era, critics of *benshi* charged that *benshi* were an undue expense. *Benshi* always countered that they were not an expense, but rather an attraction that lured enough people to the cinema to more than pay for their salaries. One portion of a theater's profits, they maintained, was generated by their eloquence. Whether poor-to-average *benshi* drew enough fans to justify their salaries is unclear, but there is no doubt that top *benshi* had huge fan followings and attracted large crowds of people to the cinema, which more than compensated for their salaries. They were not an expense, but rather a very profitable source of revenue.

For many fans, one of the great pleasures of going to the cinema was listening to the *benshi*'s *setsumei*. Good *benshi* made a silent film more interesting and enjoyable. In many ways, the *benshi*'s role is analogous to the role of a sports announcer or commentator. That is, if one understands the rules of the game, all sports can be understood simply by watching the game. Millions of people do it all the time in stadiums and at fields around the world. However, when a sport event is shown on television, there is always someone chattering away about what is going on. There is no intrinsic need for play-by-play announcers or color commentators. Spectators can understand what is happening simply by watching the moving images. If there was no voice, however, the televised images would feel eerily lifeless. Play-by-play announcers and color commentators not only make the program more interesting and entertaining, they also bring the images to life, just as skilled *benshi* did. Moreover, some skillful commentators are highly regarded as an attraction in and of themselves, just as *benshi* were.

Until now, the question has always been, Why did Japan have the anomaly of *benshi*? The emphasis in this question is on the exceptionalism of *benshi* and Japan. By breathing life into silent movies with their *setsumei*, *benshi* enhanced the cinematic experience, by making it more interesting. The question, therefore, should not be Why did Japan have *benshi*? but rather, Why did *benshi* not thrive in the West?

Most works on Japanese cinema discuss *benshi*. Writing about the first 40 years of film history in Japan would be impossible without at least mentioning them. Most film scholars, however, have focused their interests on the relationship between the aural *benshi* and the visual film text. They primarily analyze how *benshi* affected film's visual narrativity. They are seldom interested in the *benshi* themselves, and they are almost never captivated by the narrative art of *setsumei*. In short, they are indifferent to the entertainment value of the *benshi* performance of *setsumei*. This indifference stems from the fact that most film scholars are accustomed to focusing only on the visual element of cinema.

The predominant complaint lodged against *benshi* by scholars, over the years, has been that *benshi* prevented Japanese silent movies from advancing beyond the "primitive" stage—that stage in which films could not visually narrate themselves. Unlike Western silent movies, which moved beyond the primitive stage early in the century's second decade, Japanese silent films remained dependent on nonvisual sources of narrative information. Representative of this view is the influential film scholar Tanaka Jun'ichirō, who wrote, "For a long time, *setsumeisha* clearly stood out as an irregularity hanging over the development of motion pictures."[33] Writers also look upon Japanese cinema's dependence on *benshi* as the reason Japan could not export its films abroad.

Now the question is, Were Japanese films narratively deficient because producers knew *benshi* would be added to them, or were they narratively deficient in technique and thus exhibitors added *benshi* to them? The film scholar Komatsu Hiroshi concludes his article on Japanese cinema before World War I by stating, "The fact that the existence of the *benshi* helped Japanese cinema preserve its form is due to the fact that the Japanese cinema was originally not self-sufficient."[34] But, since *benshi* were always a part of motion pictures, how can one accurately assess the self-sufficiency of early Japanese cinema?

Most scholars tend not to focus on the origins of Japanese cinema's lack of self-sufficiency, but rather on its perpetuation, and most people examine *benshi* from this angle. As Aaron Gerow details in his dissertation on Japanese cinema discourse, *Writing a Pure Cinema: Articulations of Early Japanese Cinema*, until recently, the negative view of *benshi* held by Japanese scholars, such as Tanaka Jun'ichirō and Satō Tadao, was influenced by the writings of the Pure Film Movement (*jun'eigageki undō*). The Pure Film Movement was a reform movement that dominated the Japanese cinema world in the late 1910s. It attempted to westernize Japanese cinema by ridding it of anachronisms such as *benshi*. The negative picture that the Pure Film Movement painted of *benshi* holding Japanese cinema back lasted for decades, as Japanese film histories either wrote disparagingly of *benshi* or ignored their existence as much as possible.[35]

Typical of this belittlement was a special 21 page article that appeared in *Kinema junpō*, Japan's premier cinema magazine, in 1958. The subtitle of this article on the founding fathers of Japanese cinema claims that everyone from "Directors to Screenwriters, Actors to Technicians and Businessmen" will be examined. That is, everyone except *benshi*. Of the 50 biographies presented, not one is of a *benshi*. The editors of *Kinema junpō* deemed camera technicians deserving of recognition and a place in film history, but not the poets of the dark who instilled life into the pictures.[36]

Recently, Japanese scholarship has come to view *benshi* in a more positive light—as a glorious indigenous institution or as an embodiment of plebeian culture. This change of heart results, in part, from Western scholarship on *benshi*. Noël Burch's 1979 work, *To the Distant Observer: Form and Meaning in the Japanese Cinema*, is one of the first works to view *benshi* as a worthy institution. Burch rejects the idea that *benshi* inhibited Japanese cinema. Rather, he praises the *benshi* for allowing Japan to preserve "the Primitive modes of filmic representation."[37] Burch challenges the supposition that Japanese filmmakers failed to grasp Western narrative cinema; rather, he asserts that they chose to ignore it and that they could do so because of *benshi*. *Benshi* protected Japanese cinema from being colonized by Western codes of cinema, thus allowing it to develop a form of presentation different from the Hollywood model. Burch's arguments are intriguing and his praise of *benshi* welcome; however, since he did not know Japanese, the depth of his research into *benshi* was rather limited.

By reducing their examination of *benshi* to the simple dichotomy of whether they helped or retarded Japanese cinema, scholars have ignored what *benshi* added to the cinematic experience. Regardless of how *benshi* affected the visual development of Japanese movies, they made silent era performances more enjoyable with their *setsumei*. Rather than look at *benshi* in the simplistic light of good or bad, one should examine them in terms of what they added to the performance. From this point of view, I examine how *benshi* enhanced the *experience* of Japanese cinema, rather than from how they affected the *visuality* of Japanese cinema.

One Western scholar who has done a great deal of research into the institution of *benshi* is Joseph L. Anderson. In two articles, "Spoken Silents in the Japanese Cinema; or, Talking to Pictures: Essaying the *Katsuben*, Contextualizing the Texts" and "Second and Third Thoughts About the Japanese Film," Anderson details the functions of the *benshi* and provides an overall view of who the *benshi* were.[38] He does a good job examining the institution of *benshi* and *setsumei* antecedents, placing *benshi* and *setsumei* squarely in Japan's commingled performance tradition. He does not, however, detail individual *benshi*, nor does he really examine the art of *setsumei*.

Besides Anderson, several other scholars have published articles in English on *benshi*. The most notable is Donald Kirihara's "A Reconsideration of the Institution of *Benshi*," which examines the economic underpinnings of *benshi* in relation to the coming of sound.[39] Although he relies solely on English language sources, Kirihara creates a lucid picture of how *benshi* affected Japan's transition to talkies.

Aaron Gerow's dissertation, *Writing a Pure Cinema*, which focuses primarily on the Pure Film Movement and the changing image of cinema in the discourse of the second decade of the twentieth century, contains a lengthy discussion about *benshi*. Gerow particularly concentrates on the relationship between the film text and the *benshi*. He argues that "the *benshi* became an important aspect of creating a new definition of the cinematic text found in diegetic illusionism and the univocality of narration."[40] Gerow details the intertextual relationship between *setsumei* and moving image, but he does not explicitly analyze the contents of *setsumei*. He focuses on the institution of the *benshi* in relation to the reform movement and government attempts to control the *benshi*, but he does not examine the lifestyles and working methods of the *benshi*.

Of all the Japanese works that touch upon the silent era in Japan and discuss *benshi*, only a few examine *benshi* in any depth. The two most extensive studies of *benshi* in Japanese are Yoshida Chieo's *Mōhitotsu no eigashi: katsuben no jidai* (*One More Film History: The Age of the Katsuben*) and Misono Kyōhei's *Katsuben jidai* (*The Age of Katsuben*). Both works do a good job of revealing the personal history of several prominent *benshi*, but do not really explore the narrative art of *setsumei*. They also tend to rely on anecdotal and word-of-mouth, rather than archival, evidence. Yoshida's *Mōhitotsu no eigashi* is by far the more influential work: Since its publication in 1978, it has influenced most subsequent studies, on *benshi* in particular and Japanese cinema overall.[41]

In addition to these two monographs, several former *benshi* and a few silent film fans have related the history of the *benshi* era, based on their recollections. Two of the most recent additions to this growing body of works are Mizuno Eizaburo's *Nagoya katsuben ichidai: shomin ga mita mōhitotsu no gendaishi* (*The Days of Nagoya Katsuben: One More Contemporary History as Seen by the Common People*) and Waka Kōji's *Katsudō daishashin shimatsu ki* (*A Chronicle of Motion Pictures*).[42] These autobiographical tracts shed light on the silent film era and supply some interesting personal anecdotes, but they lack scholarly rigor and contain much hearsay and hyperbole. As Mizuno states in his preface, he is 90 years old and writing about the past. Although he is trying to be as truthful as possible, he acknowledges that his memory might be faulty.[43]

Most works on *benshi* tend to focus only on the institution, with few delving into the history of the *benshi* themselves. The lifestyles of the *benshi*, their workday, how they prepared for a performance, and how they delivered their *setsumei*, are just some of the subjects surrounding this significant institution that have been mostly overlooked. More important, no one has adequately explored the narrative art of *setsumei*. Those sources that do touch upon it tend to view its 40 year history as static. It was not. *Setsumei* was a vibrant art that underwent dramatic changes throughout the silent era, as *benshi* experimented with new methods of delivery and either amalgamated or discarded them, depending on how well they worked. My monograph not only details who the *benshi* were, what they did, how they did it, and how they lived, but it also brings to life the unique narrative art of *setsumei.*

2
INTRODUCTION OF MOTION PICTURES
INTO JAPAN AND THE BIRTH OF *BENSHI*

The First Motion Picture Machines

The emergence of *benshi* owed much to the nature of the early forms of motion pictures. We may thus begin our consideration of *benshi* by taking a look at motion picture machines and the entrepreneurs who first imported these machines to Japan. The first motion picture machine introduced into Japan was the Kinetoscope. Invented by Thomas Edison, the Kinetoscope was a self-contained, box-shaped, moving picture apparatus that allowed an individual viewer to watch a short motion picture. By simultaneously cranking the handle, positioned on the side of the machine, and looking through the viewer on the top, a spectator could watch roughly 20 seconds of moving pictures.

The Kinetoscope was presented to the Japanese public by Takahashi Shinji (1851–1915). Takahashi first encountered the machine at the 1893 World's Columbian Exposition in Chicago—the widely publicized event at which Edison revealed his invention to the world. Although Takahashi wanted immediately to purchase a Kinetoscope, only in 1896 was he able to buy two from the Bruhel brothers, who owned a watch business in Yokohama.[1] By mid-1897, accounts of the Kinetoscope disappear from the public record. As was true elsewhere in the world, its popularity was cut short by the appearance of projected motion pictures that could be viewed simultaneously by many people. Two competing types of machine entered the country at virtually the same time: From Europe came the Cinématographe and from the United States, the Vitascope.

The Cinématographe was imported into Japan by Inabata Katsutarō (1862–1936). In 1877, Inabata had gone to France to study at the La Martinière technical college in Lyons. One of his classmates happened to be Auguste Lumière (1864–1948), the elder of the two Lumière brothers who ultimately invented one of the first projecting motion picture machines. After graduation, Inabata returned to Japan and began working in the textile industry, eventually opening his own dyeing factory. While on a business trip to France in 1896 to examine textile and dyeing machines, Inabata ran into his old classmate, Lumière, who told him about his latest invention: the Cinématographe. Instantly enamored with what he saw, Inabata purchased the rights to distribute it in Japan. After agreeing to pay the Lumières 60 percent of all profits,[2] he returned to Japan with several machines.[3]

Inabata's first public showing of the Cinématographe was at the Nanchi Enbujō theater in Osaka on February 15, 1897.[4] Within weeks of the machine's introduction in the Kansai region, two other Cinématographes imported by Inabata were released in Kantō. One machine, which Inabata had given to Yokota Einosuke, the younger brother of a friend, opened at the Kawakamiza theater in Tokyo on March 8, 1897.[5] The other, marketed under the name of Yoshizawa, opened at the Yokohama Minatoza theater on March 9.[6]

Unlike the Kinetoscope, which could be viewed by only one person at a time, the Cinématographe projected motion pictures onto a screen—initially, about 1.5 meters wide and 1.8 meters high. Audiences of several hundred people could thus watch together. The Cinématographe was a combination camera, projector, and printer. Hand-cranked, it needed no electrical current to operate.

23

When it was used as a projector, limelight or another nonelectrical source could take the place of an electrical light.

While Inabata Katsutarō, Yokota Einosuke, and the Yoshizawa Company were busy promoting the Lumières' Cinématographe, Araki Waichi and Arai Saburō were just as busy importing and promoting Edison's Vitascope. Araki Waichi saw the Kinetoscope when he visited the United States in 1894. He planned to buy one on a return trip in 1896, but by that time the more impressive Vitascope was already available. The Vitascope had premiered at Koster and Bial's Music Hall in New York City in April 1896. Araki first viewed it in Chicago later that year and rushed to Edison's office in New York to buy one.[7]

Although marketed as "Edison's Vitascope," the projector was actually invented by Thomas Armat and C. Francis Jenkins. Edison acquired the rights to produce and sell the machine under his name, which led to the impression that it was his invention. As the film historian Robert C. Allen puts it, "The only thing Edison had contributed to the development of the Vitascope was the imprimatur of his name."[8] Unlike the Cinématographe, which was both a camera and a projector, the Vitascope was solely a projector. Both machines, nevertheless, worked on the principle of intermittent motion; that is, they both allowed each frame to remain stationary on the screen for about one sixteenth of a second, thus creating the illusion of motion.

The first official showing of the Vitascope in Japan was by Araki Waichi on February 22, 1897, at the Shinmachi Enbujō theater in Osaka. Two weeks later, on March 6, Arai Saburō held the first public showing of the Vitascope in Tokyo at the Kanda Kinkikan theater. Arai's machine was imported by Shibata Chūjirō, apparently an employee of Arai's import company.[9]

Problem Solving

The discovery of motion pictures, and financial investment in and import of the machines, were merely the first steps in the introduction of cinema into Japan. There was no guarantee that the entrepreneurs would profit from their investment, especially since motion pictures were just one of a myriad of Western wonders of science introduced into Japan around the turn of the twentieth century. Other inventions competing for attention were x-ray machines and phonographs. From the time they acquired their equipment, the initial Japanese motion picture entrepreneurs faced numerous challenges and dilemmas, ranging from mechanical difficulty to the effective marketing of their product. Their solutions to these problems left a lasting imprint on Japanese motion pictures.

Upon returning to Japan from the United States with their Vitascopes, both Arai Saburō and Araki Waichi immediately encountered a daunting technical problem. The Vitascope required direct current, which was available hardly anywhere in Japan at that time.[10] Arai overcame the problem by modifying a gas engine, acquired from friends who ran the Jūmonji Import Company, to use as a power source for the projector.[11] For the short term, Araki solved his electrical impasse by holding a preview showing of his Vitascope inside the Fukuoka Ironworks factory in Osaka. The factory had a direct current generator. The exact date of the preview showing is uncertain, but it was probably sometime in January 1897.[12] The records do not reveal how Araki powered his projector after that initial showing on the factory floor.

During the first decade after the Cinématographe's introduction, there are frequent reports of the images being projected from behind the screen. Apparently the operators were unsure how to use the projector.[13] This is curious, since one of the features that set the Cinématographe apart from its diverse competitors in this fledgling industry was its "complete package" approach to distribution. When the Lumières marketed the Cinématographe, they sent from Lyons with the machine an "operator" who worked as a distributor, exhibitor, filmmaker, and Lumière accountant.

The person sent to Japan in this capacity was François Constant Girel (1873–1952). He arrived on January 9, 1897, and stayed in Japan until December.[14] Although Inabata initially referred to Girel as his "auditor," by the end of their relationship, the entrepreneur was calling the Frenchman an "incompetent fool," because of his inability to resolve the periodic technical problems that arose with the Cinématographe.[15] Girel was evidently more interested in making movies than in projecting them and instructing the Japanese how to use the machines. While in Japan, he shot several films of everyday life for the Lumière company.[16]

In addition to overcoming technical difficulties, cinema entrepreneurs faced the problem of distinguishing their product from traditional theater and the numerous other occidental inventions entering the country. To publicize his Cinématographe exhibitions, Inabata Katsutarō hired the billboard painter Nomura Hōgoku (1854–1903). At the time, billboards were one of the primary means of theater advertising.[17] The Arai Company drummed up business for its Vitascope by hiring Akita Ryūkichi, the owner of the Hiromeya Advertising Company, to publicize its shows. Akita promoted the Vitascope by hiring a *jinta* band, to travel in a boat along the canal that ran between the Arai Company and the theater at which the Vitascope was being exhibited. Often used during the Meiji era as a means of advertising, *jinta* bands played circus-like music. The band hired by Akita also provided background music for the films. It is not clear to what extent conventional billboard and *jinta* advertising lured people away from competing exhibitions of x-ray machines and phonographs, or the traditional theater. What is evident, however, is that most early exhibitions played to full houses.

Other entrepreneurs marketed cinema by endowing it with a high-class image. Takahashi Shinji postponed presenting his Kinetoscope to the public until after he had shown it to dignitaries and officials. The crown prince, later the Taishō emperor, was in Kobe shortly after Takahashi's Kinetoscope arrived in Japan, and he viewed the machine on November 17, 1896, the first day of Takahashi's private showings.[18] When Takahashi advertised his public exhibitions, he stressed the cachet this added to his import by printing in the largest type, "Graced by His Imperial Highness, the Crown Prince."[19]

Given the high price of the machines themselves, import costs, and marketing and exhibition expenditures, most initial movie exhibitors sold tickets at prices comparable to those of stage theater. At a time when one could go to a sumo tournament for around 50 sen, visit a museum or the zoo for the entire day for under 4 sen, and attend the theater for between 25 sen and 5 yen, [20] viewing the Kinetoscope for only a couple of minutes cost between 20 and 30 sen, [21] but to see the Vitascope or Cinématographe cost between 8 sen and 1 yen. [22] Since exhibitors charged prices similar to live theater, they had to put on a show of equal value. A problem they faced in this regard was the short length of the early films. Most films were only a few tens of seconds to a few minutes in duration. Through various means, early exhibitors succeeded in lengthening their shows to up to 3 hours. [23] One strategy was to make running the projector an elaborate production. Until the Russo-Japanese War (1904–1905), several installations employed ten-person crews to run the projector. One person cranked the film, another focused the lens, a third rewound the film, a fourth threaded it through the machine. There was also someone to make sure that everything on the screen was all right, a boy to fan those working around the projector, a general supervisor, and several others with unspecified duties. [24] In an effort to clarify the picture, some exhibitors even hired a person to water the screen down between showings. [25] After the initial excitement over cinema began to wane and knowledge about how to use the machines increased, the number paid to operate the machine was pared down. [26] Usually, one or two operators were all that was needed.

Another means early exhibitors used to lengthen their shows was to extend the projection time by "looping" the film. The ends of the film were joined so that the 20 seconds to 2 minutes of film could be projected continuously for 5 to 10 minutes. Even with looping, the projection time was still only several minutes in duration. The repeated images of, for example, chickens approaching and eating feed could mesmerize audiences for only so long. One way to further enliven the projected images and lengthen the time of presentation was to hire someone to expound on how the projectors worked, who invented them, where they came from, what the film was about, and, perhaps most important, to explain the Western exotica it contained. The first men employed to perform these tasks were the founding *benshi*. A statement by one of the first patrons of the Kinetoscope affirms that such figures were an integral part of cinema exhibitions in Japan from the start.

> Only one person could view the Kinetoscope at a time, so there were a lot of people in the waiting room. In the alcove were a pine tree and an interesting model train that ran on electricity. Many people had gathered to watch the Kinetoscope. *A man stood next to the machine and explained everything.* People were called in one at a time to view the Kinetoscope, which was installed in the adjoining room. I saw a film showing Westerners standing up and wildly firing their guns in all directions. Since I was a child, I thought that the bullets being fired were causing the screen to sparkle. This film was called *The Shooting of the Westerner's Spencer Gun.* It was so interesting, that I pestered my elder brother to take me again.[27] (Emphasis added).

Performers, Pitchmen, Peddlers, and Attractions

By incorporating *benshi* into their show from the outset, the pioneer motion picture entrepreneurs transformed the nature of cinema, making the Japanese silent era distinctive in the annals of film history. As already noted, one reason why Japanese audiences readily accepted *benshi* was because they fit into the prevalent practice of commingled theater. The essential ingredient in commingled theater is a skilled orator who can enliven the visual element with entertaining speech. Cinema would take decades to achieve the perfect marriage of moving pictures and detached voice. The introductory years were a time of trial and error, when exhibitors employed various types of vocal performers. Given the fact that most exhibitors were trying to stage a production commensurate with a playhouse performance, not surprisingly, several founding *benshi* had backgrounds in traditional Japanese theater.

To provide a running commentary for his inaugural Cinématographe exhibition on February 15, 1897, Inabata Katsutarō hired Takahashi Senkichi, an apprentice of the famed kabuki actor Kataoka Nizaemon.[28] Little is known about Takahashi, who apparently provided *setsumei* for the Cinématographe on this occasion alone.[29] Records do not indicate why Inabata selected him, but the fact that Takahashi had received voice training in a traditional theatrical narrative art was probably a factor. Takahashi Senkichi, nevertheless, was not Inabata's first choice. Inabata had initially asked Ueda Hoteiken (1849–?) to provide *setsumei* for his production, but Ueda declined, on the grounds that he did not know a foreign language. A few days later, however, Araki Waichi was somehow able to convince him to provide a running commentary for the February 22, 1897, Vitascope première.[30]

Ueda Hoteiken was born Ueda Tsunejirō, to a family of Osaka merchants. He never liked the family business and left it to work as a circus barker. He later became a *gidayū katari* (ballad-drama chanter) and reportedly received the name Hoteiken from his *gidayū* master, Takemoto Tsutao. Ueda performed *gidayū* for 20 years, during which time he often served as a master of ceremonies for the Western circus-like shows that came to town.[31] Ueda's background in *gidayū*, combined with his experience as a master of ceremonies, was why Inabata Katsutarō, Araki Waichi, and perhaps even Takahashi Shinji, the importer of the Kinetoscope, wanted Ueda for their shows.[32]

Ueda Hoteiken's oration was steady and swift, and he spoke as if there was nothing he did not know. For this reason, he was nicknamed Mr. Know-It-All (*Kōmanya*). Ueda's *setsumei* for the Vitascope film *The Kiss* (1896), which arrived in Japan near the end of 1897, provides ample evidence of his skill as an orator. In the one-minute film, the famous stage actors John Rice and May Irwin embrace and kiss. Since the film was looped, the embracing and kissing was continually repeated. Araki Waichi was nervous about how the police, who were highly sensitive to issues related to public morals, and who had the authority to stop any form of entertainment containing "obscene articles, arts, and other such things that are harmful to public morals,"[33] would react to the film. Ueda resolved the problems with aplomb by explaining in his opening remarks that Westerners traditionally greeted each other by kissing, similar to the Japanese custom of slapping a friend on the shoulder.[34] Satisfied by Ueda's *setsumei*, the police allowed the show to continue, and it quickly became Japan's first hit motion picture.

Ueda Hoteiken's engaging and informative *setsumei* made him a popular *benshi* throughout his career. He was known for asking scholars about images contained within any new movies he was scheduled to narrate. The exact nature of the questions is unclear; however, given the fact that he was said to have queried shopkeepers about unfamiliar items that caught his eye as he walked down the street, we can assume that they were far-ranging.[35] During his career, Ueda trained several people in the art of *setsumei*, including Ōyama Takayuki and Eda Fushiki, two outstanding *benshi* of the late Meiji and early Taishō eras. In 1908, however, his daughter-in-law became gravely ill, and he lost his concentration and began to perform poorly. Feeling a sense of responsibility as one of the founding *benshi*, Ueda decided to retire from the profession he helped establish.[36]

When the Yoshizawa Cinématographe opened at the Yokohama Minatoza theater on March 9, 1896, Nakagawa Keiji (?–1923) gave the *setsumei*.[37] Also the son of a merchant, Nakagawa, like Ueda, hated the family business. He dropped out of Tokyo Prefectural Normal School to become a school teacher in the countryside. Later, he entered Meiji Law School, but left before finishing. For a short while, he worked for the Hachiōji court, but quit that job to travel around the nation as an itinerant artist, poet, and *gentō* performer. Bored with his bohemian life, Nakagawa joined the Jiyūtō political party, helping politicians with their campaigns and giving introductory speeches at political rallies. Eventually, disgusted by the infighting, he left politics and went to work for the Yokohama Department of Water Works.[38] While he was working there, Shiraishi Kame, the projectionist hired for the Yoshizawa Cinématographe, asked him to provide *setsumei* for the Cinématographe's Yokohama première. An old acquaintance, Shiraishi knew that Nakagawa was a gifted speaker who had provided narration for *gentō* performances. At length, Nakagawa agreed to be the *benshi*, but only for a few days.[39] He had this to say about his first days as a *benshi*:

When I was to provide narration at a Yokohama theater, I would finish up at the office just as the theater was opening, run over there, and appear on stage. When I had to provide narration in Tokyo, at first I only worked at nights, so I could go to the theater in Tokyo after finishing at the office. After the theater had closed, I would return to Yokohama on the last train. The next day, like always, I would keep my *setsumei* activity secret. After I started doing two shows—one during the day and one at night—I became an absentee worker. There was nothing else to do, because at that time there were no other *benshi*. In order to keep working for the government, I attached a medical note written by a doctor to the notice of absence I sent in. Periodically, I would appear at the office. For a long time, no one noticed that I was a *benshi*. Finally, the boss found out, and I was fired. After that, I concentrated on one thing only and left the government office to become a full-time movie *benshi*. A few months later, I moved from Yokohama to Tokyo and increasingly found my true calling in life.[40]

Nakagawa's story is unusual, because he left a respectable job to become an entertainer, at a time when employment by the government was esteemed and working in entertainment scorned.

Even though he was a "lowly" entertainer, Nakagawa Keiji performed in front of nobles and members of the imperial family—including the crown prince (later the Emperor Taishō)—on at least 19 separate occasions.[41] Later in his career, if an audience was unruly, he would solemnly declare, "I, Nakagawa Keiji, had the honor to *setsumei* before His Imperial Majesty; nevertheless, you dishonor me by making noise. You are children!"[42]

Nakagawa Keiji was one of the top *benshi* of the Meiji period. By the beginning of the Taishō period, however, he had grown old and anachronistic. During the first decade or so of motion pictures in Japan, some *benshi* provided *setsumei* that merely described what was taking place. Around 1908, however, motion pictures underwent a major transformation that caused *setsumei* to change as well. As audiences grew accustomed to the new marvel, they became bored with simple moving images of everyday life. To keep them entertained, filmmakers devised framing, editing, acting, mise en scène, and other techniques that allowed the presentation of longer narratives. These new movies required a more complex form of *setsumei*. *Setsumei* that pointed out the obvious no longer sufficed, such as the following one that Nakagawa provided for a scene in which a person was eating an apple: "It seems that this person is eating something."[43] When Nakagawa failed to adapt his *setsumei* to the changing times, his career faded away. He died in the Great Kantō Earthquake of 1923.

Although some exhibitors sought to enliven their production by hiring men like Takahashi Senkichi, Ueda Hoteiken, and Nakagawa Keiji, who had training in traditional narrative arts, selling the product to the public was as important as putting on a good show. Many of the first *benshi* thus had backgrounds in sales. Jūmonji Daigen (1870–1926), the man hired by Arai Saburō to provide *setsumei* for the March 6, 1897, Vitascope opening in Tokyo, was one such *benshi*.

Like other youth of his era, Jūmonji Daigen dreamed of studying in America and, in 1890, enrolled at the University of Michigan. Feeling that he was spending too much time talking with the 20 other Japanese students at Michigan and not enough time studying English and learning about America, he soon left Ann Arbor and moved to Chicago, where he enrolled at the Bryant and Stratton Technical School, graduating 3 years later. After graduation, he worked at several odd jobs and took part in setting up the Japanese pavilion at the World's Columbian Exposition in Chicago—the same event at which Takahashi Shinji first encountered the Kinetoscope. Afterward, Jūmonji Daigen became a representative for the Tokyo Export Association and an employee of the Japan Industrial Hall. His duties involved promoting Japanese products to Americans. He later went into business with his older brother, Shinsuke, importing from America such items as rifles, petroleum motors, fire extinguishers, motorcycles, and farm tools. Arai Saburō was a friend of Jūmonji Shinsuke, and had become acquainted with the younger Jūmonji when they were both living in the United States.[44] When Arai purchased a petroleum motor from the Jūmonji Import Company to run his Vitascope, he prevailed upon Daigen to pitch his product. Daigen obliged and fulfilled his duties admirably. Because he was so busy with work at his company, however, he performed *setsumei* only a few times.

Another early *benshi* with a pitchman background was Yokota Einosuke (1872–1943), who had received one of the Cinématographes from Inabata Katsutarō. Einosuke was the younger brother of Yokota Matsunosuke, a friend of Inabata from the United States. At the time, Einosuke was working as a spieler for an electrical show called *Mystery World*, where people could experience seeing through their bodies with the still-novel x-ray machine. Matsunosuke asked Inabata to give Einosuke the Cinématographe, in the hope that it would encourage his brother to do something productive with his life.[45] Einosuke found the transition to hawking another Western marvel of science easy and natural and quickly became one of the giants of the first era of Japanese cinema. Although he frequently worked as a *benshi* during the early part of his career, his major contribution to Japanese cinema history was in the production end of Japanese films. He founded one of the earliest motion picture companies, the Yokota Company, and later became the president of Japan's first large-scale motion picture studio, the Japan Motion Picture Company, or Nikkatsu.

According to the motion picture director Nomura Hōtei (1880–1934), his father, Nomura Hōgoku, hired the street vendor Sakata Chikuma to provide *setsumei* for the Cinématographe, when Inabata Katsutarō exhibited it in Kyoto.[46] In other words, the billboard painter Inabata chose to promote his Cinématographe enlisted a peddler skilled in vending merchandise, to help him market the new product. To give Sakata an air of prestige, as well as to distinguish his product from the rest, Inabata had him wear a European frock coat when he took the stage. The Western subject matter he was supposed to explain, however, evidently overwhelmed the peddler.

Sakata was probably the *benshi* at the 1897 Kyoto Cinématographe exhibition in which a filmed play about Napoleon was shown. Like most early motion pictures, this film was looped. According to one spectator at the performance, when the actor playing Napoleon appeared on the screen, the *benshi* became flustered and said, "This is Napoleon. Napoleon is Napoleon." Every time thereafter, when Napoleon appeared on screen, the *benshi* repeated, "This is Napoleon. Napoleon is Napoleon," much to the amusement of the audience.[47]

Although some *benshi* gave nonsensical *setsumei*, that was the exception rather than the norm. Each motion picture machine was in fierce competition with other Western inventions, traditional entertainments, and different motion picture machines. If a *benshi* continually provided poor *setsumei*, people would turn to the competition. Exhibitors of motion pictures had an incentive to supply their audiences with the best show they could arrange and quickly learned that they needed someone who not only could market their product, but also could attract people to the show. During the first decade of cinema, there was no one better at doing this than Komada Kōyō.

When Jūmonji Daigen left the profession to focus on matters at his import company, he reportedly demanded that Komada Kōyō (Komada Manjirō, 1877–1935) replace him, because he understood how to give good *setsumei*.[48] As the band director for the Hiromeya Advertising Company (which used *jinta* bands to promote the Vitascope), Komada had experience performing in front of an audience. Komada began working in motion pictures in 1897,[49] but exactly when and how he became a *benshi* is unclear.[50]

One early reviewer had this to say about Komada:

> For the two films *High Breakwater Waves* and *Poultry Raising*, the *setsumeisha* [*benshi*] made a special comment that these were the most admired works in the world, and he was correct. Komada Kōyō provided the *setsumei*. His *setsumei* was very, very truthful to the cinema, also funny, fluent, sarcastic, and without stops. The audience praised him very, very much. The reason why the audience was pleased was not because of the novelty of the machine, but because of Komada's brilliant *setsumei*, which attracted many women and children. Komada's *setsumei* helped the audience understand the advancement of scientific information very, very much.[51]

This quote, which appeared in a pamphlet about motion pictures published in 1897 or 1898, was reportedly excerpted from the *Mainichi shinbun*; however, no such article appears in the *Mainichi shinbun*. It seems likely that Komada Kōyō fabricated this positive review to promote himself and his show.

The above quote, with much tongue in cheek, uses the expression *sukoburu hijō* (very, very) three times in one short paragraph. This was Komada Kōyō's favorite expression, and he used it repeatedly in his *setsumei*. It was incorporated into his nickname, "The Very, Very Great Professor,"[52] and served as a catch phrase to advertise his shows.[53] Komada even had the kanji for *sukoburu* (頗) printed on the *haori* he wore both on and off stage.

Like all founding *benshi*, Komada Kōyō took up *setsumei* prior to the establishment of permanent theaters. Motion pictures were exhibited in rented theaters in large urban centers and in tents in outlying areas. Within a few years of entering the business, Komada set up his own touring company. Yokota Einosuke, the Yoshizawa Company, and a few others also set up touring cinema troupes. The two dominant troupes during the initial decade, Yokota's and Komada's companies, constantly competed with one another. Yokota's strength lay in the import of new films, but when it came to music, showmanship, and *setsumei*, Komada was the more powerful. Komada was also more directly involved in the actual exhibitions. He provided *setsumei*, as well as producing and marketing his shows. Yokota, by contrast, soon moved away from such aspects to concentrate on the import and production of films.

As Komada traveled around exhibiting motion pictures, he often incorporated local dialect into his *setsumei* to add to the appeal of his performance. He also performed in Western dress, which was still unusual in the outer regions of the country. In addition to attracting people to his shows with his dapper style and skilled *setsumei*, Komada also acquired a number of disciples, all of whom used the kanji for *yō* (洋), indicating foreign, Western, and European, in their stage names. In 1900, long before the glorious years of *benshi*, Komada made the profession appear so glamorous that one young person, the son of a hotel owner, went so far as to cut off his finger to demonstrate the intensity of his desire to become Komada's disciple. The boy's dream of becoming a *benshi* was short lived, however, because 2 months later, his parents dragged him back to the hotel.[54]

Komada Kōyō put on traveling exhibitions throughout the Meiji and Taishō periods. In 1924, he retired from the touring cinema business, after 27 years, and invested all of his savings in his new foreign film import company, Sekai Films. During the Meiji era, Komada's unsurpassed ability to draw audiences led to the saying: "Komada Kōyō in the east, Ueda Hoteiken in the west."[55] In earlier years, however, he faced an even more exotic rival.

When Jūmonji Daigen appeared on stage to give *setsumei* for Arai Saburō's Vitascope, he was not alone. He was joined by Daniel Grim Krouse, a twenty-eight-year-old from Philadelphia, Pennsylvania, who had come with one of Edison's Vitascopes to Japan. Krouse probably made the journey for the same reason that François Girel accompanied the Lumières' Cinématographe: He came on the pretext of helping with projection, but his real function was to keep an eye on the books. The Lumières routinely sent out an "operator" with each of their machines to help with the initial exhibition and act as an accountant; Edison did not. Why he did in this case is a bit of a mystery.

During most of Arai's early Vitascope exhibitions, Daniel Krouse stood on the stage and explained how the Kinetoscope had evolved into the Vitascope. He also discussed the "inventor of the machine," Thomas Edison, and the content of the films. Although he spoke English, a number of foreigners and educated Japanese in the audience were presumably able to understand what he said. For those who could not, Jūmonji Daigen reportedly provided a translation, in addition to his own *setsumei*.

Of all the first *benshi*, Krouse is the only one whose name appears in contemporaneous sources, as such. In 1897 and 1898, advertisements for the Vitascope routinely ran with the byline, "Technician and *Benshi*, the American Scientist: Mr. Teni [*sic*] Krouse."[56] Exploiting Krouse's exotic appeal, Arai also featured his name on predebut announcements for the Vitascope: "The American scientist Daniel Krouse, who is both a technician and a provider of *setsumei*, will

present the latest great electrical invention, the motion picture machine, from
March 6 at the Kanda Kinkikan."[57] Just by being himself—a Westerner living in
Japan—Daniel Krouse helped establish the place of *benshi* in Japanese cinema.
His popularity demonstrated that an individual possessing a certain allure, stand-
ing next to the screen, could more than pay for himself by enticing people into the
theater.

3

LAYING THE FOUNDATION:
THE EARLY DEVELOPMENT OF
BENSHI AND *SETSUMEI*

The Denkikan and Somei Saburō

One of the underlying characteristics of Meiji culture was the desire of many Japanese to catch up with the West. Compared with other aspects of Western culture imported into Japan at the time, cinema required very little catching up. The early screenings of the Lumières' Cinématographe and Edison's Kinetoscope and Vitascope in Japan are significant because they constitute the first presentation of "a Western 'performing art' in *its original form*, just as the West had produced it and as Western audiences, at the very same moment, were viewing it."[1]

For Meiji Japanese, cinema's initial attractions were the machine itself and the moving images of the West. Despite high ticket prices, Japanese flocked to see the motion pictures. Throughout late Meiji, the average price of admission was about 50 sen, with ticket prices varying between 10 sen—for third- or fourth-class tickets—to 1 yen—for first-class or special seating. With few exceptions, these prices remained consistent throughout the silent era. Aside from huge epic spectacles, such as *Cabiria* (1914) and *Intolerance* (1916), which charged 5 and 10 yen, respectively, a person could usually attend a silent film—at any time between 1896 and 1939—for well under 1 yen.

The audience was composed of a mixed crowd, ranging from the educated elite to the working class. By contrast, in the West, the elite viewed early motion pictures with disdain. A major endeavor of early exhibitors in America was to make the cinema appear respectable, so that it would attract a higher-class clientele. In Japan, on the other hand, movies were always popular among the upper classes.

During the first few years of exhibitions, motion pictures were generally shown either in rented playhouses or in tents. Bookings at a particular venue lasted from a couple of days to a couple of months. The first permanent theater for motion pictures was the 240 seat Denkikan theater in Asakusa, Tokyo, which opened the first week of October 1903. In Great Britain, by comparison, the first theater devoted to cinema—the Balham Empire—opened in the summer of 1907.[2] The first theater built specifically for motion pictures in the United States opened in 1913 (nickelodeons were merely stores turned into theaters).[3]

There are no precise records indicating how many *benshi* were in Japan when the Denkikan opened; nevertheless, one expert hypothesizes that there were only about 15.[4] The first *benshi* hired by the Denkikan were Somei Saburō (Urakawa Naruo, 1876–1960) and Miyamoto (first name unknown).[5] Little is known about Miyamoto, who left the business after a few years. Somei Saburō, on the other hand, became one of the great *benshi*. Throughout his life, he was well liked and was considered an authoritative elder statesman (*genrō*) of the *benshi* world. The celebrated author Tanizaki Jun'ichirō wrote, "In general, I hate *benshi*; however, I admire the Teikokukan's Somei Saburō. His *setsumei* is precise and to the point, while his voice is clear and powerful. Moreover, his *setsumei* does not interfere with the film. . . . In the world of Japanese motion pictures, I think that he is the only one with a good head on his shoulders."[6]

Somei Saburō was a B-grade theater actor before he went to work at an Asakusa panorama sideshow called *Kansen Tetsudō* (*Visual Railroad*). The *Kansen Tetsudō* was a ride-like attraction that attempted to present the illusion of train travel. Sitting inside a theater shaped like a train, the audience would look out their windows as panoramas of passing countryside moved by. According to Somei, "If nothing was said, it would not have been interesting, somebody needed to say something, so I spoke."[7] In later years, the panoramas were replaced by motion pictures.

Explaining that *setsumei* basically entailed pointing out what was going on, Somei later remarked that a typical example of *setsumei*, when he became a *benshi*, was, "Here is a wife. She is a very jealous person, so please play close attention to her *very, very* extremely jealous manner."[8] Although Somei did not mention Komada Kōyō by name when he commented on this *setsumei*, clearly it is Komada about whom Somei was writing. Komada Kōyō was a great entertainer, but his early *setsumei* was prosaic and simple. Somei Saburō transformed *setsumei* from a lecture form of exposition into an eloquent, animated narrative art.

Technically, Komada Kōyō and other progenitor *benshi* did not provide *setsumei*; rather, they gave what was called *kōjō* or *kōjō-ii* (oral statements, introductory remarks). Early *benshi* were called *kōjōii*[9] or *kōjōya*. *Kōjō* was very much in the form of a tour-guide-type explanation: "What you are going to see next is. . ." or "Please note. . . ." Somei called this *bamen setsumei* (surface [scene] *setsumei*).[10] When the audience saw glistening water, for example, they did not know if it was a river, an ocean, or a pond. The *benshi*'s *setsumei*, "This is a lake," clarified the images and put the audience at ease. Although this may appear simple, such *setsumei* were more difficult than it sounds.

Somei recounts that a man named Nakagawa (first name unknown) once approached him at the Denkikan and asked if he could become Somei's apprentice. Somei wanted to hear Nakagawa perform before agreeing to take him on as an apprentice. After merely instructing Nakagawa to describe what appeared on the screen, Somei allowed him to take the stage. Nakagawa took Somei's words literally, as he gave the following *setsumei*: "Now we can see a person in the window. I think she is probably the daughter of the house. Next to her there is a vase on the table. I'm not sure what the flowers in the vase are, but I think perhaps they are peonies or maybe roses. There is a cat. Perhaps it is a female cat. Because it is moving, we know it is alive."[11] The audience booed Nakagawa off the stage. Somei himself was surprised by this *setsumei*. Before this happened, he thought anyone could give surface *setsumei*. This experience showed him that it was more difficult than he thought. This example also shows that audiences were not willing to put up with poorly formulated *setsumei*. Even at this early stage, there was an art to *setsumei*.

Although a 1903 newspaper article reported, "This thing which audiences call '*kōjōii*' is just beginning,"[12] it was actually coming to an end. *Kōjō* was giving way to *maesetsu*, or introductory remarks. For the most part, *kōjō* and *maesetsu* were similar. *Kōjō* and early *maesetsu* both entailed providing a technical explanation about the projection machinery and a brief description of the content of the film. The essence of both was to give the audience the information needed to understand what was about to be projected. For example, during a *benshi*'s *setsumei* for the film *The Czar's Arrival in Paris*, the audience learned that the ruler was not the man in the superior position on the roof, but rather the man inside the carriage.[13] Both *kōjō* and *maesetsu* were performed by a *benshi* who stood on a lit stage and delivered his verbal introductions prior to the film being shown. The fundamental difference between the two was that *kōjō* resembled a lecture, while *maesetsu* was more entertaining. *Maesetsu* was a much more informal and engaging form of opening remarks. This transition is also manifested in how audiences reacted to films. Audiences did not begin applauding *benshi* until after the Russo-Japanese War.[14] This implies that there was a solemn and lecture-like air to performances, which gave way to an entertainment-like atmosphere.

The transformation of *kōjō* into *maesetsu* occurred when there was a shift in film content away from actualities to longer narrative films. *Benshi* were no longer lecturing, but were instead telling introductory stories. Early *maesetsu* contained a variety of superlative adjectives praising the film, yet dealt little with the movie's content. As films became more complex, *maesetsu* became more detailed and served as a forum for a *benshi* to display his oratorical skills. By the time of its elimination in mid-Taishō, *maesetsu* was an entertaining narrative introduction that outlined the plot of the film, whetted the audience's appetite for what was about to be shown, provided the audience with information needed to understand the film, and served as a means for a *benshi* to show off his skills as a storyteller. *Maesetsu* also functioned as the primary basis for a *benshi*'s salary, which in turn was an indication of his skill and popularity. During the first decade of motion pictures, most films were very short, and so *maesetsu* as filler lasted from 20 to 30 minutes. Over time, as films became longer, *maesetsu* became shorter. During the years 1910–1919, *maesetsu* averaged about 5 minutes in duration.

In some ways, *maesetsu* was similar to the *makura*, or opening remarks, found in *rakugo*. The *makura* served several important functions. It gave the storyteller time to let the audience settle down from the previous act and to focus their attention on him as he begin to spin his yarn. During the *makura*, the storyteller introduced the theme or subject of his story. Since *rakugo* was often one segment of a vaudeville-like program, it could follow anything from acrobats to serious heroic tales; the *makura* allowed the performer to warm up the audience. The same can be said of *maesetsu*, which allowed the *benshi* to signal the audience that a new film was about to begin. It also gave him a chance to introduce the film, and, since a variety of movies were shown on one bill, it provided him with an opportunity to change the audience's mood.

Setsumei given while the film was shown is called *nakasetsumei*, or *nakasetsu* for short. In the beginning, few *benshi* continued to *setsumei* after the film started. By 1910, *nakasetsu* had become common practice, but there were still those who felt it should only be used sparingly. According to one critic, *nakasetsu* should not be added to short films, scenic films, comedies, trick films, impressionistic films, films of fairy tales, and long films that can be understood with only *maesetsu*.[15] Until around 1918, *nakasetsu* remained less important than *maesetsu*. Audiences came to hear *maesetsu*, being less interested in *nakasetsu*. Starting in 1918, however, *maesetsu* was phased out, as *nakasetsu* became the sole form of *setsumei*. During the Golden Age of *Setsumei*, 1925–1931, what is referred to as *setsumei* was actually *nakasetsu*.

Benshi also gave *atosetsu* (remarks after the film), but these were never considered an essential part of the performance. *Atosetsu* basically entailed thanking the audience for coming. When Raidai Kamezo viewed the Cinéma-tographe in 1897, the *benshi* gave the following *atosetsu*: "The audience who entered the theater during the screening can stay here and continue to watch the program, but those who have seen all the films must leave."[16] In later years, all of the *benshi* who worked at a particular theater would sometimes take the stage after the last reel had been shown and thank the audience for coming.[17]

Somei Saburō played a pivotal role in transforming *kōjō* into *maesetsu*. Prior to Somei, men like Komada Kōyō merely explained the pictures and nothing more. By expanding the narrative scope of *setsumei*, Somei turned it into an art. Somei did not stand on the stage and lifelessly lecture the audience about the film; rather, he entertained the audience in a spirited manner, informing them about the motion picture to be shown.

Somei worked as a *benshi* throughout the entire silent era and even performed after World War II at nostalgic *benshi* recitals. He was considered one of the top *benshi* of the late Meiji and early Taishō periods. As late as 1920, one critic wrote, "The tone of his *setsumei* is outstanding. Many *benshi* try to imitate him, but no one comes close."[18] An earlier writer commented, "His speech is very fluent and articulate. People come to hear him because he makes films easy to understand."[19] What made Somei's *setsumei* so popular? As he himself said, "I give *setsumei* that contain many nuances. It is simple, but rich in meaning."[20]

In fact, Somei's *setsumei* was so moving that it once caused an escaped convict to turn himself in to the authorities. In a short article published in 1922,

Somei recounts a tale about a man who broke out of jail and entered the Denkikan to watch a film and hear his *setsumei*. The felon was so moved by Somei's *setsumei* that, after the show, he turned himself in to the authorities. Shortly thereafter, the police showed up at the Denkikan demanding to hear Somei's evocative *setsumei*.[21]

Somei's most famous *setsumei* was his *nakasetsu* for the Italian film *Antony and Cleopatra* (1914), which was released at the Denkikan on March 11, 1914.

> On his triumphal return to the city of Rome, Octavius Caesar received a grand welcome from the people of the city. At the age of forty-one, he ascended the throne as the first Roman emperor and was henceforth referred to by the honorary title of Augustus. Thus begins the hundred glorious years of the Roman Empire. The stars in the sky have moved during the months and years of the past two thousand years, but even now there are stories that remain from the lips of passing travelers. This Roman historical drama of Anthony *AND* Cleopatra takes place during the fall of the empire.[22]

Today, when so many Japanese words appear to be of English origin, it is surprising to learn that Somei caused a tremendous stir in Taishō Japan by inserting the single English word "and" into his *Setsumei*. But he did. As the *benshi* Nishimura Korakuten later recalled, "Somei was showing off the fashion of the Taishō period."[23] Although he was poorly educated, Somei fooled audiences into thinking he was a man of learning who could speak English.

Although Somei's "and" is the most famous insertion of English into a *setsumei* performance prior to 1915, other *benshi* also injected English into their *setsumei*. The *benshi* Tsunoda Shōtō was called the "American Literature Scholar," because he was so skilled at English.[24] In 1910, one critic chastised Tsunoda for reading an intertitle in English. The critic felt Tsunoda should have translated the title into Japanese, rather than inserting English into his *setsumei*.[25]

Because Somei Saburō's *setsumei* for *Antony and Cleopatra* was so good, it quickly became renowned throughout the nation. The spread of its fame was facilitated by its having been one of the first examples of *setsumei* to be recorded onto a 78 rpm SP record. As time has passed, people have come to assume that its eminence was solely because of the insertion of the English word "and." This, in turn, has resulted in the misconception that it was the first use of English in *setsumei*, but I believe that it was the "and," the lyrical beauty of the *setsumei*, and Somei's vocal skills that engendered its illustriousness.

Once, when providing *setsumei* for another long Italian film, Somei gave an apparently flawless *setsumei* for the film. Several days later, another *benshi* discovered that the numbers appearing on the intertitles were out of order. In other words, Somei had been providing *setsumei* to an incongruous film, yet audiences accepted his *setsumei* of what was going on. Somei's oratorical skills allowed him to *setsumei* an incoherent film in a satisfying manner.[26]

The Russo-Japanese War

Initially, the novelty of the moving pictures attracted audiences to the cinema. Once that wore off, interest declined. Although at first exciting, short plotless images of Western exoticism did not have sustainable drawing power. Interest in the medium was not revitalized until films pertaining to the Russo-Japanese War (1904–1905) flooded the market. The war boom lasted for several years, and, when it ended, film production had changed, enabling it once again to sustain audiences' interest. In short, filmmakers began to grapple with new styles of cinematic narrativity that allowed them to tell longer, more engrossing stories.

What lured large numbers of Japanese to the cinema in 1904 and 1905 were films about the war. By one estimate, Russo-Japanese war films constituted 80 percent of the market.[27] Some films were made by Japanese, but most were foreign; some contained actual war footage; others were "fake documentaries" using actors to reenact the events. A few films were even of other wars—such as Americans landing in the Philippines—which distributors attempted to pass off as Russo-Japanese War films.[28]

Japanese who rushed to the cinema wanted to watch films that would enhance their vision of how the war was faring. They did not want to see images that might contradict their ideals. Movies that showed the Japanese army losing angered audiences. One such film caused a writer to declare that the film was clearly made by the French, who favored the Russians over the Japanese.[29]

As a symbol of his patriotism, Hanai Hideo (Sasaki Hideo, c. 1868–?) performed *setsumei* in clothes that resembled a military dress uniform. All that was missing, as he appeared on the stage, was a sword. The police accused Hanai of being disrespectful and told him not to wear a uniform in the future. Hanai convinced the police that he was not being disrespectful, but, rather, patriotic. During his *setsumei*, Hanai would scream out: "Stand up! Hats off!" At the time, society tended to look down on *benshi* as mere entertainers, with the result that he startled audiences by making such demands. Because of rumors circulating that Hanai had just returned wounded from the war, people began to respect him. Throughout the war, Hanai was also famous for projecting a slide of General Nogi Shizuko (1848–1912) onto the screen and reading special edition newspaper articles about the war, all the while dressed in his pseudo-military uniform.[30]

As patriotic sentiment swept the nation, *benshi* added to the fervor by giving nationalistic *setsumei*. How this *setsumei* affected audiences is impossible to calculate. Nevertheless, I believe patriotic *setsumei* played a significant role in fanning the nationalist fire that swept through the nation during the war, and which resulted in riots after the war, when Japanese citizens felt the Treaty of Portsmouth had cheated their nation of its just indemnity. An example of such *setsumei* was recorded shortly after it was performed by an unnamed *benshi*.

> Everybody! Everybody in this entire audience! As you all know, in the current combat with Russia, since the outbreak of the war, we have won every battle, from the Liaotung Peninsula to the fall of Port Arthur, to the occupation of Mukden, to the great naval battle in the sea of Japan, which took place on May 27th and 28th, and which resulted in the annihilation of their Baltic fleet. That resounding victory was unprecedented and unparalleled throughout world history. There is nothing to say except hooray (*banzai*) for the Empire! For world peace and the benefit of both Japan and Russia, His Excellency, President Roosevelt of the United States of America, defined the terms of peace negotiations. Plenipotentiar-

ies of both Japan and Russia will begin peace negotiations at an early date in Washington, D.C., the capital of the United States of America. Everyone, listen to me! If the truth be told, Russia is an unprepared country; however, if we are careless, we will be taken in by their tricks and the consequences will be dire. Since we do not know whether or not the upcoming peace negotiations will end successfully, our nation must be increasingly militarily prepared, while we as a nation must thoroughly cultivate our patriotism. When His Imperial Majesty calls, we, his subjects, must be prepared to exhaust ourselves completely. In order to understand this preparation, it may be useful to watch motion pictures about our frontline soldiers, who fight hard, without concern for their homes nor themselves, but only this nation. These motion pictures are different from the eight hundred hackneyed lies that charlatan showmen try to pass off. So please keep that in mind as you watch. Furthermore, in the scenes where you see our soldiers attack, I want you all to shout out "Banzai" to cheer them on. First, we shall show *Pursuit Battle at Mukden*.[31]

What imperial subject would not be galvanized by such *setsumei*?

The *maesetsu* quoted above shows that early *setsumei* was not always simple and uninformed. The *benshi* of this *setsumei* clearly knew about world events and wanted to make sure his audience did, as well. For several *benshi*, the area in front of the silver screen served as a soapbox from which they could declare their views of the world to an audience and have those ideas reinforced with moving visual images.

One *benshi* who exploited this new forum was Takamatsu Toyojirō (1872–1952), who called himself "The Father of Educational Films." As a Meiji youth, Takamatsu dreamed of traveling to America. To raise money for the trip, he began working in a textile factory. When he was nineteen years old, he lost his arm in an industrial accident and was forced to quit his job. He received only 12 yen in compensation. At the time, there were no government or private agencies established to help the growing number of injured workers such as himself. Because of his experiences, he favored labor laws. Takamatsu went back to school and graduated from Meiji University in 1897. He then became an apprentice of the *rakugo* storyteller Sanyūtei Enyū III (1850–1907). This apprenticeship allowed him to study the art of storytelling. He performed *rakugo* for a number of years under the name "Nonkizakura Zanmai."

Takamatsu's interest in labor issues drew him into the labor movement. Takamatsu began writing for Katayama Sen's (1860–1933) periodical, *Rōdō sekai* (*Labor World*), Japan's first trade union newspaper. Later, he joined Katayama's movement, which was trying to organize labor unions in Japan. Takamatsu was one of two lecturers for the movement who traveled around the countryside discussing labor problems. Initially, he carried along a phonograph and played it while he spoke. Later, he used motion pictures as a visual accompaniment to his speeches. Takamatsu immediately realized the potential educational power of films combined with lectures.[32]

Takamatsu Toyojirō's *setsumei* was politically and socially oriented. Once, when showing a film of Niagara Falls, he gave *setsumei* about the electrical power that could be generated by harnessing the flow of water. He also commented on the Kegon waterfall at Nikko, and the different attitudes Japanese and Americans had toward nature.[33] Unsuspecting audience members probably wondered if they had come to see a film or to hear a political speech.

Providing *setsumei* to motion pictures made by someone else was restrictive, in that Takamatsu could only expound upon those topics contained within the film, and these were not always what he wanted to talk about. Thus, Takamatsu began making his own movies, the first film of which was *Shakai pakku katsudō shashin* (*Social Packed Motion Pictures*, 1903). "*Pakku*" refers to cartoons, but in this case, it does not mean animation, but rather refers to the "cartoon-like," satirical look at society he promoted. In the movie, men dressed as university students balanced themselves on large balls, each of which had the name of either a government ministry or university painted on it. The teetering students competed with one another in this dynamic and precarious society. In addition to making the film, Takamatsu provided *setsumei* for it. Because there are no extant records of his *setsumei*, we can only imagine what he must have said. Takamatsu exhibited this film throughout Japan.[34]

Takamatsu eventually caught the attention of the Meiji leader Itō Hirobumi (1841–1909), who was forming the Seiyūkai political party. Itō felt that
Takamatsu's oration could be useful in placating the natives in Japan's new col-
ony of Taiwan (he did not mind that Takamatsu's lectures were tainted with socialism). As a result, Takamatsu went to Taiwan on a propaganda mission to
mollify the Taiwanese. Takamatsu traveled between Japan and Taiwan several
times over the next few years. While in Taiwan, he performed in motion picture
shows and plays. Although he worked as a *benshi*, his primary role was as an exhibitor.[35]

Takamatsu constantly changed jobs and moved around. He never stayed
tied to one engagement for very long. Although he never gave up his ideas about
labor laws, he eventually left the labor movement. During the Meiji period, he
primarily worked as a *benshi*; in later years, he principally worked in the production and exhibition side of motion pictures. Takamatsu Toyojirō made several
films during the Meiji period. Nonsocialist *benshi* often performed *setsumei* for
Takamatsu's movies, indicating that his movies, like most silent pictures made at
the time, could be interpreted in many ways: It all depended on the *setsumei*.

"*Benshi* can kill or save a film" was an often-heard expression throughout
the silent era. In other words, if a film was bad, a skilled *benshi* could save it with
entertaining *setsumei* that would still draw people to the theater; on the other
hand, if the film was good, an untalented *benshi* could kill it with bad *setsumei*.
Throughout the silent era, most exhibitors did not care what the *benshi* said, as
long as he brought in customers and did not invite police attention. If customers
kept coming, a *benshi* could turn fiction into nonfiction and nonfiction into fiction. However, filmmakers, especially during the Taishō period, were often at
odds with *benshi*. Filmmakers argued that *benshi* changed the stories of their
films and destroyed their visual art, with *setsumei*. They complained about *benshi*
usurping interpretive control of their product. Nevertheless, during the Meiji period, few in society questioned what the *benshi* said.

The *benshi*'s freedom to *setsumei* as he wished saved the day a number of times. As mentioned, Ueda Hoteiken's *setsumei* of *The Kiss* prevented police from closing down that film. On February 13, 1908, the film *The History of the Last Days of Louis XVI: The French Revolution* was scheduled to open at the Kinkikan theater.[36] The police quickly forbade the showing, out of fear that a movie about the French Revolution might add to the turmoil plaguing the nation. An announcement in the February 16 *Miyako shinbun* read, "Due to the recognized threat to public safety and morals posed by *The French Revolution*, the film was banned; it was replaced the day before yesterday by a lengthy and tasteful production titled *Gankutsu ō (The Cave King)*."[37] But this was the exact same movie—the exhibitor merely changed the title of the film. How was it possible for an exhibitor to show a banned film merely by changing the title? Because of *benshi*. Since the police outlawed *The French Revolution*, the *benshi* could no longer *setsumei* that the film was about Marie Antoinette and Louis XVI being chased by a mob of people who wanted their heads. Instead, the *benshi* provided *setsumei* about American mountain bandits who were being chased by a mob of people helping the police. Through the skill of the *benshi* and the art of *setsumei*, Marie Antoinette and Louis XVI were saved. Long live the king!

The Theater Milieu

By drawing thousands of people to the cinema, the Russo-Japanese War provided the industry the extensive exposure necessary to impress upon the public the power and attraction of motion pictures. The war boom lasted several years and catapulted motion pictures to the fore of mass entertainment. By the beginning of the Taishō period, motion pictures had become the dominant form of mass entertainment in Japan, making it a popular art, a means of social education, a tool of scientific research, and an instrument of propaganda. Although the first theater specializing in motion pictures opened in 1903, it was not until April 1907 that the Asakusa San'yūkan opened and become the second. Over the next several years, there was a torrent of movie theater construction in Japan's major urban centers.[38] Between 1907 and 1911, over 60 theaters were built in Tokyo alone.[39] Many of these theaters, however, were little more than wooden barracks. Yamano Ichirō (Yamanouchi Kōichi, 1899–1958) later wrote about working as an apprentice at one such theater. "At the time, the Fukushinkan was known as the 'Poverty Theater.' Only about 20 to 30 customers came per day. It was a real dump of a theater. When the river in front of the theater flooded, as it often did, water poured into the theater. The ceiling leaked as well."[40]

Japan's finer movie houses sat over 1,000 people and had large areas allocated for standing room. According to one 1918 survey of theaters, the smallest sat 244, and the largest had a seating capacity of 4,221. The average seating capacity was over 1,000. Japanese theaters tended to seat many more customers than their Western counterparts. In the United States, by comparison, the majority of theaters sat under 500 spectators.[41] In addition to a large seating capacity, Japanese theaters also had a great amount of standing room, to increase their profits: they could fit more people into the theater and save on taxes, because they were only taxed on the number of seats, not the number of tickets sold.[42] The famed Shōwa-era *benshi* Ikoma Raiyū—who also managed several theaters—crammed, on occasion, 1,000 people into one of his theaters, which had an official capacity of only 450.[43]

Despite their large size, few theaters in Japan had the comfort and grandeur of their American and European counterparts. On the first floor of many Japanese theaters, rows of wooden benches were placed directly on a dirt floor. The better theaters covered their benches in velvet. Most theaters were divided into sections, with ticket prices varying, depending on where one was situated. In many cases, the better seats were located in the balcony section. In some theaters, the balcony section was covered completely in *tatami* mats. Because Japanese take off their shoes before walking on *tatami*, all theaters with *tatami* sections had a uniquely Japanese employee: a "shoe-check man." Many theaters included the byline "footwear check free" in their advertisements. This was a peculiarly Japanese attraction.

For many male patrons, one of the more pleasurable attractions was the female ushers. Movie theaters were rather dark, and, because one had to watch their step, the ushers would usually take a customer by the hand and guide him to their seat. Thus, their original name of *tehiki*, which literally means "hand-pull." Around 1910, the nomenclature changed, and they were called *jokyū* (female waiter). The term *jokyū* was first used for female cinema ushers (soon it would become the appellation for the "hostesses" who attended customers in the Taishō cafes). Most ushers ranged in age from the teens to the thirties. In the early 1920s, they earned about 50 to 80 sen a day, plus bonuses, which was a very good wage for a woman at that time. Articles frequently appeared in trade journals, comparing the looks of ushers and commenting on their love lives. Some ushers were reported to be having illicit affairs with patrons; others ended up marrying *benshi*. Generally, the best theaters hired the prettiest ushers. The most popular ushers were known throughout the city and attracted patrons to their theater. Even if a film was bad, there were still many lustful men who eagerly paid their way into the theater just for the pleasure of groping their way to their seat.

Japanese movie theaters at that time were not climate-controlled; the customers had to endure the sweltering heat in the summer and the freezing cold in the winter. Winters were slightly more bearable than summers, because the body heat of the spectators and small charcoal braziers helped keep people warm. In summer, there was nothing for people to do but sweat. Air-conditioned theaters did not appear until the summer of 1932. Many *benshi* complained about the heat and commented on having to perform while drenched in sweat. In order to stay cool—and for entertainment effect—a few *benshi* took the stage in bathing suits or loincloths.

In addition to the temperature problems in cinema houses, spectators also had to contend with the unpleasant fumes emanating from the acetylene projector and from each other. Moreover, at least until almost 1920, patrons were allowed to smoke in movie theaters. Numerous laws and ordinances required theaters to open windows and circulate the air during each performance. The 1921 *Metro-*

politan Police Order No. 15: Rules and Regulations Governing Entertainment Establishments and the Entertainment Industry, for example, stipulated, "There must be at least one five-minute intermission every hour. During intermission, the air must be circulated."[44] The date of this ordinance signifies that bad air was a problem throughout most of the silent era. Given all they had to endure when going to a movie, some people called the third-class wooden benches, situated on the first floor in front of the screen, "A Buddha's Hell."[45]

Yet, despite all of the physical discomforts associated with going to the cinema, people still went, because movies were—and still are—an escape to different places, other times, and strange worlds. For many Japanese, foreign films were a means of learning about the Occident. American movies introduced Japanese filmgoers to New York's skyscrapers, simple New England towns, and the sprawling Midwest, in addition to tramps, Casanovas, and cowboys.

Foreigners living in Japan also endured the hardships of cinema houses to watch American and European movies and at the same time, learning Japanese. In recounting how he learned Japanese, Rear Admiral Edwin T. Layton wrote, "After we were able to understand a little Japanese, [our teacher] had us go to a movie house showing American silent films. There a *benshi*—movie interpreter—gave a gist in colloquial Japanese, speaking from a dais adjacent to the screen. Conversation became much easier for us after hearing these shows repeated time after time."[46]

Throughout most of the silent era, Japanese cinema was divided into two major categories: Occidental films and Japanese films. All of the motion pictures first shown in Japan were imported, and, until the mid-1920s, the preponderance of films were imports. Prior to World War I, European films, particularly French and Italian productions, dominated the market. The United States gained preeminence—not only in Japan, but also throughout many parts of the world—only after the Great War curtailed European production. Several occidental movie stars, such as Charlie Chaplin and Harold Lloyd, become Japanese icons and trendsetters. Lloyd glasses were the rage of the Taishō era, and when Chaplin visited Japan in May 1932, he was treated like royalty.

There are two major genres of Japanese films: period dramas (*jidai geki*) and modern dramas (*gendai geki*). The term "period drama" denotes any film set before the Meiji Restoration (pre-1868). Most of the storylines for these films came from *kabuki* and *kōdan* (a type of narrative Japanese tale). The other important indigenous film style was the "modern drama." These were films about life in Meiji—and later, Taishō and Shōwa—Japan. Not uncommonly, these films were filled with symbols of "Western life," such as Rolls Royces, Western evening wear, boxing matches, pistols, and so forth. From the early 1900s, Kyoto was the center for period dramas, and Tokyo was the center for modern dramas.

In 1925, Japan became one of only a handful of nations throughout the world whose domestic films outperformed imports, and it was not until 1976 that imports, specifically American films, regained dominance in the Japanese market. In terms of sheer output, during the 1920s, Japan produced between 500 and 700 feature films a year. In fact, between 1925 and the middle of the 1960s, excluding the war years, Japan led the world in the number of feature films produced.[47]

Sometimes, during projection—especially during the early years—the film would break. When the audience inquired about what was going on, a common reply of the *benshi* was, "Like clouds gathering around the moon or the wind through flowers, motion pictures disappear."[48] In the case of Japanese films, this disappearance was especially true. Although Japan was a prodigious producer of movies, precious few Japanese silent films remain, especially ones made prior to 1925. The precarious nature of early nitrate film stock, the limited number of copies printed, and the exhibitors' penchant for showing a film until it literally crumbled, all are partly to blame. The Kantō earthquake of 1923, World War II, and other calamities that plagued the nation also played an integral part in destroying Japan's silent film heritage.

Meiji era theaters showed a mixed bill of foreign and domestic films. During the Taishō period, cinema houses began to specialize in either foreign or

Japanese films. Foreign films were always more prestigious than those produced indigenously. Not only were foreign films viewed as better, but the theaters they played at, as well as the *benshi* who provided *setsumei* for them, were viewed as superior. Theaters outside of the big cities showed mostly Japanese films, and only on rare occasions would they show foreign films. In general, students and intellectuals preferred foreign films; the working class and rural population enjoyed the domestic product.

Almost from the beginning, in Japan, motion pictures were shown theatrically on a show-by-show basis. In other words, films were not continuously shown, with the audience entering and leaving freely during the picture, as they did in the United States, where commonly heard expressions were "This is where we came in" and "Didn't we see this movie before?"[49] Instead, in Japan, customers were only allowed in prior to the commencement of each three- to four-hour performance, which contained several short films and two to three features. The maximum length of a performance was often dictated by prefectural ordinances. Throughout the Taishō period, most theaters had one or two performances a day, with a few theaters having three.

The *benshi* was usually positioned beside the screen to the left (from the audience's perspective). This allowed him to simultaneously watch the film and look at the audience. Aside from the time a *benshi* was on stage delivering *maesetsu*, the audience was unable to see him clearly, because of the dim lighting in the theater. After *maesetsu* was eliminated in mid-Taishō, spectators knew a *benshi*'s voice, but probably not his face.

Either next to the *benshi* or to the right of the screen was a lit signboard called an *andon*. The *andon* had two slots in it: one for the name of the film and one for the name of the *benshi*. The same type of signboard was used at all theaters. For short films, *benshi* could *setsumei* the entire film, but, for movies that were several hours in duration, *benshi* usually changed midway through. Whenever the *benshi* changed, the name in the *andon* was changed. Skilled *benshi* had many fans, with the result that the "changing of the *benshi*" was a time of great anticipation for the audience. When a *benshi* took the stage—and even in the middle of a performance—audience members would scream out the *benshi*'s nickname or words of praise, much as was done in *kabuki*. "The God of *Benshi*!" "Ikoma for President!" "We have been waiting for you!" were among the *kakegoe* (cries) shouted out.

Prior to 1920, all projectors in Japan were hand-cranked. By increasing the cranking speed, exhibitors were able to squeeze as many as six shows a day into the weekend and holiday schedule. A table was even printed describing how fast the projectionist should crank, depending on the number of reels to be shown and the desired number of showings.[50] Some of the revolutions per minute listed are twice the normal speed, although it is doubtful exhibitors ever went to that extreme. Tokugawa Musei (Fukuhara Toshio, 1894–1971), arguably the greatest *benshi* of all time, recalls providing *setsumei* for a holiday speed-up: "In order to compensate for the disparity in the speed, one was only a 'true *benshi*' if he could deceive each and every audience member. We became proficient and natural in the art of deception. We realized we were being fraudulent; nevertheless, it was another one of the special skills of the *benshi*."[51]

The variability in projection speed during the Meiji and Taishō eras meant that the *benshi* and projectionist needed to coordinate their activities. During the first decade of the silent era, the *benshi* signaled the projectionist by blowing a whistle, ringing a bell, blowing a horn, and the like. He blew his whistle when he wanted the projectionist to start the film, and, in the case of looped films, when to stop.

As *setsumei—nakasetsu*—matured, *benshi* increasingly seized control over the moving images. By the end of Meiji, many *benshi* had stopped using bells and whistles, which could be heard by the audience, and began pressing a button that was connected to a signal in the projection room. A series of codes existed between the *benshi* and projectionist. For example, when a *benshi* wanted to show off his oratorical skills, he would press the button once, indicating that he wanted the film slowed down. This was usually done during love scenes and tragic episodes. A *benshi* pressed the button twice and had the film speeded up, when he had nothing to say and felt that the film should be fast-forwarded to a section he deemed worthy of his *setsumei*. *Benshi* customarily pressed the button twice for action and chase sequences. Three rings signaled that the film should be shown at normal speed.[52] *Benshi* lost control over the speed of the moving images, after the motordriven projector came into widespread use, starting in Tokyo from about 1921.

Although it is unclear how widespread this practice of controlling film speed was, complaints by angered filmmakers and critics indicate that it was not a rare occurrence. The *benshi*'s manipulation of projection speed is significant, because it is proof that, by the mid-Taishō era, *setsumei* had truly become a narrative art and was no longer a simple appendage, but an essential component. Throughout film history, there has been a debate over sound's role in cinema. Purists argue that sound should not be a part of motion pictures. The moving image is all that is important; sound is little more than a superfluous appendage. Not until the 1960s and 1970s did a few film scholars begin to recognize the important role that sound plays in film. Yet, even today, the image is considered to be the cardinal element. When *benshi* gained control over projection speed, the image became subjected to their *setsumei*. Perhaps for the only time in film history, the visual element was no longer dominant; instead, the aural element was the controlling force. This control of the image is testament to *setsumei*'s strength as a narrative art. Although *setsumei* was never able to subjugate the image, in terms of drawing power, it did become a powerful attraction capable of diminishing or enhancing a film's allure.

To some film theorists, the paradigmatic motion picture is silent. Even during the silent era, however, such an ideal was never manifested in the public arena. There was no such thing as a "silent film." The noise of the projector; the sound of humans breathing, coughing, eating, and rustling about; and, most important, music, were nearly always a part of motion pictures.

Throughout the so-called silent era (a term coined for the period after talkies were invented), musical accompaniment was an integral part of Japanese motion pictures. Initially, one reason music was added was to lengthen the time of the performance. Lengthy musical performances, and *benshi maesetsu* about the movies to be shown, turned 5 to 10 minutes' worth of film into several hours of entertainment.

Orchestra size was usually determined by the size of the theater. Ideally, a large theater, seating 2,000 to 3,000 people, would have an orchestra of 12 to 25 members; a small theater, seating less than 300, might have a 2 or 3 person band or perhaps only a piano player.[53] The composition of the band depended on whether a foreign or Japanese film was being shown.

In general, foreign films were accompanied by Western music performed on Western instruments. Japanese films with a modern setting were often accompanied by a mixture of foreign and domestic instruments, including *shamisen* (three-stringed Japanese banjo), *taiko* (Japanese drum), piano, trumpet, violin, and saxophone. These mixed orchestras developed and produced a type of music called *wayō gassō* (Japanese–Western ensemble), which is unique in the annals of Japanese music. Japanese period dramas were usually accompanied by *narimono* (a type of music usually used in *kabuki*). Over time, musicians established a canon of melodies for each genre, which elicited specific emotions from the audience.

Prior to the establishment of permanent theaters, most music was haphazardly applied to films, without much thought being given to its appropriateness. With the advent of permanent theaters, music began to fit the picture better: sad music for sad scenes, happy music for happy scenes, and so on. This greatly affected the mood and atmosphere of the show. One important impetus to music's advancement was Thomas H. Ince's *Civilization* (1916), which was the first full-length film exhibited in Japan for which a musical score, lasting the entire film, was specially composed. After *Civilization*, A-grade films often had music written especially for them; B-grade films still made do with appropriate previously composed music. Sometimes, a written musical score came with the film, and other times it did not. For those films that were not accompanied by music, it was very important for the band to preview the film—just as *benshi* had to—in order to ascertain the appropriate music.

Japanese audiences learned a great deal about Western music, not only by listening to the music played while the films were being shown, but also from the "intermission music," which was performed between films at the larger theaters. This practice began in the late 1910s and lasted until around 1930. Many movie theater orchestra leaders were renowned for their intermission music. One of the most famous was the Russian, Mikail Gurigorieve (1899–?) who worked at the very ritzy—by Japanese standards—Musashinokan. In addition to his duties at the Musashinokan, Gurigorieve also found time to help organize Japan's first orchestra, the Tokyo Philharmonic, in 1914; and, in 1925, he helped to establish the Japanese Symphony Association.

Throughout the silent era, bands were invariably situated *in front* of the audience, and they only played *intermittently*. When *maesetsu* was still part of the performance, the music would begin, the *benshi* would emerge from behind the screen, and, as he greeted the audience with a bow, the music would stop. The *benshi* would then deliver his *maesetsu* from the stage. Each theater had its own entrance music for introducing the *benshi*. The Miyakoza played *Dixie Land*, the Ushigomekan used *The Star Spangled Banner*, and the Teikokukan, which showed Universal Pictures films, played the Japanese classic *Tengoku to jigoku* (*Heaven and Hell*).[54]

After *maesetsu* was eliminated, the commencement of music indicated that the film was about to start. As the audience settled down, the lights were turned off, and, inside the darkened theater, the *benshi* would assume his position behind his podium, situated to the left of the screen. Sometimes, the music would continue as the movie started; other times, it would stop and let the sound of *setsumei* open the film.

The music had to complement the film. If two people were shown taking a stroll in the moonlight, soft romantic music would enhance the effect of the pictures: loud, obstreperous music would destroy the romantic feeling. This exemplifies the essence of music's role in cinema: to deepen and strengthen the emotional impact of the visual images. Music enshrouds a movie with feeling, creating an atmosphere for the film. Just as a *benshi* can kill or save a film, so music can improve or destroy a movie.

Music and *setsumei* both enhance the emotions and impressions projected onto the silver screen, but, as Hugo Munsterberg pointed out in 1916, "Music does not tell a part of the plot and does not replace the picture as words would do, but simply reinforces the emotional setting."[55] Although the "words" Munsterberg writes about are the words contained in intertitles, his statement applies to the words of the *benshi*. For, in addition to strengthening the emotional impact of a film, *setsumei* also helped the audience grasp the content. From the *benshi*'s perspective, music without *setsumei* was insufficient; *setsumei* was essential to an audience's understanding of a film.

By stimulating the auditory sense, music and *setsumei* enhance the visual impact of the movie. If films were truly silent, the visual image would fall flat, because the brain would be distracted by the silence. When sound is added to a motion picture, the heightened sensual stimulation focuses the mind on the story being presented. The more senses that are engaged, the more enveloping the experience. For the visual image alone to transport the viewer into the diegesis (the fictional world of a film) for an extended period of time, is exceedingly difficult. Sound facilitates that mental transmogrification. The audio component, for example, makes horror movies so terrifying: Mute the sound and terror abates.

To help the audience enter the diegesis, *setsumei* and music had to work together. Each audio element had to play off the other, while taking care not to infringe upon the other's domain. When performed simultaneously, *setsumei* and music do not harmonize well with the film. At any one time, there should be either music or *setsumei*, but not both. Since most exhibitors and spectators viewed the *benshi*'s *setsumei* as the more vital component, the *benshi* was able to dictate to the band leader when he wanted breaks, what tempo he wanted the music, and so forth. From a *benshi*'s point of view, "*Setsumei* is the lord, music is the retainer."[56] *Setsumei* was generally believed to be better for slow-paced scenes such as romantic interludes, and music better for high-speed chase and fighting sequences.

One of the reasons why music and *setsumei* could not be performed at the same time—unless music was played very softly when the *benshi* was speaking—was because, throughout the silent era, *benshi* performed without a microphone. *Benshi* had to be able to project, from one corner of the theater to the other, the crying, laughing, shouting, whimpering, cajoling, assailing voices of a wide spectrum of characters, ranging from young high-pitched maidens to deep-toned, husky brutes, all with their unamplified voice. Given the size of Japanese theaters and the number of people packed into them and rustling about, the area and din over which a *benshi* had to cast his voice was immense. If loud music was playing while the *benshi* was speaking, the *setsumei* would be drowned out. This did happen on occasion, especially when the band was peeved at the *benshi* for some reason. For the most part, however, the *benshi*'s *setsumei* was the supreme aural element.

4

THE PERIOD OF EXPERIMENTATION, 1908–1914

The first definable style of *setsumei* comprised the solo performer discussing the mechanics of motion pictures, introducing the film, and, on occasion, describing the images projected onto the screen. Because of the dearth of sources, what primitive *setsumei* sounded like is hard to say; however, since it was called *kōjō*, it was probably rather like a lecture. All early *benshi* incorporated their background oratorical skills into their *setsumei*: actors used their theater voice, peddlers a merchant chant, *rakugo* performers a *rakugo* inflection, and so forth. The distinctive tone, rhythm, and cadence of the mature *setsumei* of the Golden Age of *Benshi* had not yet emerged. In terms of content, primitive *setsumei* was simple and straightforward. By contrast, mature *setsumei* contained flowery, poetic rhetoric. Although a line can be drawn connecting the founding *benshi* and the *benshi* of the Golden Age, mature *setsumei* was nothing like primitive *setsumei*. Two major periods of transformation—the Period of Experimentation (1908–1914) and the Period of Unification (1917–1925)—combined with a deluge of other influences, transformed primitive *setsumei* into mature *setsumei*.

Film historian Tom Gunning calls the early years of cinema a "cinema of attractions." The cinema of attractions was more interested in the display of curiosities than the presentation of narratives; rather than tell stories, films showed something. There was an emphasis on spectacle, demonstration, and showmanship. Then, beginning in 1907, there was a shift away from the cinema of attractions, toward what Gunning calls a "cinema of narrative integration." This transformation was nothing less than a radical paradigmatic transformation in cinematic narrativity, as filmmakers began to view and use film in revolutionary new ways. The conception of space, time, and narrative form, in films prior to 1907, was entirely different from that presented in the later "classical cinema."[1]

One of the reasons for this transformation was the desire of producers to maintain complete control over their product. In America, exhibitors sometimes employed lecturers (in effect, *benshi*) to help audiences understand the story unfolding on the screen. Production companies disapproved of this, because it gave exhibitors control over their product. Therefore, in an effort to retain control, filmmakers developed editing, framing, mise en scène, and acting techniques, all of which allowed a film to be understood visually, without the aid of a lecturer. By incorporating the narration visually into the film itself, these new methods of cinematic narrativity were able to absorb the spectator visually into the film's diegetic space—the fictional world created by a filmic narrator. That is, filmmakers began making films that drew viewers so deeply into the story that they imagined they were part of the action unfolding before their eyes and forgot they were sitting in a movie theater. In short, between 1907 and 1910, Western filmmakers established a visual narration system capable of conveying narrative information, revealing a character's psychology, indicating the continuity of film time, and creating a coherent diegetic environment. Because narration was assimilated into the film, there was no longer a need for a corporeal narrator to be positioned next to the projected image.

After the creation of the visual cinematic narrator system, the next major transformation to take place was the switch to feature-length films. Since the new filmmaking techniques allowed filmmakers to narrate visually, the natural next step was to tell longer stories. By 1914, filmmakers were fully engaged in making full-length features that utilized all of the basic filmic methods needed for visual narrativity. The extended narratives of features demanded prolonged attention and absorption, thus drawing spectators deeper into the diegetic illusion. Incredibly, at the exact time that Western filmmakers grappled with visual cinematic narrativity, Japanese exhibitors were experimenting with methods of what I term "vocal additive" cinematic narrativity. The impetus for this period of experimentation was the ever-increasing popularity of motion pictures in the years following the Russo-Japanese war. The rising demand, coupled with increased supply, resulted in fierce competition between cinema houses. In an effort to lure customers into their theater, exhibitors experimented with vocal additives. By incorporating vocal additives into the cinematic experience, Japanese exhibitors controlled how a motion picture was viewed and understood by an audience. In the West, the means of narrativity became visual, with the producer in control of the product; in Japan, the means were aural, with the exhibitor, and ultimately the *benshi*, in control. Nevertheless, the aim in both was the absorption of the spectator into the film.

During the primitive era of *setsumei, benshi* performed solo, differentiating little in their *setsumei* for foreign and domestic films. Starting with the period of experimentation, a split emerged in *setsumei*, with foreign films being narrated in a different manner than Japanese films. For over a decade, *benshi* would perform one type of *setsumei* for Japanese films and a different kind for foreign films. Throughout the silent era, foreign film *setsumei* was always performed by a solo *benshi*. All of the vocal additives described below were applied solely to indigenous films. This does not mean, however, that foreign film *setsumei* remained stagnant, or that the stream of foreign film *setsumei* flowed straight. Foreign film *setsumei* advanced, picking up and incorporating some methods used in Japanese film *setsumei*. The mature *setsumei* of the Golden Age, performed by a solo *benshi*, was a confluence of techniques. Remember that, prior to 1918, for foreign film performances, audiences appreciated *maesetsu (setsumei* given prior to the showing of a film) more than *nakasetsu* (*setsumei* given while the film was showing).

All of the vocal additives employed during the Period of Experimentation grew out of the theater tradition. Because Japanese cinema houses literally were showing "filmed plays," it was natural that they make these motion picture plays as realistic as possible. Among the vocal additives experimented with were *nagauta* (a type of lyrical narrative accompanied by *shamisen* and often used in *kabuki* theater), *gidayū* (narrative ballad common in puppet theater), *tokiwazu* (narrative ballad singing frequently found in *kabuki*), *shinnaibushi* (narrative ballad), *naniwabushi* (narrative stories), *degatari* (ballad chant), *rakugo* (humorous storytelling), and *kowairo* (mimicry, impersonation).

Momiji-gari (*Maple Viewing*, 1899) was one of the first films made in Japan. This motion picture contains several short *kabuki* segments performed by the renowned *kabuki* actors Onoe Kikugorō V (1845–1903) and Ichikawa Danjūrō IX (1838–1903). When motion pictures first appeared, *kabuki* actors felt threatened by the new medium and refused to perform in front of the camera. After much coaxing, Kikugorō and Danjūrō agreed to be filmed, but only on the condition that the photoplay never be shown publicly while they were alive. Consequently, although the film was made in 1899, it was not released until 1903. When the film was re-released at the Kinkikan on May 7, 1908, the theater incorporated *nagauta* into the performance.[2] This is the first verifiable instance of a vocal additive being attached to a motion picture. *Nagauta* was also added to the film when it was exhibited at the Fujikan, starting on August 29, 1908.[3] By incorporating *nagauta* into the performance, the exhibitors were making the cinematic experience more theater-like. Since theater too can absorb people into the drama, by making the cinema more like the theater, exhibitors were enhancing the mental mirage for a spectator of being in the illusional world of the show, rather than sitting on a wooden bench.

These experiments with *nagauta* were an important part of the development of *setsumei*. They were an attempt at *setsumei* narration and thus mark the beginning of the Period of Experimentation. Over the next 6 years, exhibitors readily attached a variety of vocal additives, singularly and in combination, to motion pictures, in an attempt to narrate the films and draw people into the diegetic space. Only after much trial and error did one method emerge as the dominant form. Although *nagauta* and many of the other vocal additives I am discussing were not technically "*setsumei*," they nevertheless played a vital role in shaping the rhythm, tone, and cadence of mature *setsumei*, and for this reason they must be thought of as an experimental form of *setsumei*.

According to most renditions of the development of *setsumei*, the first and *only* vocal additive to emerge was *kowairo setsumei*—there was no period of experimentation. *Kowairo* literally means "voice coloring." The term *kowairo* comes from the Tokugawa period, when performers called *kowairoya* went around imitating the voices of famous *kabuki* actors. The aim of *kowairo* was to cause spectators to think they were listening to the actual actors. Because many early motion pictures were filmed plays, it seemed natural to have someone add dialogue in an impersonating voice to the images appearing on the screen. One of the aims of *kowairo*, therefore, was to convince spectators that they were watching a play. *Kowairo setsumei* was also known as *kagezerifu* (hidden dialogue), because it was dialogue added from the shadows.[4] The best way to picture what *kowairo setsumei* was like is to envision a dubbed film.

Exactly when *kowairo* began is unclear. Although proof is lacking, *benshi* probably experimented with mimetic voices prior to 1908. Most authors hold that Hanai Hideo—the *benshi* who provided *setsumei* in a pseudo-military uniform during the Russo-Japanese War—came up with the idea for *kowairo setsumei* as he viewed the film *Soga kyōdai kariba no akebono* (*Soga Brothers' Hunting Scene at Dawn*, 1908).[5] The film starred an all-female acting troupe and was released at the Daishōkan on September 30, 1908.

According to the *Miyako shinbun* advertisements, however, *hayashi narimono* (a type of music found in *kabuki*) accompanied the film, and there is no mention of *kowairo*.[6] Perhaps the theater-like musical accompaniment inspired

Hanai Hideo, who at the time was the head *benshi* at the Daishōkan, to experiment with having a group of people dub dialogue for the characters appearing on the screen. Or, conceivably, since the Fujikan was located near the Daishōkan, the Fujikan's experiment with *nagauta*, several weeks earlier, might have sparked the idea for *kowairo*. Or, perhaps, there was no *kowairo setsumei* accompaniment.

At first, the actual actors and actresses appearing in the film also performed the *kowairo*, but for pragmatic reasons this later proved unfeasible. Because audiences apparently liked what *kowairo* added to the cinema experience, exhibitors needed a more long-term and viable solution. Thus the birth of *kowairo benshi*. Many of the first *kowairo benshi* were former *kowairoya* or theater actors.

Uchida Tsukibito (Uchida Inosuke, 1875–?) claimed that he became the first *kowairo benshi*, when the manager of the Shinseikan requested that he provide *kowairo*, instead of *setsumei*, for a film. According to Uchida, prior to his performance in March 1909, *kowairo* had always been performed by the actual actors of the film. They were not *benshi*, in Uchida's opinion, because they were not trained as vocal artists nor permanently employed by a theater, as he was. Uchida also states that he performed solo for quite some time before the custom of group *kowairo* emerged. Aside from perhaps being the first *kowairo benshi*, Uchida was a very minor *benshi*.[7]

The first verifiable proof of *kowairo* being added to a movie was for the film *Ono ga tsumi* (*My Crime*, 1908) on November 9, 1908, at the San'yūkan. The *Miyako shinbun* advertisement clearly states that *kowairo* was part of the cinematic experience. Because of the way the advertisement is written, who provided the *kowairo* is unclear.[8] Over the next several years, theaters regularly advertised *kowairo* as part of their show. *Kowairo* was the new attraction.

It is usually asserted that, after *kowairo* emerged, it was used for Japanese films, and that a solo *benshi* performed *setsumei* for foreign films: It was a simple and instantaneous division in the art. A few authors mention in passing that there were, on rare occasions, other vocal additives. However, *kowairo* was probably only one of several vocal additives experimented with over the next few years, as Japanese exhibitors searched for a vocal means of narrating longer, more intricate Japanese films. Although *kowairo* eventually became a widespread form of *setsumei*, the art did not instantaneously split in two. Only after a period of trial and error, *kowairo setsumei* became the dominant means for vocally narrating Japanese films.

There were two types of *kowairo*: group and single-person. Throughout the last years of Meiji and the first half of Taishō, group *kowairo* was the more prevalent form. Group *kowairo* entailed about four to six *benshi* positioned out of sight on the wings of the stage, adding dialogue in mimetic voices to the characters on the screen.[9] A theater's top *benshi* performed *kowairo* for the lead characters, and lower-ranking *benshi* provided *kowairo* for the secondary characters. A single *benshi* often had to provide the voices for two or three characters. Initially, *kowairo benshi* impersonated, as accurately as they could, the voices of the actors appearing in the film. But gradually they began to deliver their dialogue using character voices they had developed on their own. Within a few years the *kowairo* voice used by *benshi* would become highly stylized and would sound nothing like the voice of a real person. "In order to express the personalities of the characters," explained the *kowairo benshi* Tsuchiya Shōtō (Tsuchiya Michinosuke, 1870–?), "if you try to *kowairo* the actors themselves, then it is merely going to be a replica of the theater; however, motion pictures and the stage are fundamentally different. Hence, motion picture *setsumei* has to be different."[10]

Although some male *kowairo benshi* performed *setsumei* in a falsetto female voice or even a childish voice, most theaters employed women and children to *kowairo* the female and child parts. Some *kowairo benshi* were able to imitate up to eight distinct voices. Given this ability, it was only natural for talented *kowairo benshi* to begin performing solo. In general, five or six *benshi* provided the *kowairo* for Japanese period dramas, while solo *kowairo benshi* handled modern dramas.

Although *benshi* tended to specialize in one type of *setsumei* (foreign film, modern drama, period drama, and so forth), they were not locked into that style. Some foreign film *benshi* who were skilled at *nakasetsu* occasionally performed *kowairo*; in other cases, *benshi* who were renowned for their *kowairo* performed *maesetsu* and *nakasetsu*. Moreover, even at this early date, there was a confluence of techniques: *Kowairo* was sometimes incorporated into *nakasetsu*, and, conversely, *setsumei* narration was sometimes inserted into a *kowairo* performance.

The premier *kowairo benshi* was Tsuchiya Shōtō. Before becoming a *benshi* in 1910, Tsuchiya gained experience as a *kowairoya* in the Yoshiwara red-light entertainment district. Initially, he worked as both a foreign film *benshi* and as a *kowairo benshi*—further proof that there was a constant confluence of *setsumei* techniques going on at this time. Tsuchiya excelled at impersonating popular actors and became famous for providing distinct *kowairo setsumei* for several characters at one time. When he performed alone, he created the illusion of group *kowairo setsumei*. Tsuchiya's *kowairo* for modern drama tragedies reportedly brought women to tears throughout the capital.[11] The popularity of *kowairo benshi* is attributed to the eminence of Tsuchiya Shōtō.

During the early Taishō period, Somei Saburō and Tsuchiya Shōtō were the top two *benshi* in Tokyo. Tsuchiya was very upset when his rival, Somei Saburō, received praise and thunderous applause for inserting the one little English word "and" into his *setsumei*. Tsuchiya refused to be outdone by Somei and thus set out to top Somei's stunt. Having heard that Shakespeare was a famous English playwright, Tsuchiya hit upon the idea of translating one of his works. The only problem was that he did not understand English. Without fully comprehending the difficulty of the task, Tsuchiya asked one of his apprentices, who had been to middle school, to translate it. The task proved too difficult for the apprentice; nevertheless, he pretended to translate, so that Tsuchiya would continue treating him to meals.[12] Eventually, Tsuchiya abandoned his plan for topping Somei Saburō. Instead, he focused on improving his art, to the point that his solo *kowairo* gave spectators the impression they were watching a group performance. By doing so, Tsuchiya was able, in a sense, to top Somei.

Tsuchiya is most famous for his ability to *setsumei* in several clearly discernible voices. The following is his highly praised *setsumei* for the film *Konjiki yasha* (*Golden Demon*, 1912). Keep in mind that he is using different voices for each of the characters.

[*Setsumei* (narrator voice)]: This is a Japanese love story: *A Golden Demon on the Atami Seashore.*

[Kan'ichi]: Miya, tonight is the last time I will talk to you. It is January 17th, Miya—remember this date well. Ten years from now, or, for that matter, my entire life, I will never forget. How could I forget this month, this night? On this night next year, my tears will fill the sky with clouds. As my clouds fill the sky on a night like tonight, will you think that I am crying because of an old grudge?

[Miya]: Oh Kan'ichi, please do not say such sad things. In my lifetime, I could never forget you.

[Kan'ichi]: I don't want to hear this. It's a dream, a dream. It's all a bad dream.

[*Setsumei*]: Without a word, Kan'ichi puts his head down and walks on the sandy shore. Unable to control herself, Miya bursts into tears and follows after Kan'ichi. . . .

[Miya]: Kan'ichi, if I were to retire to Mount Tomiyama, what would you think?

[Kan'ichi]: What?!?! Then, from before, you have had the intention of retreating to Mount Tomiyama. You are a rotten-hearted, wicked woman.

[*Setsumei*]: Angered, Kan'ichi lifts his leg and kicks Miya in her weak back.

[Kan'ichi]: Deceived by you, I, Hazama Kan'ichi, will become a bad demon of this world. I will eat the flesh of people like you, Mistress of Tomiyama. Whenever you lift your vain face, you will have to look at the face I had when I was living among real human beings. Go and report to the uncle who helped us for so long, that, on this night at the Atami seashore, Hazama Kan'ichi became a wanderer without a destiny. We shall not meet again.

[*Setsumei*]: Kan'ichi was bearing a large grudge. He freed himself and went up the hill. Miya, falling over herself followed, after him.

[Miya]: Kan'ichi, please wait! Hazama, wait! Please. . . .

[*Setsumei*]: There is the sound of waves and a far-off temple bell.[13]

Kowairo was an important branch of *setsumei* to emerge at that time, but it was only one of several vocal additives employed. Although the other vocal additives faded away and were later erased from memories and records, they are significant because they influenced the constitution of mature *setsumei*. Moreover, the existence of a period of vocal additive experimentation demonstrates that *setsumei* did not remain static, but rather that it was dynamic and vibrant.

From the time *nagauta* was added to *Maple Viewing* in 1908, until the Period of Experimentation came to an end in 1914, a variety of vocal additives were tested, among them *gidayū, tokiwazu, shinnaibushi, naniwabushi, degatari*, and *rakugo*. Sometimes the vocal additives were used in only part of a show and *kowairo setsumei* was used for other parts. At other times, exhibitors used vocal additives in combination. *Tokiwazu, gidayū*, and *nagauta* would all be used for one film; *gidayū* and *kowairo* were used for another. The fact that exhibitors used *kowairo* in combination with other vocal additives is proof that it did not instantaneously become one of two dominant streams of *setsumei*.

Naniwabushi was one of the more important vocal additives, in terms of how it affected the tone of setsumei. The *dora koe* (scratchy or gruff) that became a distinctive feature of *setsumei* was undoubtedly inspired by the *naniwabushi* voice. They are too similar for them not to be. The main difference between the two is that, in *naniwabushi*, the voice adheres to a melody, whereas, in *setsumei*, it does not.

The distinctive music associated with each vocal additive also accompanied the film. Hence, at the same time that vocal additives were being experimented with, various genres of music were also being tried. *Setsumei* accompanied by the *biwa* (four-stringed Japanese lute), rather than the *shamisen*, for example, proved to be popular in the Kansai area.[14] In short, it was a time of aural complexity, as exhibitors searched for the mix of voice and music that best complemented the moving visual image.

Because exhibitors utilized these vocal additives to create the illusion of theater, the cinematic rendering probably sounded very much like the playhouse version. Theaters even declared this point in their advertisements: "*Gidayū*, *kowairo*, and musical accompaniment—it's just like watching a play."[15] This is further confirmed by the fact that many famous performers from the various vocal additive genres performed at the movie theaters. In other words, it was not always "*benshi*" who provided the aural element; sometimes it was actual *naniwabushi* or *gidayū* performers. Just because some of the vocal additives were supplied by people who were technically not *benshi* does not mean that they were insignificant. All vocal additives, regardless of who supplied them, were important, because they influenced and shaped the aural complexity of the *setsumei* performed in the periods that followed. Moreover, many of the "non-*benshi*" who supplied vocal additives later became *benshi*. This further perpetuated the influence of their native narrative genre on *setsumei*.

Non-*kowairo* vocal additives were neither anomalous nor insignificant. Vocal additives were only applied to Japanese films, and yet, between 1909 and 1914, non-*kowairo* vocal additives were a part of roughly 15% of all advertised cinema exhibitions. Clearly, they were not an aberration; rather, they played an important part in the evolution of *setsumei*.[16]

Japanese audiences were familiar with the storylines and cultural iconography contained within domestically produced films. They did not need matters explained to them. Instead, spectators wanted motion pictures to feel like theater. Utilizing the aural element found in traditional theater was one means of achiev-

72

ing this end. Unlike Western theater, in which the vocal element is limited to dialogue, in Japanese theater, the accompanying narration provides dialogue for the characters, reveals their emotional state, and discloses what they are thinking. Some of the vocal additives experimented with created a more theater-like experience than others; nevertheless, just like Western narrative film techniques, they drew the spectator into the cinematic experience. This is especially true for the later *kowairo*, which was added from the shadows. By vocally narrating a film, the two-dimensional images on the screen became three-dimensional images in the mind.

These experiments with vocal additives were separate from the multimedia shows called *rensageki* (chained drama). *Rensageki* emerged around the time of the Russo-Japanese war and was a combination motion picture and stage play. *Rensageki* was also known as *jitsubutsu ōyō katsudō shashin* (The Genuine Article Applied to Motion Pictures). In *rensageki*, live stage performances alternated with filmed segments of outdoor scenes and spectacles. Usually, the actual stage actors provided *setsumei* for the filmed portions. The following personal account, by the film critic Tanaka Jun'ichirō, gives the sense of what such a performance was like.

> While four or five actors performed a kind of verbal exchange on stage, a screaming women fled into the curtains. Then two or three men and women chased after her, also going behind the curtain. At that point, the stage grew dark and a white curtain descended smoothly in the downstage area. It became the scene of a park, into which the previous woman was fleeing. A fight broke out between the woman and the people following her. A passing car gave the woman requesting help a ride, and then drove away. The men began to run after her even harder. The car arrived at a wealthy mansion, and the woman accompanying the male driver went with him inside the grounds, up to the reception area. At that point, as the film disappeared and the white curtain was raised, the stage became the same reception room scene as in the movie, and the play between the man and the women from the movie continued.[17]

Rensageki was popular in the middle of the second decade of the twentieh century. Advertisements for *rensageki* shows ran regularly in newspapers and magazines. Film purists, however, opposed the mixed media productions and played a part in fashioning the rules that curbed its popularity. Although the 1917 *Metropolitan Police Order No. 12: Rules and Regulations Governing Motion Picture Entertainment* did not prohibit *rensageki*, it curtailed *rensageki*'s prominence by imposing certain regulations about where and when *rensageki* could be performed.[18] Nevertheless, *rensageki* continued to be performed throughout the silent era.[19]

The reason for this detour into *rensageki* is to clarify the differences between the types of performances on which this chapter is focused and the art of *rensageki*. At times, the vocal additives were staged in a theater-like manner, yet there were no live acting portions of the show. The Period of Experimentation was a time of vocal additives and motion pictures, not theatrical acting and motion pictures.

Like the best film techniques of Western cinema, good *setsumei* could transport a spectator into the diegetic world. Talented *benshi* did not break the feeling of being part of the film: they enhanced it. A skilled *benshi* was a poet of the dark, who could transport a spectator from his wooden bench into the world projected onto the screen. During the Period of Experimentation, many new methods, needed by *benshi* to pull off this illusion, were introduced and developed.

The usual explanation for why Japanese silent film *setsumei* was performed in one manner and foreign movies in another has focused almost exclusively on why foreign film *setsumei* was provided by a solo *benshi*. Because foreign silent pictures were alien tales full of exotica, the dominant reasoning goes, a solo *benshi* was required to explain what was going on and, in particular, to translate the intertitles. Foreign film benshi explicated rather than narrated. But when one views the problem from the angle of Japanese film *setsumei*, then other explanations come to the fore. Exhibitors only implemented vocal additives with

74

Japanese films because the vocal additives with which they were experimenting all had Japanese origins and thus blended with the films. Adding *gidayū* chanting to a Western silent picture, for example, would have been too much of a juxtaposition for all concerned.

Over time, *benshi* began to specialize in either Western films or Japanese films. In the beginning, however, the distinction was not always so clear-cut, and a number of *benshi* performed both. This intercourse between the two branches—foreign film *setsumei* and Japanese film *setsumei*—influenced the development of both. Although the art split in two, there was interaction between the major streams. There was not isolation and stagnation. All of the experimental vocal additives both affected and influenced the *setsumei* techniques used by foreign film *benshi*. Mature *setsumei* emerged, only after a period of experimentation, with a variety of vocal narrative techniques and the adoption of elements from each into one.

5

THE *BENSHI* THEMSELVES:
TRAINING, BACKGROUND, REMUNERATION,
LIFESTYLE, AND PREPARATION

Benshi Training

On July 30, 1912, after a 45 year reign, the Meiji emperor died. The crown prince, who had been one of the first people in Japan to view motion pictures when they arrived in November 1896, assumed the throne, ushering in the Taishō era (1912–1926). Two months later, on October 1, four of Japan's largest motion picture companies—the Yoshizawa Company, the Yokota Company, the M. Pathe Company, and the Fukuhōdō theater chain—amalgamated into the Nippon Katsudō Shashin Kabushiki Gaisha (Japanese Motion Picture Company), or Nikkatsu, for short. The founders of Nikkatsu modeled their company after the Motion Picture Patent Company established in 1909 by Thomas Edison. Although Nikkatsu and the Motion Picture Patent Company strove to monopolize their markets, in the end they both failed. Nevertheless, the formation of Nikkatsu marked a new era in Japanese cinema—a period in which Japanese film production grew and matured. Similarly, *benshi* and *setsumei* experienced radical transformations during the Taishō period, as they evolved into their mature forms.

Being both a producer and exhibitor of motion pictures, Nikkatsu endeavored to make the best films possible and to exhibit them in the most entertaining and alluring manner. For Japanese audiences, that meant continuing the style of performances they had grown to expect during the previous 16 years; in other words, showing films with *benshi* and *setsumei*. Nikkatsu executives, by hiring the best *benshi*, affirmed that *benshi* constituted an integral part of the cinematic experience. Among the top *benshi* working at Nikkatsu theaters in 1913 were Somei Saburō, Hanai Hideo, and Tsuchiya Shōtō. In addition to contracting the finest *benshi*, Nikkatsu established a school to train future *benshi*—the Katsudō Shashin *Benshi* Yōseijō (Motion Picture *Benshi* Training School).

Suzuki Yosaburō, a managing director at Nikkatsu, came up with the idea for the *benshi* training school, shortly after the founding of Nikkatsu. Suzuki wanted to provide audiences with the best *setsumei* possible, but that was not why he proposed building the school. He established the training center for *benshi* because he wanted to acquire greater control over new *benshi*. Suzuki felt that most established *benshi* ignored company rules and demanded high salaries. He hoped that, by training recruits in a company school, he would be able to gain greater control over them and to keep their wages low.[1]

The school opened in August 1913. Nakajima Kingorō headed the school, and Tōgō Raishū taught the students. *Benshi* needed strong voices, to be heard without amplification in the large cinema houses. According to one critic, a *benshi*'s volume was more important than what he actually said, because, if the audience could not hear the *setsumei*, then there was no point to having it.[2] Consequently, students spent long hours strengthening their voices by practicing stock *setsumei* phrases, such as "The sun sets in the west, the sun rises in the east. The temple bell rings through the air; the bell tolls. All reels have been shown."[3] This last line, "All reels have been shown," was the most common concluding *setsumei* expression during the Meiji and Taishō eras. Besides voice training, students took elective courses in Western history, world geography, and English. The variety of subjects indicates the importance exhibitors and audiences placed on *benshi* being knowledgeable informants about the Western exotica contained within foreign films.

Reportedly, over 200 people applied for the 30 available places at the Nikkatsu *Benshi* Training School.[4] The high number of applicants is a testament to the rising popularity and esteem of *benshi*. Only those people who had graduated from at least middle school could apply. All prospective applicants had to prepare a five-minute *maesetsu* for a specific film, then perform it in front of a panel of judges.[5]

Two years earlier, a commentator, writing under the pseudonym "Seigankō," expressed the need for highly educated *benshi*. Seigankō asserted that, because films featured history, geography, biography, and science, it was essential that *benshi* have a broad base of knowledge of the modern world, as well as a proper, upright character. The problem was that, when one looked at the *benshi* working at the time, few had all of the qualifications Seigankō demanded, and the ones who did possess them failed, in Seigankō's opinion, to reveal them. Seigankō went on to assert that many well-educated people, including several teachers, wanted to become *benshi*. These people were knowledgeable and possessed good character, but they lacked practical oratorical skills. What they needed, therefore, was a school to train them in the art of *setsumei*. Twenty-eight months later, Nikkatsu filled this need.[6]

Students at the Nikkatsu *Benshi* Training School were basically Nikkatsu *benshi* interns, who learned the art of *setsumei* through on-the-job training. Instead of the students paying the school tuition, the school paid the students. Students received 9 yen a month in compensation, and, if they performed on stage in front of an audience at one of Nikkatsu's theaters, they received an additional 50 sen per appearance. Within a few weeks of enrolling in the school, many students began providing *setsumei* for short documentaries and comedies. Students started with documentaries and comedies, because the comparatively straightforward and simple plot structures of those film genres made them the easiest to *setsumei*.

On October 5, 1913 (a little over a year after the founding of Nikkatsu), Nikkatsu *benshi* went on the first *benshi* strike. In Tokyo, Nikkatsu had about 160 *benshi* under direct contract at the time, and all of them went on strike. The primary causes were the workers' demands for higher salaries and better working conditions. Moreover, the very high salaries that Tsuchiya Shōtō and Emi Shuntarō received upset many *benshi*. At a time when most other head *benshi* (the top *benshi* at theaters) earned between 25 and 30 yen per month, Tsuchiya reportedly earned 100 yen and Emi 60 yen.[7]

The strikers made a great deal of noise, but were poorly organized and not well controlled. Before a week had elapsed, the strike ended, with Nikkatsu claiming victory. Nikkatsu defeated the striking *benshi* by using the students at their *benshi* training school as full-time *benshi*. By being scabs, 18 students got their big break into show business, including Ikoma Raiyū (Ikoma Etsu, 1896–1964), who went on to become one of the great *benshi*. Nikkatsu also hired apprentice *benshi* from other theaters. In the end, Nikkatsu allowed most of the striking *benshi* to return to work and made an example of the agitators by firing them—a common management strategy in Japan at the time.[8]

One result of the strike was that it clarified and facilitated a hierarchy among *benshi*: As the motion picture industry became more structured, so too did the *benshi*. The strike is also symbolic of the change from the Meiji era, of learning from the West, to the Taishō period, in which labor unrest was prevalent. Japan was entering a new era of political and cultural progressiveness and this transformation is clearly embodied in the lives and actions of the *benshi*, who in many ways personify the notion of Taishō liberalism. A final consequence of the strike was the management's decision to close the Nikkatsu *Benshi* Training School, because all of the students had been hired as full-time *benshi*.

The Nikkatsu *benshi* school was not the first school established to train *benshi*. In 1907, Umeya Shōkichi (1873–?) established the first *benshi* training school—the *Benshi* Yōseijō (*Benshi* Training School). Umeya was a very political person who actively supported Chinese revolutionaries like Sun Yat-sen and Chiang Kai-shek. While in China in 1905, Umeya began to exhibit Pathé films that he had purchased from the Singapore Pathé office.[9] He later returned to Japan and, in June 1906, founded Japan's third motion picture company. In coming up with a name for the company, Umeya, rogue that he was, appropriated the "Pathé" name and reputation, without permission, added an "M" (which supposedly came from the sound of his name) for distinction, and called his newly established company "M. Pathe." As the film historian Peter B. High noted, "Overnight, with nothing more than a single film, an operatic aura, a stolen name, and a bankroll falsely rumored to be in the millions, he shouldered his way into the keenly competitive Japanese film world."[10]

Umeya Shōkichi believed that talented *benshi* were necessary to improve the value of motion pictures, for his nine M. Pathe theaters in Tokyo. Hence, in 1907, he established the *Benshi* Training School. Umeya put up advertisements for the school, expecting only about 10 people to apply: Reportedly, over 200 applied. If the reports about the high number of applicants are true, they indicate that, by 1907, being a *benshi* had become a highly desirable job. One report even asserts that a few people quit their jobs at an artillery factory, hoping that they could enroll in the school and become *benshi*. When the school rejected their applications, they were not only disappointed, but also jobless.[11]

The head of M. Pathe's *benshi* school was Iwatō Shisetsu (Iwatō Shinsaburō, 1880–1938). Like the *benshi* Takamatsu Toyojirō, Iwatō actively worked for the Japanese socialist movement before becoming a *benshi*. Inspired by a lecture given by the socialist leader Kōtoku Shūsui (1871–1911), Iwatō joined the socialist movement as a public lecturer. In 1904, shortly after the outbreak of the Russo-Japanese war, Iwatō traveled around the country as a member of the Heiminsha (one of the main socialist organizations) giving lectures protesting the war. Sometime thereafter, he left the movement in search of a new job. At the time, many places refused to hire people associated with the Heiminsha. Becoming a *benshi*, however, was one of the few options open to these rebels, and, as *benshi*, these countercultural leftists voiced their opposition to the government.

Iwatō was a gifted speaker and excelled at *setsumei*. He was intelligent and well-read, which was rather unusual for *benshi* at the time. Shortly after he became a *benshi*, a French film titled *Akkan no saigō* (*The Last Scoundrel*) played at the theater where he worked. Recognizing that the film was an adaptation of Victor Hugo's *Les Miserables*, Iwatō had the name of the film appearing on theater billboards and advertisements changed from *The Last Scoundrel* to *Les Miserables*. To the delight of the theater owner, this change in title lured many Waseda University students and other intellectuals to the theater. In short, because of Iwatō, business increased and a "better class" of clientele came to the theater. By quickly distinguishing himself as an intelligent *benshi*, Iwatō made a name for himself and attracted the attention of Umeya Shōkichi, who subsequently hired him to head his *benshi* school.[12]

What exactly Iwatō taught at M. Pathe's *Benshi* Training School is unclear, but the training was probably not very technical and may have consisted of merely watching films and remembering each scheme. The school closed shortly after it opened. Although both the M. Pathe and Nikkatsu *benshi* training schools were short-lived, their creation is symbolically important, because it represents an explicit manifestation of *benshi* as an institution, and, by training *benshi*, the schools certified the profession.

During the Taishō period, cinema enthusiasts frequently discussed the need for *benshi* training schools and even suggested that the Ministry of Education should establish one.[13] Although schools did open from time to time, they quickly disappeared like their predecessors, because a more viable means of training *benshi* existed: the traditional master–apprentice method.

The master–apprentice system has a long history in Japan, dating back hundreds of years. It was the primary means of training in most—if not all—arts, crafts, and entertainments. Several of the founding *benshi* took on apprentices shortly after they themselves became *benshi*. In 1900, a child, one will recall, begged Komada Kōyō to allow him to become his apprentice and even gave Komada a severed finger as a symbol of his sincere desire to become a *benshi*.

At the end of the Meiji and beginning of the Taishō era, the rapidly increasing popularity of motion pictures led to a hasty expansion of the motion picture industry. The growing number of theaters all needed *benshi*, so, at that time, hundreds of people entered the profession. The glamour and large salaries of the top *benshi* began to attract people more interested in fame and fortune than in the art of *setsumei*. These aspirants believed that, if they became *benshi*, they would automatically become rich and famous. *Benshi* of this breed often lacked talent and had no love for the art of *setsumei*. They were detrimental to the profession, because they sullied the reputation of everyone else in it. To counteract the problem of inferior and pernicious *benshi*, several prominent and respected *benshi* devised means to improve the stock of *benshi*.

One such *benshi* was Izumi Sōichirō. Izumi's plan was to weed out hollow and delusive aspirants before they entered the profession. The standards he laid out and implemented are important because they reveal the qualities many people expected *benshi* to possess. Izumi began by asking a prospective candidate what motion picture he liked. If his answers indicated that he preferred movies that were popular but of low quality, then Izumi instantly rejected him. Izumi did so because he believed that the applicant's poor taste indicated that he lacked the talent necessary to make a motion picture interesting. The true art of *setsumei* is to make an uninteresting film interesting. If an applicant only liked the visually amusing, then it was doubtful he would vocally be able to make a languid dramatization entertaining.[14]

If a prospective apprentice passed the first test, which many did not, then Izumi had him read aloud a passage from a book or magazine. While the applicant read the selection, Izumi paid close attention to the applicant's ability to interpret artistically, his creative and imitative ability, his knowledge of Japanese and its purity and appropriateness, and his ability to modulate his voice. When the applicant finished reading the passage aloud, Izumi asked his opinion regarding what he had just read. Izumi assessed the candidate based on whether he had fresh, new sentiments, and whether he could analyze, scrutinize, and criticize quickly and intuitively. Finally, Izumi judged the applicant's efforts and diligence, as well as his ability to project an image of morality and propriety when performing in front of a paying audience. If the applicant failed any one of these tests, then Izumi decided that the applicant lacked the necessary skills to become a *benshi* and refused to accept him as an apprentice. Izumi encouraged other *benshi* to be as selective as he, when accepting apprentices.[15]

Most people who wanted to become apprentices introduced themselves to the *benshi* or had a letter of introduction from someone outside the theater. It was very unusual for an employee of a theater to introduce an aspiring apprentice to one of the theater's *benshi*, because theater employees knew the *benshi* personally and did not want to be held responsible if the apprentice proved troublesome. Some *benshi* taught many apprentices, others none. Unlike other Japanese arts, wherein apprentices would receive instruction under one teacher or school, without shifting elsewhere, *setsumei* allowed its apprentices to move around without being bound to one master. This was very countercultural. Occasionally, a person began his apprenticeship under one teacher and later changed to another. Sometimes people apprenticed for a particular theater; at other times, they apprenticed under a specific *benshi*.

There were two types of apprentices: the "commuter" and the "live-in." Most apprentices were of the commuter type. They commuted from home to the theater every day and only worked with their master at the theater. Unlike apprenticeships in other arts, a *benshi* apprenticeship, which lasted from a few months to several years (with 6 months to 1 year being the norm), did not provide apprentices any salary. They received free meals when they were at the theater, and at some theaters they might earn an good-receipts bonus (*ōiri*), or a portion of one, on those days when attendance was good; otherwise, they received no compensation for their toil. If an apprentice occasionally received at least a portion of a good-receipt bonus, he had enough pocket money for food and train fare.

A few apprentices chose to live with their masters. Often, these were people from the countryside who came to the city to become *benshi*. The master provided food and shelter, but the apprentice had to pay for everything else. Usually, the master would front the apprentice money. After the apprentice became a full-fledged *benshi* and began to earn a salary, he would repay his master. He was an independent *benshi* only after his repayment was complete.

Most apprentices began in their late teens or early twenties; a few were as young as 9 years old and others were well into their forties. Apprentices spent most of their time taking care of the theater and serving their masters. They usually arrived an hour or two before everyone else, to clean the theater. They had to make tea for the ranking *benshi*, polish their master's shoes, make sure that the proper name of the *benshi* and the film was in the *andon*, run to the store to buy cigarettes, and diligently perform any other chore their master ordered. No matter what a master or ranking *benshi* said, an apprentice had to do it willingly. Ranking *benshi* often hazed apprentices. Tamaki Kōsui recalls that, when he was an apprentice, he dreaded rainy days, because, on those days, his master purposely tracked mud all over the floor for him to clean up.[16]

While performing the chores assigned to him, an apprentice also had to work on his voice and pay close attention to every performance at the theater. Apprentices learned the *art of setsumei* by carefully listening to their master and the other *benshi* perform. They learned the *craft of setsumei* through vigorous voice training, which entailed projecting set phrases and tongue twisters in their *benshi* voice. Apprentices focused on enriching the pitch, tone, and loudness of their voices. Sapporo Hidematsu later commented that the voice training was so incredibly harsh that "I often felt as if my throat was going to bleed."[17]

At some theaters, an apprentice took the stage after only 1 month of training; at others, he did not take the stage for at least 6 months. After a few months to a year of performance training, an apprentice became a full-fledged *benshi*. Once one's apprenticeship was over, ability and luck determined whether or not he was successful.

Who Were the *Benshi*?

Those who became *benshi* had varied credentials, from being college graduates to grade school dropouts, newspaper reporters to *kabuki* actors, teachers to soldiers, proper gentlemen to disreputable bums. In short, people from all walks of life became *benshi*. There is, however, a discernible evolutionary pattern in the backgrounds of those who entered the profession. That is, there was a change over time in the type of person who became a *benshi*. Although exceptions existed, the following chronology generally held true: The very first *benshi* were mostly "bohemians"; next came a period in which new *benshi* came mostly from the field of entertainment; finally, the ranks became filled with students and cinema fans.

As detailed in chapter 2, the founding *benshi* came from diverse backgrounds, ranging from politically ambitious youths who had traveled abroad to street peddlers who hawked toothbrushes. One left a job in government; another left his job in advertising. Some volunteered to be *benshi*; others were asked. The one thing they all had in common, however, was a bohemian willingness to try new things. This period lasted only a few years, because the emergence of the new vocation quickly attracted professional entertainers.

The real impetus for entertainers becoming *benshi* was the fanatical interest in the Russo-Japanese War, which caused a swift and dramatic increase in the popularity of motion pictures. To keep up with the demand, the industry expanded rapidly, swelling the ranks of the *benshi*. In 1906, there were only about 30 *benshi* in all of Japan; by 1910, however, their ranks had swelled to well over 350, and, by 1917, there were an estimated 3,000 *benshi* performing with traveling cinema companies and at movie theaters throughout the nation.[18] Most of the people who entered the profession during these boom years had theatrical backgrounds. *Shimpa* actors were the most prevalent, but *kabuki* actors, *kōdan* performers, *naniwabushi* storytellers, *rakugo* comedians, *nagauta* singers, and *gidayū* chanters also became *benshi*. These entertainers brought along their training in their arts, which, in turn, shaped their *setsumei*. Consequently, *setsumei* was an eclectic mix of various vocal traditions, and, not coincidentally, it was during the Period of Experimentation that many of these people became *benshi*.

Nishimura Rakuten's (Nishimura Yoshizō, 1886–1955) background was typical of the type of person who became *benshi* at that time. When he was ten years old, he became an apprentice of the *kōdan* performer Momokawa Enrin. Rakuten's *kōdan* was more stylish than artistic. In 1906, an acquaintance suggested that he become a motion picture *benshi*. Realizing that movies were becoming increasingly popular and that his stylish demeanor was not well-suited for *kōdan*, Rakuten changed professions. He later recalled, "My first *setsumei* was very *kōdan*-like. Many people expressed emotions very objectively just with words, but I expressed emotions very subjectively with my whole body. As a result, the audience applauded me. By becoming a *benshi*, I had found my true calling."[19] Rakuten's statements further confirm that *benshi* introduced a variety of narrative art forms into *setsumei*'s developmental process.

Rakuten quickly became one of the top *benshi* of the late Meiji and early Taishō eras. Although he had no formal education, Rakuten was clever. One critic even wrote, "Rakuten's greatest fault is that he is a little too wise."[20] Rakuten's intelligence is visible in the following *maesetsu*, which he provided for a film rendition of Henrik Ibsen's *A Doll's House*.

> A student who came to Tokyo from the country wrote a letter to his family requesting that they send him Maeterlinck's *Bluebird*, Eucken's philosophy, and *A Doll's House*. If they could not find them, then money would be fine. A reply came from the country, reporting that they could not find Maeterlinck's *Bluebird*, they sent a white-eye (*mejiro*). They asked, does Eucken's philosophy mean teaching sword-fighting (*token*) at high school? And, since there was no doll house, they sent a box of oranges.[21]

Until the late 1910s, few people in the film industry were college graduates. Starting around 1915, all aspects of motion pictures in Japan came under attack from several corners of society. Responding to the criticisms, people both in and out of the film industry sought ways to improve cinema's image. One way this was done was through a general "smartening-up" of people within the industry, including *benshi*.

No concrete data exists regarding the educational backgrounds of *benshi* during the first 20 years of motion pictures, but the biographical information of people who became *benshi* at the time clearly indicates that many of them were poorly educated. Starting in 1917, in a move designed to improve the intellectual quality of *benshi*, prefectural governments throughout the country passed laws requiring that aspiring *benshi* at least graduate from "regular" elementary school. Prefectural governments, and others, wanted more intelligent *benshi*, because they worried about the ill effects that poorly educated *benshi* were supposedly having on the intellectual and moral well-being of society. The majority of *benshi*, however, had more formal education than the minimum required during the remainder of the silent era. In 1917, over 70% of the *benshi* surveyed had graduated from at least "higher" elementary school, with 12% having graduated from middle school.[22] These figures remained fairly constant throughout the silent era. A 1936 survey revealed that 73% of *benshi* had graduated from at least higher elementary school and that 10% had graduated from middle school.[23] One reason for the improved education of the *benshi* was that, starting around 1917, students and film fans began entering the profession. These were people who had grown up watching movies and who wanted to enter the fantasy world they loved.

In 1926, a group of Osaka *benshi* wrote a book entitled *Setsumeisha ni naru chikamichi (Shortcuts to Becoming a Setsumeisha)*, detailing how one could become a *benshi*. The authors stressed that, unless one had a better-than-average education, one should not become a *benshi*. Without a good education, a *benshi* would only have a shallow understanding of the content of a film and would therefore be unable to provide good *setsumei*. The authors also stressed, however, that one should not be too well-educated, because highly educated *benshi* often used obscure and unsuitable words that made their *setsumei* difficult to understand. What one needed more than a formal education was the ability to understand dramatic behavior. If a *benshi* did not know a historical fact, he could always look it up in the library; however, if he lacked the intrinsic ability to understand theatrical performance, then his *setsumei* would likely be inadequate. The authors also noted that, to become a *benshi*, one needed to possess a ready wit, proper appearance, social skills, and, most important, a good voice. Some *benshi* could not comprehend dramatic behavior, others conducted themselves immorally, and still others possessed terrible voices, yet made a living performing *setsumei*. Nevertheless, having the proper intellectual, social, and physical accoutrements made it easier for an aspirant to succeed as a *benshi*.[24]

Generally, foreign film *benshi* were better-educated than their *kowairo* counterparts. *Kowairo benshi* needed less formal education than foreign film *benshi*, because the Japanese films for which they provided *setsumei* contained culturally familiar storylines and content. Foreign film *benshi*, on the other hand, needed to know about religions, history, foreign customs and traditions, as well as a great deal about modern life. Many foreign film *benshi* also had a basic knowledge of a foreign language. The ability to read and understand the foreign intertitles appearing on the screen made performing *setsumei* easier.

The *benshi* profession provided a haven for rebels and the disabled. During the late Meiji era, many dissidents, such as Iwatō Shisetsu, the head of the M. Pathe school, became *benshi*. If the police labeled someone as a member of a seditious socialist group, as they did Iwatō, then that person would have difficulty finding a job. One's career opportunities were limited to working for the Salvation Army or an orphanage, peddling in the streets, or becoming a *benshi*. In later years, as the nation shifted from Taishō liberalism to authoritarian militarism, the profession tried to reverse its radical image by preventing rebels from joining.

Throughout the silent film era, many disabled people also became *benshi*. Since *benshi* sat in the shadows and worked with only their voices and minds, their physical disability did not handicap their performance in any way. The majority of the disabled who entered the profession had lost limbs. The unsafe working conditions and constant warfare, which Japan engaged in during the first half of the twentieth century, maimed many, thus creating a steady supply of disabled people who entered the field. For example, Takamatsu Toyojirō, the socialist *benshi* discussed in chapter 3, lost his arm when he was nineteen years old in an industrial accident. Taniuchi Matsunosuke, who worked as a showman for an x-ray machine exhibition that competed with motion pictures for spectators during the late Meiji period, lost his arm to cancer, having x-rayed it thousands of times in demonstrations. He became a *benshi* after the doctors amputated his arm. Then there is the inspiring story of Nakayama Kametarō.

Nakayama Kametarō was born in 1905. When he was a child, he lost both of his hands and his left leg in a freight car accident. Undeterred, Nakayama was determined to get an education, so he figured out a way to write using his right leg and mouth. Upon graduating from middle school, he decided to become a *benshi*, since *benshi* needed good voices, but not functional bodies. Sometime around 1925, Nakayama began an apprenticeship with Kumaoka Tendō (1894–1975) and assumed the stage name of Seidō. In 1928, he entered Tōyō University. He attended university in the day, while supporting himself as a *benshi* at night—a means by which several other university students likewise put themselves through college.[25] What became of Nakayama is unclear after he graduated from Tōyō University in 1931, but, given what he already had accomplished in his life, it is likely that he did not let his disability stop him from trying to fulfill his desires.[26]

A small number of women also became *benshi*. Female *benshi* existed throughout the silent era, but they were more prevalent in the earlier years, when *kowairo setsumei* was more prevalent. In 1917 women constituted roughly 11% of the *benshi* population; by 1926 their numbers had dropped to 4%, and by 1935 they made up less than 1/2% of the total number of *benshi*.[27] The first female *benshi* was Iioka Umeko. Nakagawa Keiji—one of the founding *benshi*—introduced Iioka to a friend, who hired her to *setsumei* the film *Kankan joshi* (*Miss Cancan*) shortly after the Vitascope premiered in Japan.[28] The film was about a woman who, while giving a speech about women's rights, suddenly screams when a rat runs in front of her. Conceivably, the exhibitor hired Iioka because he felt that having an actual woman scream would be an effective attraction.

Iioka was only the first of several hundred women who entered the profession. During the Meiji and Taishō eras, some women became foreign film *benshi*, but most became *kowairo benshi*. By synchronizing voice with image, *kowairo setsumei* strove to animate the two-dimensional images projected onto the screen. Having women provide *setsumei* for the female characters enhanced the sense of realism. Until around 1917, few actresses appeared in Japanese films. In a carry-over from *kabuki*, female impersonators (*onnagata*) played the female roles. Consequently, Japanese spectators experienced an interesting juxtaposition: female *benshi* providing *kowairo setsumei* for men dressed as women. Female *benshi* also tended to perform *kowairo* for children's roles. But women *benshi* remained an urban phenomena, being a rarity in the countryside.[29]

Although most female *benshi* provided *kowairo setsumei* for women and children's characters, there were a few who performed *setsumei* for male characters. Matsui Sumako—not to be confused with the celebrated actress of the same name—was one such *benshi*. Matsui began her theatrical career performing male roles in *Genji bushi shibai*, a form of theater that was very popular from the middle to the end of the Meiji period. In *Genji bushi shibai*, the entirely female cast acted out a play as if they were "human puppets." The authorities eventually closed down *Genji bushi shibai*, because it had become excessively erotic, evolving into a showcase for prostitutes.

Probably sometime after the authorities closed *Genji bushi shibai*, Matsui became a *benshi*. Her harsh and husky voice was not well suited for providing *setsumei* for female characters, so she began performing *kowairo* for male characters. Her forte was providing *setsumei* for Onoe Matsunosuke swordplay (*chambara*) films. Onoe Matsunosuke (Nakamura Tsuruzō, 1875–1926) was Japan's first movie superstar. In the course of a 16-year career, he starred in close to 1,000 movies. Most people in Tokyo associated Matsui Sumako's voice with Matsunosuke's. Although she had a male-sounding voice, critics often complained that she made mistakes in using male vocabulary.[30] (Male critics of female *benshi* often commented on the woman's inability to employ male vocabulary accurately. I never came across a critique of a male *benshi*'s inability to use female vocabulary—probably because most critics were male.)

Associating a *benshi*'s voice with that of the actor's became quite common in Japan during the silent film era. Mitake Suzume (Takemoto Take), a female *benshi* who provided *kowairo* for female characters, noted that most people associated her voice with that of Tanaka Kinuyo's. Audience's heard Tanaka's voice for the first time when Japan's first real talkie, *Madamu to nyōbo* (*The Neighbor's Wife and Mine*), opened in 1931. Tanaka's country accent surprised Tokyo audiences, who had grown accustomed to Takemoto's very womanly Tokyo accent.[31]

At the end of the Taishō period, a radical transformation in the art of *setsumei* resulted in the elimination of *kowairo*. Because most female *benshi* provided *kowairo setsumei*, this change eliminated their livelihood. Only a few managed to become successful non-*kowairo benshi*. One such *benshi* was Ishikawa Mitsumaru. In 1919, when she was 17 years old, she began working as a *kowairo benshi* at the Tokyo Denkikan. Around 1925, she switched from performing group *kowairo setsumei* to providing solo *setsumei*. Two years after she began providing solo *setsumei*, the Denkikan fired her, because they did not like her style of *setsumei*. Determined to continue working as a *benshi*, she moved back to Shizuoka and found a job at a local theater, where she performed solo *setsumei* until 1936.[32]

There were also a few Occidentals who worked as *benshi*. The most famous was Henry James Black (1858–1923), who worked as a *benshi* during the late Meiji and early Taishō period. The Australian-born Black spent much of his childhood in Japan. In 1878, much to the chagrin of his family and friends, he decided to become an entertainer in Japan. He tried his hand at various performing arts, before settling down to become a *rakugoka* (professional storyteller). In 1891, he assumed the professional *rakugo* name "Kairakutei." For more than a decade, he was a very popular *rakugo* storyteller. He performed in Japanese, and, through his *rakugo* tales, he introduced his audiences to Western culture and literature. By the turn of the century, young rivals within the *rakugo* world, who resented a foreigner in their midst, had, for all intents and purposes, forced Black out of the profession. But after he stopped performing *rakugo* on a regular basis, he occasionally worked as a *benshi*. At a time when most *benshi* were not advertised by name, Black's name often appeared in newspaper advertisement bylines. Even at the end of the Meiji period, a foreigner was still an attraction.[33]

Vicissitudes of Being a *Benshi*: Fame, Fortune, Sickness, and Short Careers

Many people wanted to become *benshi*, especially during the Taishō period, because skilled *benshi* were among the top-paid and best-known celebrities of the time. According to the *benshi* Matsuda Shunsui, if one asked the schoolboys who frequented the Tokyo entertainment district, in the years 1910 to 1919, who was the greatest man in the world, they would answer that the greatest man is the emperor of Japan, the second greatest is the *chambara* film star Onoe Matsunosuke, and the third greatest is the *benshi* Somei Saburō.[34] And not just schoolboys admired *benshi*. The *benshi* Nishimura Rakuten mentions that there was a poll taken at a girl's school in Tokyo near the end of the Taishō period, asking the young girls who they thought was currently the most wonderful man in the world. The girls responded that the emperor was the most wonderful, followed in order by the American film star Rudolph Valentino and the *benshi* Tsuda Shūsui (Tsuda Kintarō, 1896–1963).[35] *Benshi* often performed in front of the nobility, and, by many accounts, it appears that their fans venerated them like royalty.

Benshi constituted one of the largest groups of entertainers in Taishō and early Shōwa Japan. Cinema was the most popular form of mass entertainment in Japan at the time, and catering to the wants of the masses were hundreds of movie theaters throughout the Japanese empire. There were more movie theaters than playhouses and vaudeville venues.[36] The five main elements of the cinema that attracted spectators to movie houses in Japan during the silent era were the films, the actors, the *benshi*, the band, and the theater itself. Theaters frequently advertised with bylines such as, "Naturally, we are proud of our motion pictures. We are also proud of our *setsumei* and orchestra!" Or, "Movie, Music, *Setsumei*: We Have it All!"[37] The *benshi* was often just as important as the film, in terms of attracting customers. As one writer put it, "For many people, the *benshi*'s *setsumei* is the biggest attraction."[38] The person standing next to the screen, rather than the images projected onto the screen, often determined the entertainment value of a particular theater. Moreover, a *benshi*'s rising or declining popularity could affect the fate of the cinema house at which he worked. Fans of certain *benshi* habitually went to a theater several times a week to listen to their idol *setsumei* the same film. If moviegoers did not like the *benshi* performing at the theater where a movie opened, they would wait until the film moved to another theater, where a *benshi* whom they liked performed. During the silent era in Japan, many movie fans did not say, "Let's go and see such and such a film," rather they said, "Let's go and hear this or that *benshi*"; that is, they went to the movies, based not on what was showing, but rather on who provided the *setsumei*.

For some movie fans, the *benshi* was the cardinal element of the show. Nevertheless, the hyperbole of *benshi* fanatics should not distort the reality that, during the silent era, the motion picture was the number one attraction for the majority of filmgoers. Thus, although a *benshi*'s presence at a particular theater might sway a person to go to that theater, more often than not it was the film that initially drew customers. A frequently repeated assertion is that, during the silent era, the *benshi*'s name appeared larger than the title of the movies in advertisements. This is not true. Rarely was the *benshi*'s name printed larger than that of the film's. More commonly, but still infrequently, the *benshi*'s name was larger than the actor's. Miyoshi Masahisa is one of the few *benshi* adherents to describe the situation accurately. When musing about the glorious days of the *benshi*, he states, "In programs and newspaper advertisements, it was the *benshi*'s name that *caught my eye*" (emphasis added).[39] The printer did not enlarge the name of the *benshi*; rather, it was the *benshi* fan who exaggerated it in his mind.

Skilled *benshi*, who consistently caught the eyes of fans, often caught the attention of managers at rival theaters, who would attempt to entice them away from their current place of employment with offers of large signing bonuses (*maekin*) and huge salaries. At the beginning of the Taishō period, when day laborers earned 59 sen a day, first-year elementary school teachers earned 20 yen per month, and bankers began their careers earning only 40 yen per month,[40] Somei Saburō, Ikoma Raiyū, and Izumi Tenryō (Shirakawa Harutaka, 1894–1965) received a 3,000 yen signing bonus to move from the Teikokukan to the Fujikan. The theater gave Somei the 3,000 yen to divide as he saw fit, because he was the ranking *benshi*. Somei gave Ikoma and Izumi each 150, and pocketed the remaining 2,700 yen.[41] Being less-experienced *benshi*, Ikoma and Izumi had to accept the radically uneven split offered to them by one of the most respected elder statesman of the art of *setsumei*. Theaters offered signing bonuses only to top *benshi*. The bonus was usually several times higher than the salary the *benshi* would earn once they began working at the new theater.

In 1917, upon completion of 3 to 6 months of training, a male *kowairo benshi* earned a starting salary of between 12 and 15 yen per month; females earned between 8 and 10 yen.[42] For those who were talented—male or female—their salary could rise quickly. The female *benshi* Hanayagi Yoneko began working as a *benshi* sometime around 1913, when she was only nine years old. Although she was popular, she left the business several years later. When she quit, her salary was 80 yen per month. There were very few professions in early Taishō Japan in which a thirteen-year-old girl could earn so much money while still remaining chaste.[43]

Foreign film *benshi* generally earned more than *kowairo benshi*, because they typically performed solo. Until around 1920, a foreign film *benshi*'s ability to give *maesetsu* determined his salary. After 1920, his salary was based on his ability to give *nakasetsu*, or what became known as *setsumei*. After *kowairo se-*

tsumei disappeared at the end of the Taishō period, all salaries were based on the *benshi*'s ability to provide solo *setsumei*.

During the Taishō and Shōwa periods, the average *benshi* earned between 50 and 80 yen per month in base salary. Head *benshi* usually earned between 100 and 200 yen, with a handful of top *benshi* earning well over 500 yen. Ikoma Raiyū is reported to have earned 1,000 yen per month in 1920.[44] *Benshi* earned as much as, if not more than, Japanese studio actors. According to a 1927 report, star actors earned about 200 yen, with a few earning as much as 450 yen. The majority of actors, however, received monthly salaries of only 20 to 30 yen.[45] One advocate of *benshi*, recognizing this as just, pointed out, "It is the *setsumeisha* who cements the connection between the film and the audience. He is the one who brings the film to life and unites the audience with the film. Thus, he should be paid more than actors, who are merely filmed and projected on to the screen. . . An actor is merely a very tiny element in a motion picture show; at best, an element like the wind, clouds, and trees."[46]

Benshi supplemented their base salaries with a number of bonuses. The two most common bonuses were the money for noodles (*soba-dai*) and good-receipt (*ōiri*) bonuses. Head *benshi* and band leaders reportedly received 1 yen a day "with which to buy noodles"; everyone else received 50 sen.[47] Managers paid out good-receipt bonuses whenever the box office receipts exceeded a certain amount. The theater did not have to be full for there to be a good-receipt bonus. In 1933, at the better Tokyo theaters, the system worked something like this: Over 1,200 yen in ticket sales resulted in a 1 yen bonus, with each additional 500 yen in sales resulting in an additional 50 sen. At Japan's finest theaters, especially at holiday times, a *benshi* could earn as much as 30 yen a month from good-receipt bonuses. If a film became a huge hit, the theater paid out good-receipt bonuses every day during the run, which could last 60 or more days. Smaller theaters paid smaller bonuses. Yet, at most small theaters, the good-receipt bonus still netted *benshi* an additional 4 to 5 yen a month. Some *benshi* also received from half to a full month's salary as a year-end bonus.[48]

Many top Tokyo and Osaka *benshi* often guest-performed outside their respective cities. One place that was especially lucrative for *benshi* to perform was Hokkaido, Japan's northernmost island. Hokkaido theaters lured *benshi* to perform there with enormous salaries. One theater, for example, offered Kunii Shikō a 3,000 yen signing bonus and 350 yen per month salary to come and perform.[49]

In addition to the money the theater paid them, *benshi* could supplement their salaries by various means. Fans, female ones in particular, sometimes placed money by the podium next to where a *benshi* was performing, as a gratuity, and, in the case of love-struck fans, as a token of affection. Because *benshi* were skilled elocutioners, people often asked them to host special functions and receptions, or to provide speeches for them. In 1930, Ikoma Raiyū gave 23 campaign speeches for the Minseitō Diet member Endō Masamato. Ikoma charged Endō only 100 yen per speech; in other cases, his enormous popularity enabled him to charge as much as 200 yen per speech. Ikoma earned more giving one speech than most Japanese earned in an entire month. Occasionally, however, he had to wait quite a while before he received his remuneration. Endō Masamato claimed in court that, because of excessive spending during his campaign, he would not be able to pay Ikoma for over 9 months.[50]

Although *benshi* earned high wages, the job was demanding. *Benshi* generally performed only 20 minutes to 1 hour during each show, which averaged between 3 and 4 hours; nevertheless, each theater had two to three shows a day, and as many as seven or eight during the busy holiday seasons, with the result that *benshi* had to remain at the theater all day. Moreover, since theaters usually showed new films every week, *benshi* had to spend many hours each week preparing new *setsumei*. There were many other onerous aspects to the profession, such as the low number of days off, lack of health and housing benefits, unsanitary working conditions, and the lack of job security.

Cinema was an industry without holidays, and, since *benshi* were an integral part of motion picture exhibition, they had few—if any—days off. During the 1932 Nikkatsu strike, *benshi* demanded that they be given two holidays per month, and more than five holidays in the summer.[51] The final settlement awarded the strikers 2 days off per nonsummer month and 3 days off during the summer months of June, July, and August.[52] Because the strikers demanded that they be given 2 days off per month, it is logical to conclude that, before 1932, most *benshi* had only one or, more likely, no days off per month. Theater managers showed films every day and expected their *benshi* to come to work and *setsumei* their films.

The four main health ailments suffered by *benshi* were respiratory disease, nervous breakdowns, stomach problems, and "diseases of the pleasure quarters."[53] Japanese silent era cinema houses were unsanitary and filled with noxious air emanating from the projection room. Theaters were also filled with the tobacco smoke from the pipes, cigarettes, and lungs of the spectators. Articles and editorials frequently appeared in newspapers and magazines demanding that something be done to improve the unhealthy conditions.[54] In an attempt to clean up the air, prefectural governments repeatedly passed ordinances requiring that theaters frequently circulate fresh air into the theater. In passing such legislation, the government was mainly concerned with the health of the customers who sat in the theater for a couple of hours every now and then; it was not concerned about the *benshi* and other theater employees who worked in the theater for 10 hours a day. Many *benshi* suffered terrible respiratory ailments as a result of their regular exposure to polluted theater air.

Many *benshi* also smoked, despite the fact that they were narrative artists whose livelihood depended on their voices. When asked what he liked, Ikoma Raiyū responded, "I like cigarettes. I smoke about sixty a day."[55] Smoking that many unfiltered cigarettes and still being able to project one's voice throughout the theater was quite an accomplishment. In the end, however, heavy smoking destroyed many *benshi*.

Benshi faced incredible pressure to perform well every week. *Benshi* could achieve unbelievable popularity very quickly, but that popularity could vanish just as fast, if the *benshi* did not constantly work to maintain a high-caliber *setsumei*. They continually had to develop new material and hone their acts, because, as one critic put it, "There was no product greater than a *benshi* that peaks in the evening and is thrown away in the morning."[56] The never-ending stress of having to perform well and keep abreast of new trends resulted in many nervous breakdowns.[57]

    Benshi who did not steadily provide quality *setsumei* had short careers. Sadly, many of those who consistently performed at a high level had their careers cut short by the physical demands of *setsumei*. Many entertainers reached their prime in their forties and remained at the top of their profession well into their fifties. Most *benshi*, however, wore out in their thirties and retired before they reached forty. Of the 233 *benshi* reported to have worked in Kumamoto between 1911 and 1937, 140 worked a year or less, 79 worked between two and five years, 7 worked between six and ten years, 6 worked between eleven and fifteen years, and only 1 had a career longer than sixteen years.[58] In other words, only about 3 *benshi* in 100 stayed in the profession longer than ten years.

    The ephemeral nature of a *benshi*'s career and popularity can also be discerned from the ranking charts known as *banzuke*. Today, the only *banzuke* with which most people are familiar is the one used in the sport of *sumo*. In prewar Japan, however, *banzuke* existed for everything from hot-spring resorts to entertainers such as *benshi*. *Banzuke* ranked *benshi* both locally and nationally; some ranked all *benshi*; others ranked only the top *benshi*. *Banzuke* often arranged and ranked the *benshi* according to categories, such as foreign film *benshi*, period drama *benshi*, up-and-coming *benshi*, and female *benshi*. On some *banzuke*, there was a space at the bottom reserved "to publicly admonish ill-behaved *benshi*"—in other words, those *benshi* who had run off with their large signing bonuses.

    Yoshizawa Shunmu issued the most famous and celebrated national *banzuke*, beginning in 1916. *Benshi* cared a great deal about their ranking on a *banzuke*, not only because it was a reflection of their talent, but also because a higher rank increased their bargaining power with theater managers. One's skill and popularity formed the basis for one's ranking; however, as Ōkura Mitsugi remembers, giving Yoshizawa a little "tip" could also be beneficial. One day, Ōkura met Yoshizawa in the street and Yoshizawa said to him, "Ōkura, my friend, for an entertainer, one's reputation should be prized more than money. One must treasure one's name. If you fork out a little money, I will promote you to *Komusubi* (fourth highest rank). Recently, your popularity has increased, and if you can find it in yourself to generously give over ten yen, by next year you should be an *Ōzeki* (second highest rank). What do you think of that?"[59] Being the miser that he was, Ōkura refused to tip Yoshizawa. Even so, he remained at the top of the *banzuke*. Despite the apparent corruption involved in the rankings, they still reflected the skill and popularity of the *benshi*.

When one examines *banzuke* issued in different years, the ephemeral nature of most *benshi*'s careers becomes apparent. Names at the bottom of one *banzuke* may appear near the top of the next and disappear by the one after that. It was the rare and exceptional *benshi* who perpetually ranked at the top.

There were two main reasons for the fleeting careers of most *benshi*. First, the job was mentally demanding. If a *benshi* wanted to keep his job, he continually had to develop new and popular *setsumei*. Second, the job was physically demanding. Working every day in a polluted environment took its toll on many *benshi*; the strain of projecting their voices throughout the large theater claimed others. But what truly caused many *benshi* to be as glorious and ephemeral as fireworks was the wild and hedonistic life that the majority chose to live.

From Hedonism to Buddhism: Lifestyles of the *Benshi*

In reflecting upon his days as a *benshi*, the great *chambara* film *benshi* Kunii Shikō (Aebe Yoshinosuke, 1894–1966) wrote, "I know that I am not just speaking for myself when I say that the thirty golden years of *katsuben* life were thirty years of liquor, women, and gambling."[60] Takemoto Shōko (1894–?) put it this way: "It was a time when one could take the stage drunk and drag geisha or girls from the neighborhood into the dressing room to play, without worrying about getting fired. Today, that wonderful occupation is nothing but a glorious dream."[61]

The Taishō period was a time of relative political and cultural liberalism in prewar Japan. As the political atmosphere at the top relaxed and became slightly more open and democratic, the cultural milieu in which most citizens sought enjoyment and release from the hardships of daily life became more carefree and open. Party politics replaced the oligarchic rule of the Meiji era, and *moga* (modern girls) and *mobo* (modern boys) listened to American jazz music. The *benshi* were paragons of Taishō liberalism. Most *benshi* lived life to its hedonistic fullest, with drinking and cavorting with women being two prevalent diversions. High salaries and celebrity status provided *benshi* with the means and freedom to be as self-indulgent as they wished.

Many *benshi* lived flamboyant lives and liked to show off by coming to work by rickshaw and wearing outlandish clothes. During the Taishō and Shōwa periods, some *benshi* continued to perform in frock coats—a custom that began in 1897; others started wearing flashy kimonos or Western suits with a red or white flower in their lapel. Usually, foreign film *benshi* wore Western dress and Japanese film *benshi* wore kimono or *hakama*. Some *benshi* wore imported foreign suits costing over 100 yen, which they bought on credit; others had suits tailor-made.[62] Clothing stores frequently displayed copies of suits they made for the *benshi*[63]—an indication of how *benshi* were cultural icons who others wanted to imitate.

Although they performed only a couple of hours a day, *benshi* had to be at the theater all day; hence, they spent much of their day in the dressing room. Most *benshi* spent their free time talking, smoking, playing games, chasing after women, and drinking. Most *benshi* drank in moderation during working hours and heavily after work. If a *benshi* drank during work, he had to feign sobriety when he appeared on stage. Many *benshi* were quite skilled at this, but a few were unable to hide their inebriation. Some theaters had rules against drinking during working hours; ingenious *benshi*, however, found ways around such prohibitions. In 1917, when the Denkikan issued regulations against drinking inside the theater, one *benshi* poured liquor into a medicine bottle. When anyone inquired about what he was drinking, he retorted, "My heart medicine."[64] As long as a *benshi*'s drinking did not adversely affect his *setsumei*, most managers and government officials looked the other way.

Although many *benshi* were alcoholics, some still had outstanding and long-lasting careers. In fact, the man considered by most aficionados to be the greatest *benshi*—Tokugawa Musei—was an incredible lush. Tokugawa Musei was born Fukuhara Toshio, in 1894. In elementary school, whenever rain canceled gym class, Musei became the center of attention. Other students gathered around him to hear him repeat ribald *rakugo* yarns he had heard at the vaudeville theaters that he occasionally attended with his father. Even at a young age, Musei was a talented storyteller. That he would become one of the most respected narrative artists in twentieth-century Japan, however, was not an idea that entered young Toshio's mind. Toshio was planning to attend Tokyo Imperial University and enter the government upon graduation.

In 1912, Musei took the test to enter the First High School for the first time and missed passing by only one question. He failed the next time he took it as well. One of the reasons he failed was that he was having an affair with his neighbor's wife, a woman by the name of Shige, who later went on to a short but successful career as an actress, under the name "Izawa Ranja." Just before he was to take the test for the third time, Musei decided he wanted to become a *rakugo* performer. His father, who worked in politics and did not want people to know that his son was an entertainer, suggested that he work as a *benshi*, since they did not have to show their faces. His father did not realize that *benshi* provided *maesetsu* on lit stages before they drifted off to the shadows to provide *setsumei*. Nevertheless, Musei heeded his father's advice and became a *benshi*.

On August 10, 1913, Fukuhara Toshio became the apprentice of Shimizu Reizan and began working under the stage name "Fukuhara Reisen." Toshio showed incredible potential and impressed his master; he was not satisfied with

101

the working conditions, however, and stormed off in pursuit of a higher salary. After 2 years of working for short periods of time at various theaters throughout Japan, he finally settled down at Tokyo's Aoikan theater, where he assumed the name under which he would work for the rest of his life: Tokugawa Musei. Tokugawa derived from the name of the theater, which literally means "hollyhock theater." Hollyhock was the symbol for the Tokugawa family. He took on the name "Musei" because he had a "dream voice," the meaning of the characters for Musei (夢声).[65]

Musei was skilled at unifying his *setsumei* with the music and the film. His *setsumei* became a part of the whole, and was calm and to the point. He was admired by all, but especially by the intelligentsia. The political scientist Maruyama Masao declared, "Musei is a genius. I can't imagine films like *The Cabinet of Dr. Caligari* separated from Musei's *setsumei*."[66] Besides being one of the greatest *benshi*, Musei was also the most prolific, having written close to 100 books and a similar number of articles. Many of these works are invaluable for the information they provide about the author, the period in which he performed, and the art of *setsumei*.

Tokugawa Musei accomplished a great deal in his life and achieved great heights in terms of power, respect, and influence, all despite his alcoholism. He started drinking around the time that he graduated from middle school, and within a few years he was drinking as much as a bottle of whisky a day. During his life, he was hospitalized seven times because of alcohol. He frequently performed drunk and sometimes passed out at the *benshi* dais. On other occasions, the moving pictures made him so dizzy that he felt like vomiting. Once, when providing *setsumei* for the film *Dr. Mabuse*, he had a particularly bad run-in with the audience. He had started drinking especially early that morning and took the stage drunker than usual. His slurred *setsumei* provoked audience members to scream out, "*Benshi*, speak clearly." Musei tried to, but could not. He was simply too drunk. Someone screamed out that Musei was a fool (*baka*). Musei replied, "The person who screamed out that I was a fool is more of a fool than I am." When the intertitle "You ignorant people, I am a god; you cannot resist me. In the end all you can do is obey my words" appeared on the screen, Musei said, "You are all fools. I am great, like a god. You ignorant people, no matter what you do, compared with my greatness, you are all trivial. Oh, you ignorant fools." Several audience members took offense at these remarks and screamed out, "Kill him!" To which Musei replied, "Go ahead and try, I am a citizen of the empire of Japan and I am protected by the Imperial Constitution." In response to these remarks, someone threw a bottle that hit Musei in the head and knocked him out. The police were called in to restore order in the audience. Despite the difficulties that Musei's drunkenness created, he possessed more talent and intelligence than many other *benshi*, and most audiences loved him.[67]

Although Tokugawa Musei occasionally let alcohol get the better of him, he was somehow able to continue performing at the highest level. And, despite occasional problems, such as the *Dr. Mabuse* incident, his drinking did not really effect his livelihood. Others, unfortunately, fell victim to liquor and were forced out of the profession. Some ruined themselves by spending all of their money on liquor; others became incapable of providing intelligible *setsumei*. A few *benshi* even drank themselves to death. In 1918, Ichikawa Mugō (1890–1928) wrote his brother, "The amount of *sake* I drink has increased because there are so many things that stress me out."[68] Ten years later, his alcoholism reached the point that he drank a bottle of ink one day, in the hope that its alcohol content would settle him down. It settled him down permanently, for the next day his fellow *benshi* found him dead, lying in a pool of vomited blood. He was thirty-eight years old.[69] In addition to killing some *benshi*, excessive drinking was the primary cause of the stomach ailments that plagued so many in the profession.

Another occupational hazard many *benshi* experienced was sexually transmitted diseases. One critic asserted that 8 or 9 male *benshi* out of 10 were sex maniacs (*shikima*), and, by most accounts, he appears to have been right.[70] All types of women—from high-class *geisha* to low-class streetwalkers, from wives to schoolgirls—cavorted in dressing rooms with the *benshi*. A few *benshi* even had beds in their dressing room so that they would not have to go far to satisfy their sexual desires. Given the number of women who chased after them, it was not surprising that *benshi* had numerous relationships. Although some *benshi* paid for their sexual pleasures, most did not need to, because female fans constantly threw themselves at their feet. Female fans often placed 50 sen to 1 yen tips and love letters before their favorite *benshi* while they performed, and chased after them when they left the theater. One magazine even reported that many schoolgirls gave up their virginity to *benshi*.[71]

One of the most notorious "lady-killing" *benshi* was Tsuda Shūsui—the *benshi* voted the third most wonderful man in the world by a group of Tokyo high school girls. Tsuda continually had women vying for his affection. Enraged fathers and husbands complained to the police that Tsuda was a sexual deviant stealing the virtue of their loved ones. The police dragged Tsuda in for questioning on numerous occasions and revoked his *benshi* license three times.[72] Even so, he was a highly skilled and talented *benshi*. Once, when giving *setsumei* for a five-reel film, the projectionist left out reel four. Tsuda pretended not to notice and continued performing. When the film was over he said, "The projectionist made a mistake and left out reel four." Tsuda astonished the audience by giving a seamless performance even through the projectionist's error.[73] His charm and charisma attracted women, but his mastery of the art of *setsumei* pleased both sexes.

Although the hedonistic and flamboyant lifestyles that *benshi* lived seemed attractive to many, it incurred the wrath of others. The author Nagai Kafū held *benshi* in particular contempt. He viewed *benshi* with the same abhorrence with which he viewed rickshaw pullers. In his 1918 semiautobiographical short story *Ame shōshō* ("Quiet Rain"), a wealthy company director abandons his geisha mistress after he learns of her affair with a *benshi*. For this man, and Nagai, it was impossible to "imagine anyone who could have the bad taste to get worked up over a *katsuben*."[74] Evidently, Nagai had not met Tsuda Shūsui. The author Dazai Osamu also wrote negatively about *benshi*. In *Zensō o omou* ("Thinking of

Zensō"), a woman suggests a particular outfit for her husband to wear, at which point the husband scornfully responds, "If I walk out in that, I'll look just like a *katsudō benshi.*"[75]

The drunken and sybaritic lifestyles in which many *benshi* engaged were a reflection of the times. Nevertheless, the negative publicity inflicted upon the profession, by the antics of a few excessively wild *benshi*, upset many of those who took their job seriously.[76] Although some *benshi* imbibed too much, and others fornicated to excess (and still others did both), not all *benshi* were hedonistic. Many took their job seriously and partook of libations and lascivious pleasures only after work. Some *benshi* restrained their self-indulgent tendencies, and a few totally refrained from the hedonistic lifestyle of their fellow *benshi*, choosing instead to live very moral and principled lives. One such *benshi* was Fujinami Mumei (Hara Shinpei). Audiences nicknamed him *go-seijin* ("The Saint"), because he was a virtuous and devout Nichiren Buddhist. Had audiences known more about Mumei's diligent research and preparation for each show, they might have nicknamed him "The Scholar."

Preparing for the Show

The fact that *benshi* performed on stage for only a few hours each day made the job look easy to outsiders. In reality, each performance hour required several hours of preparation. Generally, theaters changed movies every Friday, and *benshi* previewed new films on Thursday nights following the last show. They usually previewed a movie only once or twice before they had to provide *setsumei* for an audience. Critics complained that a *benshi*'s preview of a motion picture was insufficient and resulted in mistakes that the audience could easily notice.[77] The critics were correct that the *benshi* did make mistakes on opening day, but, if they were skilled in the art of *setsumei*, they could conceal their blunders. Moreover, if one screening was insufficient for *benshi*, it is unlikely the audience themselves would have noticed their mistakes upon their first viewing.[78]

For many *benshi*, Fridays provided an opportunity to experiment and become familiar with a new film. Some *benshi* came to work early on Friday mornings, to practice before the theater opened. During the years in which *kowairo setsumei* was prevalent, *kowairo benshi* had to practice as a group, synchronizing their *setsumei*. Because the aim of *kowairo setsumei* was to create a theatrical illusion, it was vital that the *benshi* synchronize their dialogue with the moving images and that *benshi* know when they had to give their lines. When *kowairo benshi* were in harmony with each other and the movie, the illusion generated was magical. However, when *kowairo benshi* were not in harmony, the impression given was undoubtedly similar to the one a contemporary viewer garners from a poorly dubbed 1960s or 1970s martial arts film.

For *benshi* who provided *setsumei*—*maesetsu* or *nakasetsu*—Fridays became the day on which they worked out the kinks in their *setsumei*. Some *benshi* had people critique their first performance, so that they could improve subsequent shows; others sneaked incognito into the audience seats right after their performance to listen to criticisms of their *setsumei*. If a *benshi* worked at a second- or third-run theater, he could preview the motion picture that was going to come to his theater the following week, by going to a first-run theater where the film was premiering. This allowed him to preview the movie and to listen to a top-ranking *benshi*'s *setsumei* for the film.

There were times, however, when a *benshi* was too busy to preview a film. When this happened, he had to perform cold, or what *benshi* called *mizuten* (doing without seeing). If a *benshi* were literate, he could read through either the "dialogue script" that came with the film, or a fellow *benshi*'s script before providing *setsumei* for the film he had never seen. If a *benshi* were illiterate, he could ask a fellow *benshi*, who had read one of the scripts, to explain it to him. Sometimes, *benshi* provided *setsumei* for motion pictures about which they had never seen or read anything. That was true *mizuten* and required incredible skill to manage successfully. Tsukada Kiyū was one *benshi* who never liked previewing a film. He often provided *setsumei* for films he had never seen. Tsukada was able to convince audiences that he knew what he was talking about by having one of his apprentices sit in the shadows and read the script to him while he performed.[79]

During the first two decades of motion picture production in Japan, there was little emphasis on having a good script written before shooting. Most films were made in an ad-libbed manner, with an emphasis on getting the picture done quickly. Concerning film production early in the second decade of the twentieth century, Kinugasa Teinosuke, a female impersonator (*onnagata*), who later became a famous director, recalled, "There was no practice or rehearsal. Everyone performed thinking only of their own movements. It was not necessary to memorize any dialogue. The director prompted us by standing next to the camera and reading the dialogue. If we made a mistake, it did not matter, because when the film was shown, the '*benshi*' would skillfully emend any contradictions."[80] Only in the late 1910s did Japanese filmmakers begin insisting on detailed and well-written screenplays.[81]

The early scripts that film companies supplied *benshi* were often not the ones used in film production. According to Kobayashi Isamu, the M. Pathe film company supplied the first dialogue script sometime around 1907. Iwatō Shisetsu, the head of the M. Pathe *Benshi* Training School, apparently wrote the script.[82] Not until soon after 1910, however, did companies began regularly supplying *benshi* with dialogue scripts. The dialogue scripts the *benshi* received only contained the title, the staff, the cast, a brief plot summary, and a transcript of the film's intertitles. In the case of foreign films, distributors began providing *benshi* with scripts that contained translated intertitles, beginning around 1915.

Spectators and critics often unjustly blamed *benshi* for improperly translating foreign intertitles. *Benshi* could indeed be accused of not verifying that the scripts they used contained perfect translations of every intertitle; because they did not usually translate the intertitles themselves, however, audiences should not have reproached them for incorrect translations. The film companies provided *benshi* with the faulty scripts, and the companies, not the *benshi*, needed to improve the translations contained in the *benshi* scripts. By one estimate, there were as many as 50 mistakes in each translated script of a feature film.[83]

Most distributors hired translators for foreign intertitles. Partly because film companies circulated only a limited number of prints, and partly because *benshi* were there to provide *setsumei* that contained translations of the intertitles, distributors never filmed, printed, and inserted translated intertitles into their foreign films. In other words, Japanese intertitles never appeared in foreign films.

In 1925, the people who translated foreign intertitles into Japanese earned about 100 yen per month, but it was a demanding and thankless job.[84] Film companies often rushed the translators, forcing them to deal not only with complex foreign slang, puns, alliteration, and cultural allusions, but also with the Japanese censors. After a translation of the intertitles was made, the finished product was turned into a book and presented to the police or Home Ministry to be censored. Although the vast majority of translations were accurate, the handful of incorrect ones attracted the attention of intellectuals who possessed the linguistic ability to detect discrepancies. The following examples of "incorrectly" translated intertitles reveal, however, the difficulty of translating foreign intertitles that were full of dialectal usages and colloquialisms.

Original intertitle: He is the Kipling of the movie world.
Japanese translation: He sells movie tickets.[85] (Kipling sounds like "selling tickets" in Japanese—*kipu uru*.)

Original: So this is Paris! Wee Wee! Hot dog!
Translation: This is Paris! It's hot, really hot![86]

Original: Don't say "pop me." I don't want from you no streetwise freshness.
Translation: Call me "father." Don't you think you should use a more respectable word like that.[87]

Original: Rocking chair
Translation: Rock chair (*iwa no isu*)[88]

Original: Here is your pay on your discharge, and the sooner you are gone, bag and baggage, the better for all parties.
Translation: Here is your pay on your discharge, and soon after you leave this house your bags will be sent to you.[89]

Original: The lesson—the French Revolution, RIGHTLY overthrew a BAD government.
Translation: The lesson to be learned from this movie is that the French political strife was caused by a tradition of bad governing and the consequences of this were worse.[90]

This last translation is from D. W. Griffith's *Orphan's of the Storm* (1921). The translator interpreted the intertitle in this manner to appease the censors, who were highly sensitive to anything that might inspire or provoke public agitation against the government.

When a *benshi* previewed a film, he checked to make sure that the dialogue script he received from the film company was correct. For Japanese films, that meant confirming that the script contained transcriptions of all the intertitles. For foreign movies, that meant making sure that the transcribed translations made sense, and, if the *benshi* knew a foreign language, that the translations were correct. As Somei Saburō pointed out, however, "There are very few benshi who understand English, so, if there is a mistake in the translation, we can't always discover it."[91]

Benshi provided *setsumei* for a film in one of three ways: they relied on a script, they ad-libbed the entire performance, or they used a mixture of reading from a script and ad-libbing. Some *benshi* felt compelled to adhere closely to their script, but others liked to improvise everything. The majority, however, did a combination of the two.

Benshi mostly used the scripts that companies sent them as a base upon which to construct their *setsumei*. Some *benshi* made a minimum of written changes, because they planned to improvise at length. Those *benshi* who relied more heavily on their scripts wrote lengthy and detailed additions. How the *benshi* enriched the intertitles and how they differed from each other is clearly revealed in the following presentation of *setsumei* from the film *The World and Its Women* (1919). In the left column is the translated intertitle that appeared in the script supplied by the distribution company. The next two columns are the corresponding *setsumei* that two unknown *benshi* wrote down and, presumably, performed.

1. Prince Orbeliana's fief in Kavkaz Russia	On Prince Orbeliana's fief in Kavkaz, Russia, there were oil reserves.	In Kavkaz, Russia, there was a Prince named Orbeliana. The family was in possession of a fief, and there were oil reserves within this family's fief.
2. Prince Michael Orbeliana has entrusted the American engineer to develop an oil field on his property	The American engineer Robert Warren was entrusted to develop an oil field.	The American engineer Robert Warren was entrusted with drawing up plans on how to develop the reserves.
3. The American engineer Robert Warren	One day, the Prince visited the house of the engineer on urgent business.	One day, the prince visited the engineer's house on business.
4. The Prince's heir, Prince Michael Orbeliana	He brought along his heir, Michael Orbeliana. While he went inside, the heir stayed behind on the horse-drawn carriage.	He rode there with his heir, Michael. The young child waited in the horse-drawn carriage while the Prince went inside on business.

110

| 5. The engineer's daughter, Marcia Warren | Meanwhile, the engineer's daughter, Marcia Warren, had climbed up a tree. While teasing a dog, she blundered and fell. The heir, who was still in the carriage, quickly dashed off. He looked at her condition and surmised that nothing was really wrong.

While looking at him, she asked, "Who are you?"

"I am Michael Orbeliana. . . ah. . . Prince. . ." | Meanwhile, the engineer's young daughter, Marcia Warren, had climbed a tree in the garden and was teasing a dog. Michael, the young child who remained behind in the carriage, was bored. While he was looking about to and fro, he noticed the engineer's daughter, who was the same age, teasing the dog. He looked at her wholeheartedly. For some unknown reason, the girl blundered and fell from the tree. Surprised by this, he dashed off to there.

"Are you hurt anywhere?"

"I'm not really hurt, but my lower back hurts."

Since she had never seen him before, she asked, "Who are you?"

"I am Michael Orbeliana. . . I'm a Prince." |

6. If you are a real prince then why aren't you wearing a crown?	"If you are really a prince, then why aren't you wearing a crown?"	Remembering the image of the prince that people talked about, she inquisitorially asked, "If you are really a prince, then why aren't you wearing a crown?"
	After the boy and girl had been talking for some time, the elder prince said he was going home. Then he got in his carriage and went home.	After the boy and girl had been talking for some time, the elder prince finished up his business and went to his carriage. However, since his heir was not there, he called out to him. Hearing his father's voice, the young Michael quickly dashed off in the direction of the carriage. He returned home with his father.
7. Father, is that child really a prince?	The girl was confused by her conversation and asked her father, "Father, was that boy really a prince?"	The girl thought that the conversation she just had was strange and she wanted to know whether he really was a prince. Just after her father had seen the prince off and while he was still at the threshold she asked him, "Father, was that young boy really a prince?"[92]

When providing *setsumei*, *benshi* generally read aloud the intertitles, in the case of Japanese films, or translations of the intertitles, in the case of foreign films. Yet, as the above example shows, *benshi* often embellished these intertitles. The above script also reveals how *setsumei* was a combination of dialogue and explanation.

After a *benshi* performed a particular *setsumei* a certain number of times, he became so familiar with the material that he no longer needed a script. For most motion pictures, however, the majority of *benshi* used scripts to help them through their performance, especially at the beginning of the week, when they were less familiar with the material. But *benshi* had to be careful not to rely too heavily on the script, because, if he merely looked down and read his entire *setsumei* word for word, he risked falling out of synchronization with the movie. This was a problem for less skilled *benshi*.

The lack of harmonization with the movie, which resulted when an unskilled benshi read his script verbatim, was a shortcoming for which critics chastised *benshi*, especially *kowairo benshi*. One of the aims of *kowairo setsumei* was to create a "theatrical illusion." If the *kowairo* dubbing was not synchronized with the pictures, the effect was lost. Hearing the voice of a young peasant girl as the mouth of a burly samurai warrior moved on the screen did not engender a diegetic illusion. Glaring mistakes such as this caused a few critics to declare that, "reading from scripts should be eliminated."[93]

Given the problems that reading one's *setsumei* could produce, very few *benshi* actually read their scripts word for word. Most just used them as a guide they could consult from time to time. Each performance, therefore, tended to be slightly different. Although the basic structure of a *benshi*'s *setsumei* for a particular film remained the same from performance to performance, the phraseology, emphasis, and tone differed. I present three versions of Satomi Yoshirō's *Tsubaki hime* (*Camille*) *setsumei* alongside one another, so that the reader can see how each rendition of a particular *setsumei* remained fundamentally the same, and was nevertheless distinct. This *setsumei* was popular among the intellectuals of the time.

Winter has come. It is the last day of a passing year. Silently, it becomes colder. Her body thins day by day.		Winter has come. It is the last day of a passing year. Silently, it becomes colder. Her body thins day by day.
"My breathing appears to be blocked. Nanine, could you please open that window and leave it open? Wow, all of a sudden it has begun snowing heavily.		"Could you please open this window? Wow, all of a sudden it has begun to snow heavily.
"Today is the last day of December. I wonder how he is?"		"Today is the last day of December. It is my friend's wedding day. If only I could move, then I could be celebrating by their side.
Having vaguely heard that Armand, with his wounded chest bandaged, was in Southern Europe's Italy, she wrote her final diary entry to him.		"Armand, I am thinking of you like always as I write this diary entry.
"Since two or three days ago, my condition has seriously changed and because of this I do not think I have long left. Outside the snow is silently falling and I am as lonely as a desolate graveyard.	"Since two or three days ago, my condition has quickly changed and because of this I do not think I have long left. The snow is falling silently outside and I am lonely. There is not a single person by my side.	"Since two or three days ago, my condition has seriously worsened and because of this I believe I do not have long left. Outside it is silently snowing, and it is as lonely as a graveyard.

114

"As I write in this diary entry, there is not a single person by my side. Armand, where are you? I have heard that you are so far away from Paris.	"Armand, as I write this letter, where are you? I have heard that you are so far away from Paris.	
"You have forgotten about me, Marguerite, haven't you? I'm so forlorn.	"You have forgotten about me, Marguerite, haven't you? I'm so forlorn.	"You have already forgotten about me, haven't you? I am so forlorn.
"Even if I die, it will be no loss to the people of the world. I was a useless ornament, a toy, nothing more than a pale, ephemeral, phosphorescent glow. If I die like this, I will have not the littlest regret. In this lonely life of mine, I am thankful to you for making such happy times, and I will never forget what you did for me.	"But within this lonely lifetime, you gave me some happy times. I will never forget your kindness. I have already confessed about what I did sometime ago in my last letter to you. It seems that people consider everything a woman like myself says as a lie.	"As a woman, I was a useless decoration, a boring toy, nothing more than a pale, ephemeral, phosphorescent glow. If I die like this, I will have not the smallest regret. In this lonely life of mine, I am thankful to you for making such happy times, and I will never forget what you did for me.
"My death will make it very clear to you the deeds I did sometime ago.	"Soon happiness awaits me in death, so I gladly pray for that.	"My death will make it very clear to you the deeds I did sometime ago.
"As I have been writing, breathing has become even more difficult. Armand, please return to my side just one more time, I can't wait any longer. I've begun to cough, red blood is coming out. No, I am happy. I'm really happy."	"As I have been writing, breathing has become even more difficult. Armand, please come back. Please come back quickly. I can't wait any longer. I've begun to cough—ugly, red blood is coming out.	"As I have been writing, breathing has become even more difficult. Armand, please return to my side just one more time."

While the pen was moving, many creditors had jostled together by her side.	"No one is looking after me, yet by my side many creditors have gathered."	While the pen was moving, many creditors had jostled together by her side.
Lionized as the most beautiful belle of Paris and called the Camellia Princess, Marguerite Gautier would not be meeting Armand again, for she is now quietly, quietly on her way to heaven.[94]	Lionized as the most beautiful belle of Paris and called the Camellia Princess, Marguerite Gautier, would not be meeting Armand—who was rushing back—again, because she was finally and ephemerally going to heaven.	Lionized as the most beautiful belle of Paris and called the Camellia Princes, Marguerite Gautier would not be meeting Armand—who is rushing back to see her—again, for she is now quietly, quietly climbing up to heaven.[95]
	Alexandre Dumas' masterpiece literary work, the brutal *Camille*, is concluded.[96]	

If a *benshi* wanted to perform well, he had to prepare. To provide quality *setsumei*, *benshi* needed to understand the complete story, background, setting, and characters of the movie. Unless he was exceptionally smart and talented, he could not simply rely on previewing the film and reading the script provided by the distributor. He had to do additional research and preparation; otherwise, his *setsumei* would suffer. *Benshi* had to think about what they wanted to say in their *setsumei*. They had to make sure that their *setsumei* fit the film and that it would appeal to the audience. Many *benshi* searched libraries or asked scholars for information about certain objects, places, and ideas contained within the motion pictures. If the film was based on a literary classic, then the *benshi*, if he was diligent, read the original work, or, at the very least, skimmed it. At one theater, a priest came by every Saturday and talked about the Bible; for foreign film *benshi*, knowing about the Bible was essential, not only for religious movies such as *The Ten Commandments* and *King of Kings*, but for other movies as well.[97] *Benshi* needed to do extra research, because the details made their *setsumei* more interesting.

When a *benshi* did not prepare well enough, his *setsumei* revealed his ignorance. One *benshi*, who did not research why the actors in a filmed version of *Romeo and Juliet* were all wearing tights, for example, gave the following *setsumei*, "As for the English court at that time, because of financial difficulties, men did not wear pants. They were naked from the waist down."[98] In contrast, Fujinami Mumei, the *benshi* that audiences nicknamed "The Saint" because of his devotion to Buddhism, researched his *setsumei* in incredible detail. He thoroughly examined the geography, historical context, and characters within the films he had to *setsumei*. If Western mountains appeared, he would deviate from the storyline to inform the audience about the mountains.[99]

What is unclear is which type of *setsumei*—accurate or inaccurate—was more prevalent. That critics sometimes chastised *benshi* for blundering indicates that *setsumei* were not always perfect. At the same time, the advice that experts gave *benshi* could itself be deficient. Musō Byōe implored *benshi* to be cognizant of the difference between Western and Japanese customs when providing *setsumei* for foreign films, because, if one did not understand these differences, then one could not provide *setsumei*. To exemplify his assertion, Muso writes about the differences between Japanese and Western husbands. "In Japan, husbands are autocratic; however, in Western culture, there is no autocratic husband. Rather, in the West, a husband is enslaved to work for the benefit of his wife."[100] If a *benshi* gave this *setsumei*, some might argue that it was incorrect; others would argue that it was correct. Determining the accuracy of a *benshi*'s *setsumei*, therefore, was often subjective. Consequently, one must assess criticisms of inaccurate *setsumei* judiciously.

The high salaries and wild lifestyle of many *benshi* lured people from all walks of life into the profession. After paying one's dues as an apprentice for 6 months to 2 years, luck and skill determined whether one would succeed as a *benshi*. For many, the demands of the job were too overwhelming, and they quickly burned out. Aside from the introduction of talkies in the 1930s, however, nothing the *benshi* had to endure at work was as menacing as the twin attacks from the government and reformers that took place during the Taishō period.

6

GOVERNMENTAL ATTEMPTS
TO CONTROL THE *BENSHI*

During the late Meiji period, as motion pictures became increasingly popular and assumed a dominant role in entertaining the public, concerns grew over their effect on society. Some claimed—as many do today—that movies were having a detrimental impact on public morality and therefore warranted governmental control. The debate over cinema heated up in 1911, as a furor broke out over the French serial *Zigomar*. The first installment premiered at the Tokyo Kinryūkan on November 11, 1911.

The serial was based on the story of police detective Polin's efforts to capture Zigomar, the master criminal of a hundred disguises. In each episode, Zigomar miraculously managed to elude capture. The following *setsumei* by Yamano Ichirō recreates an atmosphere for this important film and demonstrates the nature of serial film *setsumei*.

> The screen is now black—pitch black, in fact—as the trees and plants sleep in the dead of the night. As they said in the past, it is the bewitching hour. A flash. Were those the eyes of a giant serpent? No, that's not it. What it is will surprise you. It is a great invention of human labor. A modern convenience. It's a flash-

light—flash, flash, unrestricted and free. Under cover of darkness, one suspicious-looking person in black clothes is stealing into the vault of the Bank of Paris. Secretly, surreptitiously, stealthily on tiptoes, it's the menacing man of Paris, the one who instills fear, the leader of the Z-group, none other than Zigomar. He's just about to. . . If he can just get the vault open. . . Suddenly. . . Zigomar is cornered, as the night watchman unexpectedly jumps out. Expecting Zigomar would come, Polin had carefully made plans and disguised himself beforehand. In the dark, where one cannot recognize anything nearby, Justice and Injustice scuffle together in a great fist-fight of personal combat.

(Musical interlude)

Suddenly the lights came on. It is truly scary, for where is Zigomar?!?! Polin looks out the open window; the moonlight faintly falls on the pavement; there a black figure is dashing away. You scoundrel! The fleeing figure is none other than Zigomar. Polin screams, "Wait!" But Zigomar is not that stupid. He runs swiftly, without answering. At a Paris train stop, he nimbly jumps onto the train. The steam whistle blows. Next stop, Shinbashi.[1] If only it was such a carefree situation. Thundering loudly, the train rushes along the rails. Only one step behind—how very vexing. Wait! Look! With lightning speed, detective Polin nimbly, in a death-defying stunt, gets on the rapidly moving train. Hey, you rascal Zigomar. You coward. I am detective Polin, so you better come out, come out wherever you are. Surprised and astonished at the enormity of being discovered, Zigomar quickly climbs onto the roof of the train. Polin follows. There, on top of the speeding train, the two are once again fiercely wrestling in violent combat.

(Musical interlude)

However, regrettably, Polin is unable to subdue Zigomar. In an instant, Polin falls off. Sadly, he is seriously hurt. He was like a moth approaching a candle. Reveling in his success, the rascal Zigomar cynically laughs in the eye of the fallen detective Polin. Where is the train going that Zigomar is on? What will be detective Polin's fate? Unfortunately, this week's episode has come to an end.[2]

What frightened people throughout the world about *Zigomar* was the glorification of crime through the character of an upper-class criminal. Critics in Japan asserted that *Zigomar* films were corrupting the morals of youth who imitated and mimicked their hero, Zigomar. Motion pictures began serving as a scapegoat for those who sought to blame something for the ills of society. On October 5, 1912, the *Tokyo Asahi shinbun* launched a multi-part editorial attacking the *Zigomar* films. A week after the editorials began, the Japanese authorities banned *Zigomar* and all similar films.[3]

The increased attention that the *Zigomar* debate brought to the medium eventually resulted in increased governmental controls on cinema. When moving pictures first entered Japan, the medium fell under the same legislation that regulated public shows (*misemono*).[4] Not until the end of the Meiji era did prefectural governments start debating the need for legislation aimed specifically at motion pictures and their exhibition. A significant part of the new legislation focused on controlling the *benshi*.

Many authorities believed that, since *benshi* were interpreters of images, they could potentially be a dangerous and harmful influence on spectators. They believed it was essential that the *setsumei* for the moving images be delivered in a virtuous manner. The authorities understood that spectators needed help in understanding films. They hoped that, with proper guidance supplied by the *benshi*, audiences would interpret movies in an ethical way. If a film like *Zigomar* glorified evil, then the *benshi* had to ensure that his *setsumei* glorified good, so that the audience would leave the theater with an appropriate impression. The government tried to regulate and control the *benshi*, to guarantee that they provided only proper *setsumei* that would help audiences read films in a correct and sanctioned fashion. Governmental actions were supported and influenced by a reform movement, known as the Pure Film Movement (*jun'eigageki undō*), which sought to purify Japanese cinema of its anachronisms. The Pure Film Movement is examined in the next chapter.

Benshi Examinations and Licensing

Benshi played a central role in interpreting motion pictures, and some officials felt it crucial that *benshi* provide *setsumei* in an ethically appropriate manner. Not all *benshi* emphasized the righteous aspects of a particular story, even when the plot was moral. Many believed, therefore, that the state needed to control the *benshi*, to ensure that they provided ethical *setsumei*. One critic worried that, even with "an especially good movie, a *benshi* can corrupt an audience."[5] Moreover, although some viewed the wild and hedonistic life that many *benshi* lived with envy, others viewed it as a plague on society that needed to be cured. Concerned over *setsumei* being excessively perverse, female fans chasing after *benshi*, and other influential effects of *setsumei*, the authorities in various parts of the country began instituting regulations aimed at controlling the *benshi*. Film companies, concerned members of the public, and even some *benshi* who felt that the excessively wild antics of a few were denigrating the good name of the profession, supported the government's actions. The primary weapons used to keep base and vulgar people out of the profession, and to ensure that *benshi* gave befitting *setsumei*, were governmental licensing and testing. The authorities hoped that licensing would ensure the good character and intelligence of *benshi* and improve the content of *setsumei*. As one critic put it, "It is said that a foolish person can mislead ten thousand people. Licensing will correct audiences' misunderstandings and allow them to understand correctly."[6]

In spite of the remonstrations over *Zigomar* and the subsequent calls for controlling the *benshi*, almost all prefectures dallied in passing comprehensive and enforceable legislation that governed *benshi*. Occasionally, prefectures issued internal guidelines (*naiki*) for controlling *benshi*, but they were closer to recommendations than stringent laws. In Osaka, the *Katsudō shashin torishimari naiki* (*Motion Picture Regulation Guidelines*), issued in July 1911, forbade those *benshi* from performing who had committed illegal acts. The guidelines also "banned" certain kinds of *setsumei* and movies, such as those that dealt with adultery, revealed how to commit criminal acts, could induce children to be mischievous, or were labeled immoral. Nevertheless, these were only "guidelines" and the police never strictly enforced them.[7]

One of the most significant pieces of silent era legislation directed at motion pictures was the 1917 Tokyo *Keishichō meirei 12 gō: katsudō shashin kōgyōjō torishimari kisoku* (*Metropolitan Police Order No. 12: Rules and Regulations Governing the Exhibition of Motion Pictures*). Contained within this ordinance were a variety of regulations. They prohibited the use of barkers, required that fresh air be circulated into the theater for at least 5 minutes every half hour, and stipulated that, "whenever an inspector from the police station wants to inspect a show, the movie theater must supply him with a seat."[8]

Concerned that virtuous girls could be attacked by mashers inside the darkened theaters, sections of the law also stipulated that men and women sit separately.[9] The authorities applied the law only to cinema houses and not traditional playhouses, because they viewed cinema as a more base and dangerous form of entertainment. The segregation of the sexes lasted until 1931.

The 1917 law also divided movies into two categories: "open to all" and "no one under fifteen permitted."[10] Worried over the effects that movies like *Zigomar* were having on children, the authorities wanted to ensure that children did not see potentially deleterious films, by prohibiting their access to them. As with gender segregation, this ordinance applied to cinema alone; the police did not issue similar regulations for the theater. Cinema owners and managers vociferously opposed this regulation, because it cut into their business. Children made up a large part of the motion picture audience, and, under the new regulations, most films were classified as "no one under fifteen permitted." Opposition by the movie industry and fans forced the police to repeal this segment of the 1917 regulation in November 1919.

For *benshi*, the most important aspect of the 1917 ordinance was the mandate for a *benshi* licensing system.[11] Article 20 reads, "A person who wishes to *setsumei* motion pictures in front of the public must submit a resume and apply through the local metropolitan police station for a license (*menkyō*)."[12] Just as one needed a license to practice law or medicine, henceforth, a *benshi* needed a license to perform *setsumei*.

Initially, to receive a *benshi* license from the police, a prospective applicant had to submit a resume. The police then ran—or at least, they were supposed to run—a background check on the candidate before issuing the license, which was valid for 3 years. During the inaugural registration period in August 1917, one official speculated that about 80% of those *benshi* currently working would be granted a license; the police would prohibit the other 20%, or roughly 145 *benshi*, from performing *setsumei* in front of an audience.[13] Confirming or denying this statement is impossible, based on the extant data. Nevertheless, evidence indicates that the Tokyo Metropolitan Police did prevent some *benshi* from performing in Tokyo.

Ideally, a Tokyo *benshi* would no longer be able to earn a living without an affirmation from the authorities of the "impeccability of his ethical character."[14] According to Article 26, any *benshi* who provided *setsumei* that was "harmful to public safety and public morals," or who conducted himself in a "dubious and inappropriate manner," would have his license revoked.[15] Lest a *benshi* forget this, the authorities often printed it on the actual license. On Hasegawa Shōichi's Hiroshima license, item six, under "Matters that Require Attention," states, "If, through words or actions, a *setsumeisha*, when doing *setsumei*, is perceived to threaten or harm public safety and morals, or if improper conduct or other improprieties are perceived, we have the right to order the *setsumeisha* to stop performing and can revoke this license."[16]

Ideals, however, are often hard to achieve. Licensing raised the overall quality of *benshi*, but it did not eliminate all the scoundrels. Popular *benshi* were stars, and, as with celebrities today, the authorities frequently had difficulty controlling and disciplining them. One of the reasons that *benshi* licensing was sometimes ineffectual was because many of the *benshi* who were governed by the regulations disliked them. The trial of the *benshi* Minamikaijin (Hirota Kiichi) is a testament to that distaste and reveals the ambivalence that some *benshi* held for the licensing system. On October 24, 1922, the police inspector at the Tokyo Ushigomekan theater fined Minamikaijin 1 yen for performing without his license. Minamikaijin was indignant and hired a lawyer to fight the charge. He claimed that he had a license, but that he left it at home that day. The light fine did not bother Minamikaijin. What troubled him was the persecution of the *benshi*. Minamikaijin argued that, since *benshi* were custodians of a popular art form, the regulations covering *benshi* were out of date, ridiculous, and harsh.[17] Nevertheless, despite remonstrations like Minamikaijin's, and other minor acts of *benshi* defiance, licensing helped the authorities gain some control over the majority of *benshi*.

The licensing, after conducting a background check, was only the initial step in the government's efforts to control *benshi* and improve their character. The next step was to require all *benshi* to pass a written examination. Although people had talked about testing when the licensing system was first implemented in 1917, it did not begin until the summer of 1920. After August 1920, each Tokyo *benshi* had to pass a written examination that tested both "academic subjects" and "common knowledge," before he could receive his license. Several *benshi* antagonists wrote the following poem in honor of the occasion.

> I'm not very bright,
> So the answers I can't really write.
> Damn! Damn! There is no time!
> Failing this thing doesn't scare me.
> So I'm not frightened, but I don't want to flunk.
> For if I am fired, there won't be any rice,
> And if there is no rice, I won't have a life.
> Nothing, nothing, nothing, I won't have a thing—
> Zippi-di-do-da-zippi-da-ding.[18]

The Tokyo Metropolitan Police administered the first *benshi* licensing examination on August 6, 1920. The first question on the exam asked *benshi* to explain "what effect motion picture *setsumei* has upon an audience." The next question required that *benshi* "write down the articles of the *Rules and Regula-*

tions Governing the Exhibition of Motion Pictures that they knew." In the third and final part of the examination, applicants had to elucidate the following terms: "public safety and public morals," "the Yellow Peril," and "rewarding good and punishing evil."[19] Subsequent tests all asked similar questions, with particular emphasis placed on an understanding of the effect *benshi* and their *setsumei* have on an audience, and on knowledge of the laws governing *benshi*. In this way, the government strove to ensure that *benshi* were cognizant of the important role that they played in society, that they understood the responsibility that came with their position, and that they continually bore in mind the laws implemented to control them.

During the first examinations in August 1920, several of the applicants fainted, and a few female candidates burst out in tears, from the stress. Among those who did not pass the inaugural examination was the consummate *kowairo benshi* Tsuchiya Shōtō. Yet, despite the fact that he reportedly got a zero on the exam, he still received his license, because he was such a highly regarded master of the art of *kowairo setsumei*.[20] In licensing Tsuchiya and others who failed the examination, the Tokyo Metropolitan Police undermined the stringency of the law. Moreover, according to some accounts, it was easy for established *benshi* to cheat on the exam.[21] What these examples show is that, during this period of relative political liberalism in Japan, the government's approach to some segments of society was much stricter and more oppressive on paper than it was in reality. There were ways to circumvent the law without landing in any trouble, especially if one was famous.

Over the years, there were many *benshi* who failed the examination and consequently did not obtain a license. In this way, the authorities forced dozens, if not hundreds, of *benshi* out of the profession. As the number who failed the licensing examination mounted, editorials from *benshi* advocates and opponents appeared in newspapers and trade journals. This cleansing of the profession pleased the foes of the *benshi*. Opponents asserted that the examinations proved that the *benshi* were ill-trained and stupid. One critic wrote, "Most *katsuben* could not answer the questions on the *katsuben* test that any twelve- or thirteen-year-old could answer."[22] The author used the derogatory term *katsuben* to emphasize his disdain for the profession.

One anonymous advocate of the *benshi* countered that the problem lay with the test. *Benshi* did poorly, with none earning a perfect score on the exam, because the questions were too ambiguous. Question one asked, "What effect does movie *setsumei* have on an audience?" According to the *benshi* supporter, this question was so broad and nebulous that it was like asking what effect the sun has on the earth. The adherent continued his criticism of the test by pointing out that, although everyone in Japan used the terms "public safety and public morals" and "rewarding good and punishing evil," remarkably few people could adequately define them. Asking the *benshi* to do so, then ridiculing them for not being able to, he concluded, was unjust.[23] Iwatō Shisetsu scoffed at the critics of *benshi* with the following words: "If there was a test for politicians and many failed, I do not think all politicians would be forced to quit. It would be problematic to expel so many politicians just because of their test results. We can say the same thing about the large number of *benshi* who failed their test."[24]

The *benshi* testing and licensing system lasted until the end of the silent era in many parts of Japan. It was not until 1936 that the Tokyo Metropolitan Police finally terminated the Tokyo licensing system.[25] A few years earlier, in 1930, the Tokyo Metropolitan Police declared that, as of September 1930, all licenses would be good forever.[26] To protect the current *benshi* from losing their jobs, they made the test for new applicants even more difficult.[27] In 1931, only about 25% of those who took the test passed it.[28] The authorities also updated the test to reflect the changing mood of the nation. Here are two of the multiple-choice questions that appeared on one test from the 1930s:

1. The left-wing movement is:
   a. A partial movement, not with two parts, but with only one part.
   b. A type of physical exercise.
   c. An opposition movement.

    2. A government or study group newspaper (*kikan shinbun*)
      a. Writes about electrical motorcars.
      b. A civilization newspaper. A speed newspaper.
      c. A newspaper that society is permitted to see.

If a *benshi* marked the wrong answer, either through carelessness or ignorance, he not only failed the exam, but also incurred a good deal of unnecessary trouble with the government.[29]

After Tokyo enacted *Metropolitan Police Order No. 12*, several other prefectures established similar licensing regulations. In 1918, Aichi prefecture passed a piece of legislation that was nearly identical to Tokyo's 1917 ordinance.[30] By 1921, 11 prefectures had *benshi* licensing systems, some with testing, others without.[31] As of 1926, 15 prefectures had implemented a testing and licensing system, 14 had a simple background check licensing system, and 18 others had no licensing requirement.[32] By January 1932, 26 prefectures had testing and licensing, 13 had background check licensing, and only 9 did not require a license to perform *setsumei*.[33]

A *benshi* needed a license for each prefecture in which he wished to perform. Some *benshi* had licenses from several prefectures. If a *benshi* failed to obtain a license in one prefecture, or if the prefectural police prohibited him from performing in their prefecture, his only legal choice was to try to obtain a license from another prefecture or move to a prefecture that did not require a license. For this reason, in 1926 the Home Ministry discussed plans to centralize *benshi* testing and licensing under its authority. These discussions, however, never materialized into actual legislation. Licensing remained under the jurisdiction of prefectural governments throughout the silent era.

In Tokyo, both *kowairo benshi* and foreign film *benshi* had to pass the same examination. Each passed under the same police scrutiny and received identical licenses. In trade journals, people wrote about the need to license *kowairo benshi* and foreign film *benshi* separately, because they each needed to know different things. *Kowairo benshi*, for example, did not need to know where

Rumania, Nikolayevsk, or Los Angeles were (actual questions from the second Tokyo exam) in order to provide *kowairo* dialogue for Japanese period dramas.[34] Despite repeated remonstrations, Tokyo police continued to issue a universal *benshi* license. In Osaka, the prefectural police noted how many *kowairo benshi* and foreign film *benshi* took their examination. They also announced that those who did poorly on the exam should limit themselves to *kowairo setsumei*. However, whether the Osaka police issued separate licenses is unclear.[35]

One applied for a license only when ready to become a full-fledged *benshi*; apprentices did not have to be licensed. A *benshi* had to renew his license every 3 years. In places where passing the examination was a prerequisite for licensing, a *benshi* had to take the examination each time he renewed his license. The authorities, however, were often more demanding of new applicants. *Benshi* who already possessed a license could do poorly on the examination and still renew their license, but a prospective *benshi* had to do well on the test to receive his initial license.

Benshi objected to being forced to pass an examination once every 3 years, especially given that other professionals, such as doctors and lawyers, only had to pass a test once. One *benshi* commented that becoming a *benshi* was more difficult than becoming a lawyer, because lawyers only had to pass one examination, and *benshi* had to pass an exam once every 3 years.[36] *Benshi* also complained that having to pass a written exam was unfair, since they earned their living vocally. Moreover, they asserted that testing their academic knowledge was not a good determinant of how skilled they were at *setsumei*. A genius could kill a film with poor *setsumei*; an academic failure could give awe-inspiring *setsumei* to a bad film. For *benshi*, *setsumei* was an art that required artistic talent, not testable knowledge. Even if a *benshi* passed the test and received a government license, his success depended on his skill in impressing his audience. As one observer noted, "Skill is much more important than knowledge."[37]

Initially, *benshi* were the only performers whom prefectural governments screened, tested, and licensed. All other narrative artists and entertainers could perform without a license. The government originally licensed *benshi* alone, because it viewed them as having a greater influence on society than other entertainers. Testing and licensing validated the *benshi* and confirmed their cultural importance as the true mediators of cinematic understanding.

In 1921, the Tokyo Metropolitan Police enacted *Keishichō meidai 15 gō: kōgyōjō oyobi kōgyō torishimari kisoku (Metropolitan Police Order No. 15: Rules and Regulations Governing Entertainment Establishments and the Entertainment Industry)*. This new piece of legislation updated the 1917 *Order No. 12* and was the first comprehensive piece of entertainment industry legislation since *Police Order No. 41* became law in 1900. Under *Order No. 15*, all performers (*gigeisha*) henceforth had to be licensed. What is most significant about this new ordinance is the government's placement of *benshi* into a category separate from all other performers. Article 76 states, "A performer (*gigeisha*) is defined as a person whose vocation is to appear in and perform in theatrical performances (*engeki kōgyō*), spectacles/sideshows (*misemono kōgyō*), and vaudeville (*engei kōgyō*). A *benshi* (*setsumeisha*) is defined as a person whose vocation is to appear in motion picture entertainment and *setsumei* motion pictures."[38] Articles 77 through 80 detailed the rules and regulations governing the licensing of performers; Articles 81 through 87 governed the *benshi*. The rules and regulations governing performers and *benshi* were virtually identical, although those applied to *benshi* were slightly more stringent. The regulations pertaining particularly to *benshi* were much more specific in requiring that a *benshi* keep the police informed about where he was working and that the *benshi* to whom the authorities issued a license always carry his license, and no one else's, with him when he performed. The authorities prohibited *benshi* from performing without their license on their person, but other performers were not subject to such a regulation.

The government deemed it necessary to single out *benshi* and to write separate articles within the legislation specifically for them, because they regarded motion pictures and *setsumei* as highly influential. Because it was the *benshi*'s job to help the audience to interpret the moving images, it was imperative that *benshi* elucidate them in a manner the government deemed appropriate. Thus, to assure that the *benshi* providing *setsumei* at a particular theater was sanctioned and licensed by the police, the police enacted regulations that specifically kept track of individual *benshi*. In the eyes of the state, *benshi* were not just performers, they were something more: They were highly influential social educators.

Benshi as Social Educators

In 1909, the *benshi* Eda Fushiki wrote, "*Setsumeisha* must be cognizant of the fact that they are social educators (*shakai no kyoikusha*). . . . Now that I am a *setsumeisha*, I try to give morally upright *setsumei*: *setsumei* with an educational value."[39] By 1917, writers compared the importance of *benshi* as social educators with that of teachers as school educators and fathers as family educators.[40] A few years later, one editorial went so far as to say that *benshi* were more important than school teachers, because they educated more of the public than teachers did.[41] A few people argued that *benshi* were not social educators, but rather, entertainers, since cinema entertains and does not educate. Nevertheless, to most observers, *benshi* taught, sitting next to the silver screen, as surely as teachers instructed in front of a blackboard.

In 1920, some people began calling on the Ministry of Education to fund a school to train *benshi* to be appropriate social educators skilled in the art of *setsumei*. Although the ministry never established such a school, it did try to mold the character and intellect of the *benshi*, so that *benshi* conformed to the government's ideals about what a social educator should be. The government was also worried about the effect motion pictures was having on the public, and they wanted to ensure that, in the future, the effect would be as positive as possible. During February 21–28, 1921, the Ministry of Education sponsored the first "*Setsumeisha* Training Symposium" in Tokyo.[42] Representative *benshi* from theaters throughout the nation attended, as did members of the Ministry of Education and other officials. *Benshi* hoped that, by working and cooperating with the government in symposia such as this, they would be able to alleviate the mounting pressures from the state and from critics. Speakers gave lectures on topics that included "Public Virtue and Modern Trends of Thought," "Social Education and Motion Pictures," and "*Setsumeisha* and the Public."[43] On the last day, there was a grand performance in which all the *benshi* in attendance participated.

As they discussed the important role *benshi* played as intermediaries between the film and the audience, lecturers at the symposium summarized many of the ideas that had been circulating in the trade journals over the previous several years. Lecturers noted that it was important for *benshi*, as intermediaries, to act responsibly and to *setsumei* in an appropriate fashion. Lecturers also propounded specific techniques and approaches that they wanted the *benshi* to follow.

One participant stressed the need for *benshi* to adhere to the one film–one meaning (*ichiga ichigi*) theory, which said that each film had only one overriding theme running through it and that it was imperative that the *benshi* stick to that one central idea. Neither *benshi* nor the audience should have two contrary ideas about the picture. If there was a forking point in the movie, the *benshi* must choose "the right way" by adhering to the one film–one meaning precept. If, for example, a scene in a motion picture appeared socialistic, but the overall plot is not about socialism, a *benshi* must not veer off into any socialistic dialogue, but rather must stay focused on the principal idea of the movie.[44] The problem with this theory was finding that "one true meaning." Ideally, filmmakers made films with only one meaning, yet this was rarely the case. They often endowed each scene with two or three meanings. Hence, spectators could interpret motion pictures in myriad ways. By claiming that there was only one appropriate way to interpret a lengthy movie, authorities were making a fanciful attempt at trying to control the minds of the masses. Filmmakers continued to make complex movies, and *benshi* continued to *setsumei* them with complex interpretations.

In one exceptionally nationalistic speech, the speaker argued that education outside the classroom was extremely important and that *benshi* occupied the central position in that education. He expounded on his belief that the Japanese were insular people and needed to learn about the outside world, especially about the United States, if they were going to become a strong nation. Since the Meiji Restoration of 1868, Japan had striven to "catch-up" to the West militarily and economically. During the Meiji era, Japanese traveled throughout the world, studying the outside world and bringing back to Japan what they perceived to be "the best of the West." By the 1920s, Japan had "caught up" in many ways. Yet, as the words of this participant indicate, many Japanese still felt that there was more they needed to learn. "In order to advance into the future, we need to educate our youth. Advancing into the future is going to be a desperate struggle both militarily and nonmilitarily. We are all going to have to struggle and fight together, including us social educators [i.e., you *benshi*]."[45]

Tachibana Takahirō, the head censor for the Metropolitan Police Censorship Department, commanded *benshi* not to give obscene *setsumei* or to describe sexual matters in detail. He also instructed *benshi* to make sure that during their *setsumei* they did not inform the audience about how a criminal in a movie committed his crimes. Moreover, he suggested that *benshi* not give excessively detailed *setsumei*, because when a *benshi* talked continually he increased his chance of slipping censored ideas into his *setsumei*. Tachibana also cautioned against editorializing. He contended that editorial comments could mislead the audience. To elucidate this argument, he cited the example of a *benshi* who gave the following *setsumei*. "The foreign minister said that, as for the League of Nations, the intimacy deepens daily and that no international problems have arisen; however, at the peace conference, America insisted on armament limitation, with herself greatly increasing the size of her navy. *Japan now perceives this as nothing less than her own destruction!*" This enticed a blue-collar worker to scream out in rough language, "Who are these damned Yankees?" In this instance, Tachibana maintained, the *benshi* caused problems by going beyond simply explaining what appeared on the screen.[46]

Tachibana, among others, also entreated *benshi* not to circumvent censorship by giving *setsumei* that negated what the censors were trying to do. In Ta-

134

chibana's opinion, there were two reasons why a *benshi* tried to undermine the censors: Either the *benshi* did not study the film or he was thinking only about pleasing the audience in a manner that would endear him to them, thus increasing his popularity and wealth. Tachibana then went on to give specific examples of how *benshi* circumvented censorship. Several *benshi*, for example, came straight out and said, "Sections of this film you are about to watch are difficult to understand, because they have been censored." Obviously, when a *benshi* did this, censorship became undermined. Others tried to reinsert through their *setsumei* scenes that the censors had cut. According to Tachibana, although some *benshi* complained that films were difficult to understand after he and his fellow censors cut them apart, if a *benshi* clearly outlined the story in his *maesetsu*, it would not be that difficult to understand.

Government Censorship

The censorship of motion pictures in Japan was always much more severe than the censorship of any other form of mass entertainment. The state always considered cinema more influential and potentially more dangerous. When asked by a *benshi* why censors cut scenes out of motion pictures, but allowed the same scenes to remain in plays identical to the film, a censor replied, "Because plays are shown in bright theaters on a large stage, the audience's attention is spread out and is not focused on one place. Motion pictures, on the other hand, are shown in dark theaters. The offending scenes are blown up, are bright, and the audience focuses only on them. Consequently, motion pictures give a deeper impression."[47]

One could also argue that the authorities focused on motion pictures because cinema was the foremost form of mass entertainment. Within 6 years of entering Japan, motion pictures had captured 26% of the theater entertainment market. By 1912, the last year of the Meiji period, that figure had risen to 57%, and by 1925 it had risen to 71%.[48] In 1931, one foreign commentator observed, "Motion pictures are like opium to the Japanese."[49] For those concerned with maintaining public morals and public safety, such a popular, powerful, and intoxicating medium needed supervision and controls.

The censoring of cinema was not something limited to Japan. Concerned citizens in New York, London, Paris, and throughout the world were just as worried as those in Tokyo that films that showed thieves, loose women, drinking, gambling, and other immoral acts were a bad influence on spectators, especially the young. The uproar of the righteous over cinema's role and influence in society forced governments and filmmakers to try to regulate the medium. Although the arguments were often the same, the criteria and methods that the film industry and governments used in censoring cinema varied from place to place. In Japan, efforts to censor the *benshi* were integrated with efforts to censor the films they described.

From the very first exhibitions of moving pictures in 1896, police throughout Japan had the authority to censor films. According to the 1891 *Police Order No. 15: Rules and Regulations Governing Public Entertainments*, the police could prohibit any show that contained "obscene articles, arts, and other such things that are deemed harmful to public morals."[50] To safeguard the public against moving images and *setsumei* that might be detrimental to public morals, police could inspect and halt any exhibition that violated the law and that any officer deemed offensive.[51] Under the mandate of this law, any patrol officer walking his beat could enter a theater at any time and immediately censor a film.

Before the 1917 *Order No. 12* came into law, censorship in Tokyo varied from ward to ward, and often censor to censor, officer to officer. *Order No. 12* established the model that a number of prefectures followed. This regulation centralized censorship under prefectural control. Nevertheless, censorship varied from prefecture to prefecture, and every time a film moved to a new prefecture, that prefecture's police censored it. Hence, one could watch a film in six different prefectures and on each occasion watch the film slowly dwindle away.

In 1925, *Home Ministry Decree No. 10: Motion Picture (Film) Censorship Regulations* nationalized motion picture censorship under the jurisdiction of the

Home Ministry. Henceforth, exhibitors had to pay the Home Ministry to censor the film at a rate of 5 sen for 3 meters of film. This worked out to about 5 yen per film. Once the Home Ministry stamped a film with its seal of approval, which was valid for 3 years, the film could circulate around the nation without further censoring. Movies no longer had to gain approval every time they moved to a new prefecture. However, under the new system it was no longer possible to see an uncensored or less-censored film.

The basic criteria used in censoring a film were obscenity, cruelty or brutality, immorality, lèse-majesté, and anything else that fell under the rubric of "public safety and public morals." In Japan, this included kissing scenes. Although mixed bathing was an accepted practice in Japan, and although the government garnered income from licensed prostitution, most motion picture censors in Japan feared that kissing scenes would have an undue influence on public morality. Consequently, censors usually excised kissing scenes.

Japanese censors also inspected the scripts that film companies distributed to *benshi*. During the 1910s, censors often ascertained the propriety of a motion picture, based on the *benshi* script. Before a *benshi* received a script, which contained little more than the title, cast, a brief summary, and a transcript of the intertitles, either the prefectural censor or the Home Ministry had to stamp it with their seal, for example, "Passed Inspection by the Aichi Prefecture Public Security Department." Some prefectural censors also stamped "Text Not Harmful" onto the script. The problem with censoring *benshi* scripts was that *setsumei* was not simply a verbatim reading of the script. *Benshi* used the scripts as a base upon which to build their poetic rhetoric. Therefore, to guarantee that *benshi* and their *setsumei* did not adversely affect the spectators, the police employed more direct means of supervision and restraint.

Police officers patrolled the theater district, and any officer in uniform could enter a movie free of charge. Situated in the back of Japanese cinema houses was a seat or box with a placard in front of it that read "Inspector's Seat." This is where the inspector, or an officer who happened into the theater, sat, to ensure that the film, *benshi*, and audience maintained public morals and safety. If a *benshi* said anything inappropriate, the inspector would interrupt the performance and verbally warn the *benshi*. If the *benshi* continued in an improper manner, the inspector would halt the performance. From his seat on stage, however, a *benshi* could instantly tell whether or not an officer was sitting in the specially marked area within the darkened theater and thus knew when not to say anything that might land him in trouble. On occasion, the *benshi* Hayashi Tempū liked to vex the inspector by pointing into the audience during his *maesetsu* and declaring, "There is a dead body over there!" After the officer jumped up in astonishment and looked around, Tempū would continue, ". . . said the mysterious gentleman who lodged the complaint in the movie you are about to see."[52]

As with the licensing of *benshi* prior to 1925, censorship of *benshi* and *setsumei* varied regionally. In some areas of the country, police prohibited *benshi* from using certain words in their *setsumei*. The Osaka police forbid the following words: *masuizai* (anesthesia), *hakuretsuyaku* (explosive), *yūkai* (kidnapping), *gōdatsu gōkan* (pillage and rape), *kakumei* (revolution), *seppu* or *kissu* (kiss), and *dorobō* (burglar). To get around this proscription, *benshi* used euphemisms such as *nemuri kusuri* (sleeping medicine), *atsuki kuchi zuke* (hot mouth touching), and *kano akkan* (that scoundrel).[53]

If a *benshi* made an unfortunate slip of the tongue while providing *setsumei*, the police would either reprimand him, fine him, revoke his license, or throw him in jail. A tale that accurately reflects both the censorial and *benshi* milieus at the end of the Taishō period appears in a sequence of scenes from the 1957 film *Katsuben monogatari* (*The Tale of the Benshi*), which revolve around the *setsumei* "Ishikawa Goemon and Crown Prince Hirohito." In *The Tale of the Benshi*, a young apprentice named Chiba Juntarō has to provide *setsumei* for a newsreel of Crown Prince Hirohito's 1921 trip to Europe. In reality, these films premiered at several special public showings held in parks throughout the nation with upwards of 150,000 people in attendance. They were the most sensational newsreels ever shown in Japan up to that time. Fortunately for Chiba, he did not have to provide *setsumei* for such a large crowd. At one point in the newsreel, the crown prince looked around at the beautiful scenery. As he took in the scenery, Chiba announced, "My, what a glorious view." These words may seem rather innocuous, but the phrase was deeply associated with Ishikawa Goemon (d. 1594), a master thief who was repeatedly glorified in *kabuki* and *bunraku* plays, as well as in *rakugo* yarns. Immediately after the apprentice uttered these words, the theater inspector halted the performance and dragged Chiba off to jail. For putting the words of an infamous thief into the future emperor's mouth, the government charged Chiba with committing lèse-majesté and sentenced him to 29 days in jail.[54]

The Japanese authorities kept a close eye on cinema throughout the Japanese empire. Shin Chul is one of the last surviving Korean *benshi*. He was born Shin Byonkyung, in 1925, and as a child he worked as a janitor in a movie theater. When he was fourteen years old, one of the popular *benshi* at the theater was absent, thus providing Shin with a chance to perform. Having watched and listened to *benshi* for years, Shin understood the art of Korean *setsumei*. Shin provided *setsumei* for the Korean film *Arirang* (1926), which was about the March 1, 1919, Independence Incident and Korean resentment of the Japanese occupation. In the last scene of the film, the Korean hero kills a fellow countryman who has been working as a spy for the Japanese. Thereupon, the Japanese police arrest the hero. During this climatic scene, as the hero is being taken away, instead of providing the befitting *setsumei*, "Please take care of my father and sister!" Shin unconsciously inserted his own sentiments as he declared, "*Nippon no keiji yarō*" (You fucking Japanese police!). The Japanese military police (*kenpetai*), who were in the theater to ensure that the audience behaved itself and that the *benshi* did not say anything against the Japanese Empire, stopped the show, took Shin out back, and thrashed him.[55] Despite the anticolonial slant of the story, this movie was also released in Japan, with the title song becoming very popular. Because *benshi* could manipulate how spectators understood the filmic text, Japanese audiences merely thought that *Arirang* was a sad tale about an individual; they did not relate it to the March 1 Independence Incident.[56]

Despite the apparent severity of police rules regarding propriety, *benshi* often gave lewd *setsumei*, without any repercussions. The king of obscene *setsumei* was Ōkura Mitsugi. Ōkura was born into a very poor family. As a child, he never imagined that he would live in a house with *tatami*, because his father—as he saw him—was a lazy, drunken good-for-nothing. As an elementary schoolboy, Ōkura sold *natto* (fermented soybeans), before and after school, to help support his family. He eventually dropped out of school and, after failing at several factory jobs, became a *benshi*. He was only thirteen years old. He worked diligently to perfect his craft and eventually became a top *benshi*. Ōkura was known as the "Chaplin *benshi*," because he dressed up as Charlie Chaplin's Tramp when he provided *setsumei* for Chaplin films.[57] Unlike other *benshi*, who spent their money on *sake* and women, Ōkura saved everything he made. By the time he was twenty-five, he had saved 30,000 yen. He eventually invested all of his money in movie theaters, and by 1935 he owned around 35 theaters—the most owned by any individual in Japan.[58] Ōkura had become a top *benshi* and a movie mogul. After the war, he became the president of the Shintōhō film studio. He even sat next to the crown prince during the 1957 premier of *Meiji Tennō to Nichi-Ro daisensō* (*The Emperor Meiji and the Great Russo-Japanese War*). His is a true rags to riches story. He was also one of the lewdest *benshi*.[59]

But women loved his ribald *setsumei*. According to one report, on the days that Ōkura did not perform at the Meguro Kinema, female attendance was off 60%.[60] Women were often so moved by his *setsumei* that they could not help but put their hands inside their kimonos to satisfy themselves when he performed. In fact, he was so popular with women that geisha paid to go out with him.[61] This despite the fact that (or perhaps because of the fact that) his *setsumei* was extremely explicit. Ōkura gave the following *setsumei* for a scene in which a wife was crying by the side of her deceased husband. As the chaste woman raised her head slightly, Ōkura remarked, "I've become a bit itchy, sleeping alone is so unsatisfying." During the comedy *Odoriko Sari* (*Dancing Sally*), when the virtuous head of an orphanage looked admiringly at the children, Ōkura provided the *setsumei*, "Although they are only twelve- and thirteen-year-old girls, whenever they see a man, they have the urge to do him."[62] Nishimura Korakuten recalls that Ōkura once told him that he was going to give a special *setsumei* for all the ladies who were in attendance that day. According to Korakuten, Ōkura's *setsumei* went something like this: "The big hole is open wide. The man and woman go in and out, in and out, aah, they are spent, they couldn't hold it any more. In the area around the hole weeds are growing luxuriantly."[63] Although the police often reprimanded Ōkura for "harming public morals," they never revoked his license and he continued providing lascivious *setsumei*. Why the police never revoked his license or jailed him is unclear, although his celebrity and wealth may have protected him.

Setsumei such as Ōkura Mitsugi's scared the authorities into enacting governmental controls aimed at preventing *benshi* from providing *setsumei* that might be harmful to public morality. However, given that, throughout the silent era, Ōkura continued to provide lewd *setsumei* that could be considered harmful to public morals, the effectiveness of these rules and regulations comes into question. Evidence indicates that the licensing and examination system improved the intellectual stock of *benshi* and helped keep some disreputable characters out. However, there is also evidence showing that *benshi*, especially top-ranking ones, often ignored the rules. Moreover, the continual remonstrations that appeared in books and magazines indicates that the problem was never eradicated. At a time when the Japanese imperial government was cracking down on left-wing radicals, *benshi* thrived as countercultural heroes who lived life to its hedonistic fullest, while circumventing governmental controls.

7

THE PURE FILM MOVEMENT'S
ATTACK ON THE *BENSHI*

The Need to Reform Japanese Cinema

In addition to the government's assault against *benshi*, they also came under attack from a group of motion picture reformers set on rectifying Japanese cinema. In fact, a major impetus for the state's regulatory actions against the *benshi* was this captious onslaught by a band of filmmakers, fans, reporters, and critics who became known as the Pure Film Movement. The fundamental aim of the Pure Film Movement was to improve Japanese motion pictures and to free them of "impurities" such as *benshi*. While European and American filmmakers were making epics, such as *Anthony and Cleopatra* (1914), *Civilization* (1916), and *Intolerance* (1916), Japanese filmmakers were still producing what many perceived as "low-quality" frivolity, such as Matsunosuke films. Ideally, in order for the Japanese to make movies equal to those produced in the West, Japanese cinema needed to liberate itself of its impurities. Once it did, it could create "pure film."

Contemporary sources often claimed the movement began in June 1918, with the release of Kaeriyama Norimasa's film *Sei no kagayaki* (*The Glow of Life*).[1] However, for years prior to the release of this motion picture, Kaeri-yama—considered by many to be the leader of the movement—and other critics had been complaining about the alleged inferiority of Japanese cinema. Thus, the movement is more accurately dated 1915–1925. These dates are by no means in-clusive, but they incorporate the period of heaviest criticism, as well as the period in which members of the Pure Film Movement actively engaged in making films that matched their ideals. Also, during this decade, other Japanese motion pic-tures underwent a radical transformation as a result of the Pure Film Movement.

Members of the Pure Film Movement viewed Japanese films as being dis-gracefully inferior to foreign films. In the eyes of the reformers, European and American cinema had matured over the years, but Japanese cinema had stagnated and remained childlike. Intellectuals were ashamed of their domestic product and felt that all aspects of Japanese cinema needed improving, from script writing to directing, from acting to film techniques, and from editing to exhibition methods.

In 1916, a writer named Toshio listed six reasons why foreign films were much better than Japanese films. First, people in Japanese movies appeared too small on the screen, because three-fourths of the screen was empty space. In other words, Japanese cinema lacked close-ups and mid-shots. Second, Japanese actors' facial expressions were too formal. Since cinema was the medium for pantomime, facial expression needed to be more expressive and exaggerated. In England, where there were no *benshi*, people could understand a film just by watching the actors. Toshio argued that it would be great "if Japanese films could also be understood without *benshi*. Let's make Japanese motion pictures truly silent theater." Third, there were no actresses in the vast majority of Japanese motion pictures. Although some smaller companies employed actresses, the larger and more popular companies still used female impersonators. Fourth, the storylines of films were very unsophisticated. The plot structure was weak. To-shio complained that it was not that Japanese culture lacked good stories, but merely that filmmakers were using inferior ones. Fifth, the intertitles were too simple. Japanese movies needed intertitles that could help the audience understand what was unfolding on screen. Intertitles also needed to be more poetic, like the ones in foreign films. Sixth, the intertitles needed to be artistic and aesthetically pleasing.[2]

Contained within these six points were the central positions of the Pure Film Movement. Ideally, reformers hoped that, by improving the Japanese product, they would be able to export it abroad and compete with American and European filmmakers on the world market. They also hoped that the profits received from exports would, in turn, help the industry modernize. However, before Japanese film companies could begin exporting their product, they needed to overhaul Japanese cinema. To many reformers, along with improving filmic techniques at the level of camera set-ups, close-ups, and editing, Japanese cinema needed to rid itself of the two major theatrical anachronisms that played a central role in the Japanese cinematic experience: female impersonators and *benshi*.

Female impersonators had been used in Japanese theater for centuries, particularly in *kabuki*. Although *kabuki* started in 1596 as an all-female form of entertainment, by 1629, the government prohibited women from participating in it, because it had become a front for prostitution.[3] Consequently, men began dressing in female costumes and playing the female roles. Female impersonators quickly became an appreciated component of *kabuki* and are still an integral part of *kabuki* today. When filmmakers began making photoplays in the early 1900s, it seemed only natural to use female impersonators. Actresses appeared only on rare occasions in minor productions. In 1908, an all-female cast starred in the first film to which *benshi* attempted to apply *kowairo setsumei*. Actresses began performing in more major productions around 1915. At first, actresses merely played bit parts as geisha, bar girls, dance hall girls, and other minor characters. Only gradually did they begin assuming lead roles. By 1918, as the appearance of actresses on screen increased, people began to call for the elimination of all female impersonators. The title of one 1918 trade journal article clearly summed up

144

the sentiments of the majority of contemporary movie fans as it declared: "Let's Use Actresses in Movies!"[4]

Actresses—many of whom came from *shimpa* and opera theater—quickly replaced female impersonators, and by 1923 the anachronism had been completely removed from Japanese cinema. The Pure Film Movement succeeded in one of its goals. The movement also improved acting quality, introduced the use of scripts, and incorporated a variety of new cinematographic techniques, such as the use of close-ups and certain types of editing, into film production. They did not, however, succeed in eliminating the *benshi*.

The Pure Film Movement attacked *benshi* from a variety of angles and for a myriad of reasons. Some critics felt that *benshi* were holding Japanese cinema back and preventing it from maturing. Others attacked *benshi* for their hedonistic lifestyles, their arrogance, their apparent lack of education, and their use—as some saw it—of foolish and inappropriate language to mislead the audience and degrade the movie. In Takeda Kōkatsu's opinion, the fact that people from other nations did not need *benshi* to understand motion pictures, but the Japanese did, was "a disgrace to the great Japanese empire."[5] The Pure Film Movement's attack was brutal, as when some pronounced, "Both *benshi* and rabid dogs should be exterminated."[6] In the end, *benshi* and *setsumei* suffered some bruises and had to adapt to a changing environment, but survived the assault. In fact, the Pure Film Movement's assault actually fortified the *benshi* and refined the art of *setsumei*.

The arguments used in the assault on *benshi* are complicated and include theoretical discussions over the use and necessity of *benshi*, foreign film *setsumei*, *maesetsu*, *kowairo setsumei*, music, and intertitles. Some people argued for the abolition of all *benshi*, others only for the elimination of *kowairo benshi*; some discussed the need for *benshi* reform, and others maintained that motion pictures should be completely silent. Complicating the debate was the critics' inconsistent usage of key terms. A writer might advocate the elimination of "*benshi*" at the beginning of a piece, but then talk about how he liked "*setsumeisha*" at the end of the same piece, without ever defining what he meant by "*benshi*" and "*setsumei-sha*." One person might employ the word "*benshi*" to mean "foreign film *ben-shi*," but another might use "*benshi*" to signify "*kowairo benshi*" and "*setsumei-sha*" to denote "foreign film *benshi*."

The inconsistent use of cinema-related vocabulary results, in part, from the general transformation of terminology that the Pure Film Movement instigated. Reformers learned to use different words to distinguish their new product from what it replaced. Pure Film Movement filmmakers did not make *katsudō shashin* (moving pictures), but rather *eiga* or *eiga-geki* (movies). The word *eiga* had been used for many years prior to the Pure Film Movement, but only came into wide-spread use at that time. By the end of the Pure Film Movement, "movies" had replaced "moving pictures" as the dominant locution in the trade journals and in general parlance. Similarly, *gendaigeki* supplanted *shimpageki* in signifying modern dramas. The expression *jidaigeki* came to replace the term *kyūgeki* in de-noting period dramas, as a more realistic and fast-paced sword-fighting style re-placed the traditional impressionistic and ballet-like *tachimawari* sword fighting that filmmakers had borrowed from *kabuki*.

For Kantō *benshi*, *setsumeisha* became the politically correct idiom; for Kansai *benshi*, *kaisetsusha* (one who explains) was the preferred locution. The previously prevalent appellation *katsuben* became a derogatory term, used mainly by those who hated the institution of *benshi*. *Benshi* were no longer "orators" but "explainers." In the eyes of many, *setsumeisha* were honorable social educators, but *katsuben* were low-life degenerates; *setsumeisha* were more than entertainers, they were artists. Even the 1917 Tokyo law distinguished *setsumeisha* as a cate-gory distinct from all other performers.

Many critics used the word "eliminate" in their writings, even though they were advocating "*benshi* reform." Over the years, people have tended to focus on this discourse of *benshi* elimination, with the result that today many sources assert that the Pure Film Movement's goal was to eliminate the *benshi*. Actually, very few members of the Pure Film Movement called for the elimination of all *benshi*;

most merely wanted to reform the institution of *benshi*, by limiting and controlling the *benshi*'s command over the filmic text.

Kaeriyama Norimasa led the charge against the *benshi*, as a part of the drive for producers to regain authority over their filmic text. Kaeriyama was born in 1893, and fell in love with movies at an early age. While still in middle school, he began submitting articles to *Katsudō shashinkai*. He quickly became an influential critic and attacked Japanese cinema for its anachronistic underpinnings. Kaeriyama noted that, when a person listened to a *kōdan* storyteller, they imagined in their minds the images he described. The hand gestures and expressions of the storyteller were like moving pictures that left a distinct impression on the audience. A skillful *benshi*, Kaeriyama contended, was just like a *kōdan* storyteller. Customers went to *see* a film, but when they listened to the *benshi* "*the film images become subordinate to the setsumei.*"[7] To critics like Kaeriyama and to filmmakers throughout the world, the image should always be paramount rather than subordinate. In Japan, however, spectators were not consuming the product supplied by film companies, but rather the performance given by the *benshi*. As a mediator between the filmic text and the audience, *benshi* affected the spectators' reading of the films. They had usurped control over the textual meaning of movies, taking it away from the producers. This angered many of those on the production end of the industry.

From top city *benshi* to country *benshi*, it was the nature of the profession to wield interpretive power over films.[8] *Benshi* seized control over the text in several ways. The customs that most perturbed critics and producers were some *benshi*'s habits of physically editing a film himself or dictating to the producer what type of films to make. One critic remembers going to a film in 1920 or 1921, where a *benshi* unabashedly said, "Since there are a bunch of brats in the audience tonight, I have removed one reel."[9] The *benshi* was annoyed with the audience and used his power to radically change the structure of the film. At other times, *benshi* edited films to fit their *setsumei*. When the rapid scene changes of the serial *Black Box* (1915) disrupted Yanagi Shigai's normal style of *setsumei*, Yanagi reedited the Universal picture to match his *setsumei*.[10] Instead of changing his *setsumei* to fit the film, he changed the film to fit his *setsumei*. For obvious reasons, those involved in making motion pictures resented the power *benshi* wielded over their product. The *benshi* derived much of their power from their popularity; thus, the more popular a *benshi* was, the more power he possessed. Reformers wanted to limit the effect *benshi* had on their text and reassert their authority over how audiences read their product.

To many filmmakers, *kowairo benshi* were the worst abusers of *benshi* power. According to Tanaka Eizō, a director of the era and a member of the Pure Film Movement, *kowairo benshi* demanded that films contain no more than eleven or twelve scenes. *Kowairo benshi* preferred movies with few scene changes because, the fewer times the scenes changed, the easier it was to *kowairo setsumei*, i.e., dub dialogue. Long scenes with few cuts were easy to *kowairo setsumei*; short scenes with many cuts rendered the synchronization of dialogue with moving mouths extremely difficult. *Kowairo benshi* also complained about the use of flashbacks and other editing techniques that complicated the structure of a film. Through their complaints, *kowairo benshi* exerted pressure on production companies and influenced the shape of the final product.[11]

Not only did *benshi* pressure producers to make films that fit their *setsumei*, but major movie theaters, too, pressured producers to cater to their needs. Theaters such as the Daishōkan and Fujikan even employed people called *kanzuki sakusha* (writers attached to the theater) to write movie scripts that harmonized with their *benshi* and clientele.[12] In fairness to the *benshi*, not all directors were opposed to *benshi*. Several directors willingly and on their own initiative made movies with specific *benshi* in mind and in consultation with *benshi*.[13]

The fact that *benshi* could physically change a film, and could dictate to a production company what type of film to make, clearly indicates the kind of power they possessed. *Benshi* were not insignificant cinematic appendages, but rather a central component to the motion picture experience that affected the fashioning of movies and influenced how audiences understood films. *Benshi* were an important attraction that audiences paid to hear, and the more popular a *benshi* was, the more freedom he had with his *setsumei*. This freedom to interpret and *setsumei* motion pictures in disparate ways upset filmmakers who had surrendered control to the *benshi* over how audiences read their picture. The *benshi*'s *setsumei* had just as much, if not more, influence over how a person read a film as the moving pictures themselves. *Benshi* determined the conclusive textual reading of a film, because they literally had the final say. As long as *benshi* provided *setsumei* that conformed to the filmmaker's intent, there were no major problems. Unfortunately, *benshi* sometimes provided *setsumei* that radically differed from the filmmaker's design and altered how audience members interpreted the text. A major goal of the Pure Film Movement was for filmmakers to reclaim control of the moving image from the *benshi* and to secure their dominance over how spectators comprehended their motion pictures.

To fully understand the controversy over the existence of *benshi*, one must place it within the much larger discussion about what constituted a "pure film." The debate was not just focused on *benshi* but also included a heated disputation over the role of music and intertitles. Although the reformers reserved their most vitriolic attack for the *benshi*, to understand the forces at work here, one must also look at the attack on music and intertitles.

The most strident members of the Pure Film Movement argued that pure film should be just that: silent moving pictures without *benshi*, without music, and without intertitles. To these men, the best way to watch a film was in silence. According to Kaeriyama Norimasa, "You cannot call a film that merely lacks *benshi* a pure film, because an ideal pure film not only does not have *benshi* attached to it, but also lacks music and intertitles."[14] Other critics asserted that it was only the true film connoisseur who could appreciate a pure film. For the cinema aficionado, the ultimate cinematic experience was watching and understanding a series of moving pictures in complete silence. Most reluctantly conceded, however, that the plebeian spectator needed an aural component. Some reformers held that, as the aural element, music alone was best; others preferred music and *setsumei* together. The *benshi* and movie commentator Takeda Akira maintained that it was only after places of exhibition added aural elements to a film that the "power of the movie" emerged.[15] A few *benshi* fanatics who opposed the reformers even clamored for *setsumei* unaccompanied by music.

The reformers garnered many of their theories about pure film from Hugo Munsterberg, a Harvard University professor who became infatuated with cinema after he was introduced to it in 1915. Within a year of discovering motion pictures, Munsterberg wrote *The Photoplay: A Psychological Study* (1916), the first theoretical treatise on spectatorship.[16] Munsterberg's untimely death in 1916, combined with growing criticisms of his purported pro-German sympathies, limited *The Photoplay*'s influence in the United States.[17] Nevertheless, the work was very influential in Japan, particularly for the profound effect it had on the thinking of Kaeriyama Norimasa and other Pure Film reformers.

Munsterberg argued that the power of film must come from the pictures themselves. For Munsterberg, intertitles and music were accessories that needed to be limited, if not eliminated. In writing about intertitles, he stated, "The photoplay of the day after tomorrow will surely be freed from all elements which are not really pictures. . . . [We must make] plays which speak the language of pictures only." As for music, Munsterberg believed that it must always be subordinate to the pictures, because it does not tell part of the plot, but merely "reinforces the emotional setting." Throughout his work, Munsterberg stressed that the primary power of cinema lies in the content of the pictures themselves, and that motion pictures must be understood without words. The "words" Munsterberg discussed were usually intertitles, but he also discussed the spoken word that sometimes accompanied films in America. In particular, he wrote about experimental contraptions, such as the Kinetophone, which tried to synchronize a voice recorded on a phonograph record with the moving images.[18]

> The condemnation of guiding words [intertitles], in the interest of the purity of the picture play as such, also leads to earnest objection to phonographic accompaniments. . . . Even if the voices were heard with ideal perfection and exactly in time with the movements

150

> of the screen, the effect on an esthetically conscientious audience
> would have been disappointing. A photoplay cannot gain but only
> lose if its visual purity is destroyed. If we see and hear at the same
> time, we do indeed come nearer to the real theater, but this is de-
> sirable only if it is our goal to imitate the stage. Yet if that were
> the goal, even the best imitation would remain far inferior to an
> actual theater performance. As soon as we have clearly understood
> that the photoplay is an art in itself, the conservation of the spoken
> word is as disturbing as color would be on the clothing of a marble
> statue.[19]

Munsterberg's theory that aural accompaniment destroys the visual purity of a motion picture was one of the principal assumptions that the reformers of the Pure Film Movement incorporated into their writings denouncing *benshi* and *setsumei*.

Takeda Kōkatsu was one of those who believed that only music was necessary and that *setsumei* was superfluous. In a theoretical discussion of the role of *benshi*, he reasoned that intertitles and music explain the film, and that *setsumei* clarifies the intertitles and music. In as much as *setsumei* does not explain the film directly, it is nonessential and should be eradicated.[20]

Arguing for the power of *setsumei*, Matsuki Kyōrō, one of the top Kansai *benshi* during the Taishō era, asserted that music only had an indirect effect on the audience, and that *setsumei* had an immediate and direct effect. Matsuki maintained that music alone could not impart an understanding of a movie, but that *setsumei* by itself could.[21]

Those who favored music hoped that the efforts of the Pure Film Movement would limit the power of *benshi* and strengthen the position of music. They were tired of music playing second fiddle to *setsumei* and hoped that the battle taking place would end with a victory for music. Although music improved and gained greater prominence, it never transcended *benshi* and their *setsumei* in importance. What resulted, however, was a better harmonization between the components, which led to an improved diegetic illusion.

The key to a successful diegetic illusion is that the audience remain unaware of the elements involved. When any one of the components, be it aural or visual, draws attention to itself or is inconsonant with the other elements, the illusion is lost. For example, when music is incongruous with a scene, or when a *benshi* provides *setsumei* that is discordant with a film, or when his inebriation or antics distract attention from the screen, the diegetic illusion is unattainable. Only when all the parts blend harmoniously into one is the audience transported into the diegetic world.

As Aaron Gerow explains in his work on the Pure Film Movement, one of the goals of the reformers was to internalize the *benshi* "within the enunciative system of a film rendering themselves invisible and supporting the illusionism that the text spoke itself."[22] In other words, they wanted to create a believable diegetic illusion, by making the audience unaware of the *benshi*'s presence. The writings of *setsumei* theorists of the so-called Golden Age of *Benshi*, reveal that this goal was achieved and it became a cardinal ingredient in the art of *setsumei*. In describing how to *setsumei*, Tokugawa Musei stated that a *benshi* must not *setsumei* directly to the audience. "*Setsumei* must appear as if the force is emanating from the screen, just as if it were a billiard ball bouncing off a cushion."[23] The ideal *setsumei*, therefore, was one that fused the aural and visual components into one, because, when that happened, the "audience melted into the film."[24]

Although the end results of *benshi* becoming more invisible and *setsumei* less obtrusively conformed to the ideals of some reformers, the means used to achieve those ends were not always determined by the reformers. The *benshi* played an active role in reshaping their position within the cinematic presentation. The reformers merely attacked the *benshi*. The *benshi* weathered the assault, fortified their position, and restructured their art.

One of the weapons used by reformers in their war against *benshi* was intertitles. Grounded in the presumption that *benshi* merely provided a verbal reading of what visually unfolded on the screen, some people believed that *benshi* could easily be replaced by intertitles. Since intertitles could visually provide the words that *benshi* supplied orally, then the use of intertitles, *benshi* foes reasoned, was a way to supply narrative information within the visual text and without *benshi*.

The presence of *benshi* initially caused Japanese cinema to be slow to adapt to the custom of using intertitles. Japanese films did not need intertitles, because they had *benshi* to supply the necessary information. Films had two basic kinds of intertitles: spoken titles (dialogue) and explanatory titles (narrative information). American and European filmmakers began experimenting with intertitles at the turn of the century; by 1906, the nickelodeon trade paper, *Views and Film Index*, was urging that intertitles become a standard fixture, which they quickly became.[25] Dialogue intertitles did not appear in Japanese films until the 1910s.[26]

To Japanese cinema purists, neither *setsumei* nor intertitles should be a part of a film. One critic even proclaimed that the existence of *benshi* and intertitles was not only an affront to the story and the art of motion pictures, but an insult to the audience.[27] Theoretically, a movie should transmit all of the information needed to understand it through acting, camera work, and editing alone. For the pragmatists who realized that conveying all of the information necessary to follow a film without any words was nearly impossible, the issue of the better means of transmission, visual or aural, became the focus of heated debate. Those on the producing end tended to favor intertitles, because they could control them, ensuring a uniform product. Intertitles negated the necessity of *benshi*, and, without *benshi*, the means by which the site of exhibition could alter how spectators interpreted the product were greatly reduced. Most reformers also favored intertitles, because, as they argued repeatedly, cinema was a visual medium.

Opponents to intertitles argued that listening to the *benshi* was easier than reading the intertitles. Moreover, listening to *setsumei* was effortless; reading intertitles required mental exertion. Arai Saburō, the man who introduced the Vitascope into Tokyo in 1897, complained that reading intertitles was very tiring and was like "reading a novel while watching a play."[28] Many also argued that simply watching with the eyes did not have the same impact as watching and listening. The aural element of *setsumei* enhanced the visual images in a way that written text could not.

According to the Pure Film advocates, the one caveat to using *benshi* was ensuring that they provided proper *setsumei* and that they did not diverge from the text. If *benshi* read the filmic text in an appropriate and approved manner, they could help audiences read a film correctly. In particular, *benshi* could ensure that audiences interpreted the single meaning of the film properly.[29]

In addition to the debate over whether *benshi* or intertitles was better, a separate discussion focused solely on the relative merits of intertitles, without any connection to *benshi*. Some wanted to increase the number of intertitles; others wanted to eliminate them. This deliberation mirrored the larger debate concurrently taking place throughout the world. The number of articles published in Japan on this topic rivaled, if not exceeded, those concerning the disputation over *benshi*.

Most people who argued against intertitles did so from an artistic point of view. They held that intertitles disrupted the artistic flow of the pictures, and that having fewer intertitles would force a perfect style of motion picture to emerge. In short, intertitles acted as a crutch that prevented cinema from standing on its own. Those who favored intertitles claimed that even great pantomime and film techniques could not always communicate narrative meaning. Reformers like Kaeriyama Norimasa believed that the key was to avoid overuse of intertitles, because, when numerous, they became just as disruptive and annoying as *benshi* and *setsumei*.[30]

Contrary to Kaeriyama's hopes, intertitles assumed a prominent position within Japanese cinema. At a time when American filmmakers were moving away from intertitles, Japanese filmmakers embraced them. Nor did the utilization of intertitles eliminate the custom of *benshi* and *setsumei*. Intertitles caused the profession and art to reform, but they could not efface them. *Benshi* merely incorporated the intertitles into their *setsumei*. A *benshi* did not read the intertitles; he played off of them, using them as foils for his *setsumei*. The *benshi* added to abbreviated intertitles, and abbreviated lengthy ones, and, when an inter-title was simple and without taste, spiced it up and added flavor to it.

Attacking *Kowairo Benshi*

Kaeriyama Norimasa dreamed of introducing Japanese motion pictures to the rest of the world; however, before he and his fellow reformers could do this, Japanese films needed to improve. In particular, he felt that it was imperative that they become truly silent. Kaeriyama theorized that only a picture that communi-cated its meaning through pantomime and film techniques, without the aid of spo-ken words, could be exported to people throughout the world, and the only way for pantomime to improve was for films to become silent.[31] To many reformers, therefore, the biggest factor inhibiting Japanese cinema was the *benshi*, particu-larly *kowairo benshi*. Because *kowairo benshi* supplied dialogue for Japanese films, there had been no incentive to improve them to the point they could speak for themselves. As one critic frankly declared, "Because of *kagezerifu* [*kowairo setsumei*], our motion pictures are prevented from becoming more interna-tional."[32]

In order to export Japanese movies, they needed to become more like the American and European motion pictures that dominated the Japanese market at the time, but reformers did not want simply to copy them.[33] When they said that they wanted to mimic Western cinema, that meant understanding the superiority of Western movies and applying that knowledge to Japanese films. It also meant studying Japanese cinema to learn what was holding it back. The one thing that most critics agreed was hindering the advancement of Japanese cinema was *kowairo setsumei*.

The addition of *kowairo setsumei* to Japanese motion pictures made the film more "theater-like." Spectators constantly declared that "it was just like watching a play." In the theater, dialogue was essential, because understanding could not be imparted through editing and framing. Motion pictures, on the other hand, did not need to rely on dialogue, because they could communicate information through editing and framing. Japanese cinema resembled stage plays too closely.

This connection with theatricality was not limited to the site of exhibition. It permeated production methods. During the 1910s, directors relied on dialogue-based scripts, and they often read the dialogue aloud while filming. Production focused on dialogue, which audiences could not hear, rather than on the acting, which they could see. Actors should have been focusing exclusively on their movements, but many were thinking of their lines. Moreover, to allow the *benshi* to dub their dialogue, directors utilized long actionless scenes.[34] Producers had to eliminate these anachronisms if they wanted Japanese cinema to improve. Ideally, with better pantomime and careful editing, Japanese movies would be able to tell a story without the crutch of *kowairo setsumei*.

Ironically, the first endeavor to do away with *kowairo setsumei* was reportedly attempted by the *benshi* Iwatō Shisetsu in 1912. Iwatō tried replacing *kowairo setsumei* with intertitles and foreign-film-style *setsumei*. At the time, audiences viewed his experiment as a hindrance and it quickly disappeared.[35] Six years later, filmmakers of the Pure Film Movement tried this modification again.

Kaeriyama Norimasa was not a filmmaker; he was a critic and theoretician. In 1918, however, he had an opportunity to put his theories into practice. With financial backing from Tenkatsu, Kaeriyama made *Sei no kagayaki* (*The Glow of Life*). Kaeriyama shot this film on location, used actresses in place of female impersonators, employed close-ups and realistic acting, and polished it with complex editing. As an added touch, he printed his intertitles in both Japanese and French. One reviewer raved, "It uses methods exactly like those used in foreign products. Even without *setsumei*, one can understand the film."[36] Despite this, the film never played without *setsumei*. It was, however, one of the first Japanese films shown without *kowairo setsumei*, since *kowairo setsumei* became the dominant form of *setsumei* attached to Japanese films.

From the time he first began to plan the movie, Kaeriyama pledged to ensure that it "used dialogue titles instead of *kagezerifu*."[37] In Kaeriyama's opinion, when *benshi* added *kowairo setsumei* to a motion picture, the balance of power between the visual and the aural was 50–50, and the *benshi* was just like a *kōdan* or *rakugo* storyteller, in terms of his aural sway. When *benshi* provided foreign film *setsumei*, however, the balance of power shifted to 70–30, with the visual element clearly in command.[38] For Kaeriyama, therefore, it was imperative that the visual element of his movie be supreme, and, to prevent *kowairo setsumei* from being applied to his films, he insisted that they be released at a theater that specialized in foreign films. Tenkatsu initially refused to comply. The battle between Tenkatsu and Kaeriyama lasted for months and delayed the release of *The Glow of Life* and Kaeriyama's second film, *Miyama no otome* (*The Maid in the Mountains*). In the end, however, the company observed his wishes. Kaeriyama later wrote that, if he had exhibited his films with *kowairo setsumei*, the entire aim of the Pure Film Movement would have been rendered meaningless.[39] Although Kaeriyama often theorized and wrote about watching a pure film in total silence, he was also a pragmatist who came to appreciate the benefits that certain types of aural elements could bring to cinema. Like many other members of the Pure Film Movement, Kaeriyama was open to the benefits of foreign-film-style *benshi*, but hated and wanted to eliminate *kowairo benshi*.

One problem that movie companies faced, as they tried to release their new films, was hostile resistance from *kowairo benshi*. In March 1919, Nikkatsu released Tanaka Eizō's new film *Ikeru shikabana* (*The Living Corpse*). This film employed many of the editing theories of the Pure Film Movement; moreover, in an effort to do away with *kowairo setsumei*, Tanaka inserted a tremendous number of dialogue intertitles. When the preeminent *kowairo benshi*, Tsuchiya Shōtō, saw the film at the Asakusa Yūrakukan, he had a fit. Tsuchiya immediately complained to Nikkatsu, with whom he was under contract, that the bewildering number of cuts and complex editing in *The Living Corpse* made the film nearly impossible to *kowairo*. He gave Nikkatsu an ultimatum: Either make a film he could *kowairo*, or he would have to leave Nikkatsu. Tsuchiya's threat terrified the Nikkatsu executives, because he was one of Nikkatsu's biggest attractions. A few days after Tsuchiya's ultimatum, the Nikkatsu head office issued a letter to their filmmakers, directing them to lengthen the scenes in their films and to make these films according to their "regular methods."[40]

Not only *benshi* objected to Pure Film Movement films. Audiences and critics often complained that they smelled like butter (*battā kusai*). In other words, they were too foreign, not only in technique, but also in content. These movies frequently contained Japanese in Western dress, living in American-style houses, sitting in European furniture, and eating with forks and knives. Curiously, *benshi* often acted in these films that tried to do away with their profession. Naitō Shiren, Sugirua Shirō, and Shiraishi Shikō, for example, all starred in Tōmas Kurihara's *Amateur Club* (1920).

Attacking Foreign Film *Benshi*

Some reformers advocated that foreign film *setsumei* replace *kowairo setsumei* for Japanese motion pictures; others called for the elimination of foreign film *benshi*. Many felt that the rambling chatter of the *benshi* destroyed the feeling of the motion picture. Too much irrelevant prattle distracted from the visual image and tampered with the plot. In defending his occupation, Tachibana Kōyō declared, "*Setsumeisha* are needed to translate foreign intertitles. Without *setsumeisha*, foreign films would be unsatisfying."[41] Other supporters of foreign-film *benshi* tried to fend off the critical onslaught with similar arguments, which emphasized the indispensable role *benshi* served as translators of foreign intertitles and, to a lesser extent, as teachers of foreign exotica.

Predominantly, intellectuals loved foreign films, and, from their perspective, having *benshi* translate the foreign intertitles, which they could read and translate for themselves, was totally superfluous. Tokugawa Musei countered this argument by asking, "For those who say that *setsumeisha* are unnecessary, what percent of a theater's audience do they think can read all the intertitles? Can these naysayers grasp the meaning of every intertitle in the short time that it appears on the screen?" Musei concluded his justification by proclaiming that he believed that, in the future, *benshi* would exist in foreign countries as well, because *benshi* enabled foreign filmmakers to tell more complex stories.[42]

Benshi adversaries countered that, if all the *benshi* did was translate intertitles, they were not really entertainers, but rather translators (*hon'yakusha*).[43] One critic suggested that one way to get rid of *benshi* and reduce the need for intertitles would be to provide audiences with detailed programs that explained everything a spectator needed to know to understand the film.[44] Others asserted that, if *setsumei* was simply an oral reading of translated intertitles, it would be better to replace the projected foreign intertitles with translated Japanese intertitles that everyone could read. This would eliminate the need for *benshi* and preserve the visual art of motion pictures. To strengthen their argument regarding the elimination of *benshi*, many reformers stressed that inserting translated intertitles would be less expensive than using *benshi*.

Recent scholars have tended to disagree. Several have argued that, because the Japanese usually imported only one print of a film and circulated it around, it was cheaper to use *benshi*. In their opinion, the cost of making new intertitles, filming them, and editing them in was "probably greater" than that of relying on *benshi*. Others have asserted that "the *benshi* was a much less expensive alternative," because distributors could not spread the cost of producing intertitles out over several cheaply produced copies.[45]

I contend, however, that, in terms of aggregate expenditures, inserting intertitles into just one print was probably less expensive than it was to employ *benshi* as verbal intertitle translators for every showing. Inserting intertitles into a motion picture was a one-time proposition, but maintaining *benshi* was a daily expense. Although the Japanese frequently distributed only one print, films often circulated for months and years. After a movie opened in Tokyo, it traveled around the empire. That the Home Ministry's seal of censorial approval was valid for 3 years suggests that motion pictures circulated for lengthy periods of time. Based on cost per day, the longer a film circulated, the less expensive the cost of inserting titles became and the more expensive the cost of the *benshi*.

Despite the meager data available, making a general comparison of cost effectiveness is possible. The expense of translation was the same, regardless of whether the company used intertitles or *benshi*. Companies already employed people to translate the foreign intertitles for *benshi*. Therefore, if companies wanted to insert translated intertitles, they would not have to incur the extra cost of translating the titles, since they already bore that expenditure. For comparison's sake, let us assume that a film was 5,000 feet in length (about 1 hour, depending on projection speed), and that one-fifth, or 1,000 feet, consisted of intertitles. Assuming a very high estimate of 30 sen per foot for the combined cost of negative stock, positive stock, and labor to make and edit the new film titles, it works out to a total cost of 300 yen for inserting Japanese intertitles into a foreign film.[46] Top *benshi* earned that much or more in a single month. Consequently, if the film played at a theater with a *benshi* who earned 500 yen per month and it had a run of over 3 weeks, inserting titles, rather than employing *benshi*, would be less expensive. However, if we make a conservative assumption that *benshi* earned on average 60 yen per month, then, if the film circulated less than 5 months, it was less expensive to use *benshi*; if it circulated over 5 months, it was cheaper to use intertitles. The calculation hinges on how long the film circulated. A few hit films circulated for 5 or 6 years, but most had much shorter runs.

One factor that is even more important than how long a film circulated is the relative drawing power of intertitles versus *benshi*. The above explication is focused solely on the out-of-pocket cost of *benshi* and intertitles, and assumes that both served the same single function of imparting to an audience the information needed to understand a film. It does not account for the entertainment value of each medium; nor does it take into consideration the ability each medium had to attract customers into the theater. In other words, it omits the income generated by intertitles and *benshi*.

When reformers, who disliked *benshi* to begin with, argued against *benshi* in favor of intertitles, they presumed that no one came to the cinema to hear *benshi*. I argue that many *benshi* were major attractions who paid for themselves.

Many people attended the cinema just to hear *benshi* perform *setsumei* for the film; but surely no one went to a movie just to see intertitles. If exhibitors replaced *benshi* with intertitles, they might save on payroll; nevertheless, in the end, they would lose at the box office. In short, the gross cost of intertitles might be less than *benshi*, but the net cost would undoubtedly be higher.

As the Pure Film Movement debate heated up, both *benshi* and reformers advocated that movies be shown without *benshi* and *setsumei*—be it foreign film *setsumei* or *kowairo setsumei*—to determine whether or not *benshi* and their *setsumei* really did attract customers. As Tokugawa Musei saw it, "At these theaters, people who believe that *benshi* are definitely not needed, and those who blindly follow the crowd in rejecting the *benshi*, could gather and fully appreciate the movies to their heart's content."[47] A few theaters took the challenge. All such efforts, such as Shōchiku's attempt to show *Haha izuko* (*Where Is My Mother?*) at the Konparukan in 1923, failed at the box office.[48] That there is no record of a financially successful theater that showed motion pictures without *benshi* indicates that *setsumei* was an important attraction that exhibitors and audiences could not do without.

Regardless of which was more cost-effective, foreign film *benshi* still needed to defend themselves against those who claimed that all they did was translate titles. Some resorted to the defense that listening to *setsumei* was more pleasurable than reading intertitles. Others emphasized that *setsumei* required much more than simply reading or translating intertitles. Between 1918 and 1920, the Konparukan theater even advertised that there was "absolutely no *setsumei* of titles" during its shows.[49] This suggests that creative *setsumei* that veered from the titles was a major selling point. *Benshi* had to use intertitles as a base upon which to expand their *setsumei*. If *setsumei* were simply the reading or translating of intertitles, it would lack interest, and audiences could easily do without it. When performed by an expert, *setsumei* was an art that incorporated intertitles into an invisible oral narrative that carried audiences into the diegesis and guided them pleasurably through the intricacies of the motion picture. Intertitles could not do that.

Many Pure Film Movement movies, including those by Kaeriyama, failed at the box office, in part because of the poor quality of the films and in part because of audiences' unwillingness to accept the radical changes they introduced. Attempts to export these films also failed. Nevertheless, by the end of the 1920s, most of the changes advocated by the Pure Film Movement had become an integral part of Japanese cinema. The Pure Film Movement succeeded in introducing parallel editing, close-ups, and other filming techniques. It also initiated the use of the screenplay and replaced female impersonators with actresses. The dreams of those who advocated a purely silent cinema, however, never materialized. Sound, in the form of music and voice, continued to be an integral part of Japanese cinema. The Pure Film Movement debated the relative merits of music, intertitles, and *benshi* for years, focusing much of their attack on the *benshi*. Nevertheless, they failed to eliminate the *benshi*, because they underestimated the entertainment and attractive power of *setsumei*. Reformers focused almost exclusively on the aural and informative aspect of *setsumei*, while ignoring its entertainment value. Spectators enjoyed listening to engaging *setsumei* and relied on it to help them enter the diegetic environment. The *benshi*'s insightful comments and ready wit were elements of the show to which Japanese audiences had grown accustomed. It did not eliminate *benshi*, but the Pure Film Movement served as a catalyst for a radical reorganization of the art of *setsumei*, which took place during the Period of Unification.

8

PERIOD OF UNIFICATION, 1917–1925

During the Period of Experimentation, exhibitors and *benshi* experimented with multiple vocal techniques, in search of the best method of entertaining and informing an audience. They tried to incorporate many traditional narrative arts into the performance, before settling down primarily with group and solo *kowairo setsumei* for Japanese films and solo descriptive *setsumei* for foreign films. During the Period of Unification (1917–1925), *benshi* synthesized the disparate forms into one, so that, by the time of the Golden Age of *Benshi*, all *setsumei* conformed to the established form of presentation. As a result, all *benshi* adhered to a similar structure of presentation, while varying in how they performed their *setsumei* within that homogeneous form of presentation.

Much as motion pictures improved, to become an "art form," during the Pure Film Movement, *setsumei* also advanced into a bona fide art. By calling attention to the various roles the *benshi* played in a cinematic exhibition, the Pure Film Movement forced people to reexamine the institution of *benshi* and the role of *setsumei*. As a result, the *benshi* restructured *setsumei* into a purer art form, and people began acknowledging that *setsumei* was no longer a mere adjunct to motion pictures, but rather an art form in its own right.

164

Elimination of *Maesetsu*

An integral part of a movie showing in Japan during the first 20 years of exhibition was *maesetsu*, or opening remarks. A *benshi* would stand in the middle of the stage, introduce himself, and give a general outline of the movie about to be shown. *Maesetsu* was more important than *nakasetsu*, or *setsumei* given during projection, and it set the tone for the entire performance. People often based their perceptions of a theater on *maesetsu*, and it was a *benshi*'s ability to give amusing *maesetsu* that determined his salary. Initially, exhibitors added lengthy *maesetsu* as a means of lengthening the performance, in order to give greater justification for the high ticket prices. As films got longer, the length of *maesetsu* decreased, but it still remained the most valued part of the vocal performance.

To show how *maesetsu* introduced a picture and set the tone for the show, I present the following *maesetsu* from the serial *Zigomar*. An audience attending the performance by Yamano Ichirō, which opened chapter 6, would have heard this *maesetsu* before hearing that *nakasetsu*.

> Thank you for coming today. On behalf of the theater, I, Yamano Ichirō, humbly welcome you. Efflorescent Paris? London? The moon cried? A little cuckoo. In the town of Paris, France, mysterious incidents are now occurring, at banks, companies, opera houses, and millionaire mansions. An apparitional band of thieves, who move like the wind, audaciously leave a "Z" mark at the scene of their crime. Who are these Zs? Here, the famous detective Polin will try to uncover this secret. Zigomar, the leader of the Z-group, will be in disguise, then detective Polin will be in disguise. Will Zigomar win, or Polin? Clever competition in a battle of intelligence with sparks flying; a strong wind is blowing, rain must be coming. As for the victor, will it be Justice? Or Injustice? I won't talk about the content, for it is a Pandora's box. Westernization (*bunmei kaika*)—using electricity, machines moving—we can say it is feverishly at work in this picture. So let's give a tremendous round of applause, and please enjoy.[1]

Maesetsu was not limited to foreign films: It was also an integral part of Japanese films. Tsuchiya Shōtō, the *kowairo setsumei* specialist who supplied the *setsumei* for *Golden Demon*, recounted in chapter 4, gave the following *maesetsu* for *Hototogisu* (*A Little Cuckoo*, 1922), before he participated in providing group *kowairo setsumei* for the film.

> You are all waiting impatiently to see Yamazaki Naganosuke, Kubota Kiyoshi, and Wakamizu Midori star in a special work from Mukōjima. It is a grand, dramatic tragedy. Cry, cry, until you cannot cry anymore. If you are a parent, listen! If you are sentimental, watch! In any world, there are many tear-filled tales like this one. The main characters of this story are twenty years old—mere budding flowers. The college student, who is in the thoughts of a retired person from a great family, who is suffering the conflict between duty and emotion, who by chance is walking below, and who is wearing a university cap, saves a woman. If I speak for too long, you will lose interest in the show, so I will stop talking about the content. I, the bald Tsuchiya, will make the greatest effort of my life to *setsumei* the scene on the beach. You with a sword by Masamune and I with a rusted sword. You can cut and I cannot. To make you comfortable, I will sing a little bit of a beach song during the show. I will work together with the other young people who work here. In other words, we will provide *narimono kowairo* for the film. (Sound of wooden clappers.) Let's begin.[2]

Although *maesetsu* was the central part of the performance, not everyone liked it. Critics complained that previewing the action caused one to lose interest in the events when they appeared on the screen.[3] Fans of motion pictures argued that they came to see the film, not listen to an opening monologue.[4]

The impetus for the elimination of *maesetsu* came with Thomas H. Ince's *Civilization* (1916), which was released in Japan on March 26, 1917, at the Teikokukan. This was a major motion picture event. The film opened with an enlarged orchestra of over 20 members, and exhibitors raised ticket prices, with the best seats costing 5 yen. After a week at the Teikokukan, the film moved to the Aoikan.

A film of this stature required great *setsumei*. At the Aoikan, two of the best in the business, Fujinami Mumei and Tokugawa Musei, had the task of supplying sublime *setsumei* for this movie spectacular. Curiously, this was the first movie for which Tokugawa Musei worked as the head *benshi* at the Aoikan. Having a chance to preview the film thoroughly before they had to provide *setsumei* for it, the two *benshi* discussed how they wanted to handle this epic. What concerned them most was that the first reel of this ten-reel film was composed entirely of intertitles. The two reasoned that, since this reel of intertitles contained most of the information normally given in *maesetsu*, providing *maesetsu* would appear redundant. Fujinami wanted to jump right into the *nakasetsu*, without providing needless *maesetsu*. Musei likewise thought that beginning the show as the curtain opened to the film would artistically captivate the audience. Fujinami provided the *setsumei* for the first seven reels and Musei provided it for the last 3 (and 2 other comedies). As the curtain rose in the darkened theater and the English intertitles appeared on the screen, Fujinami provided his translated interpretation of the intertitles, heralding the end of *maesetsu*. The show received rave reviews.[5]

For three weeks, *Civilization* played at the Aoikan without any *maesetsu*, and no one complained. The audience did not have much trouble adjusting to films without *maesetsu*, because they had become film-savvy over the years. At the same time, motion pictures and *setsumei* had improved to the point that all the information needed for understanding what was unfolding on the silver screen could be conveyed through the moving pictures and *nakasetsu*. Audiences no longer needed preliminary knowledge. When another *benshi* asked Tokugawa Musei how audiences would understand serial films without *maesetsu* informing them about what happened in the previous week's episode, Musei replied, "Explain what happened last week in the *setsumei*."[6]

After *Civilization* moved on to another theater, the Aoikan continued to show films without *maesetsu*. The practice then spread, first to other foreign film theaters in Tokyo, next to Japanese film theaters in the capital, and finally throughout the country. By August 1920, *maesetsu* had been eliminated from Osaka, and by January 1923, it was no longer part of regular performances in any major urban center.[7] *Maesetsu* never completely disappeared from the countryside, however, because one could still on occasion hear a shortened form of it in rural theaters, and, on rare occasions, urban *benshi* revived it for special nostalgic performances.[8] Still, for all intents and purposes, *maesetsu* was eliminated.

With the elimination of *maesetsu*, the content of *setsumei* changed. *Benshi* had to incorporate background and outline information into their *setsumei* that was formerly provided prior to the film. They had to lead people through the story by skillfully explaining what was unfolding, while giving the background to what was happening and hinting at what was to come. Not an easy task.

At the same time that *maesetsu* disappeared, the word "*nakasetsu*" became extinct. *Benshi*'s salaries were no longer based on their ability to introduce a film, but on their ability to entertain during the film. Since *maesetsu* was no longer a part of the show, *benshi* no longer had to show their face to the audience. They no longer had to wear formal or flashy clothes, and, by not having to worry about appearing tipsy onstage, could now perform in a higher state of inebriation.[9] The real benefit of eliminating *maesetsu*, however, was that it improved the diegetic illusion: *setsumei* was now fully conjoined with the film.

Elimination of *Kowairo Setsumei*

Kowairo setsumei strove to create a realistic diegesis, by providing dialogue from the shadows. *Kowairo* literally means "voice coloring," and, in the contemporary literature, it was the term most often used with the type of *setsumei* that accompanied Japanese films. *Benshi* who provided *kowairo setsumei* technically performed shadow dialogue (*kagezerifu*). During the Period of Unification, *kowairo setsumei* disappeared as a separate branch of *setsumei*. It became amalgamated into the foreign film form of *setsumei*.

Since the Period of Experimentation, foreign film *benshi* usually incorporated some *kowairo setsumei* into their running commentary. After the Period of

Unification, this became the standard form for all *setsumei*, as *kowairo setsumei* became fully integrated into foreign film *setsumei*. In other words, a *setsumei* of the Golden Age was a seamless narrative mix of explanation, reading of intertitles, and dubbed dialogue performed by a solo *benshi*.

Between 1914 and 1923, *kowairo setsumei* was the type of *setsumei* applied solely to Japanese films. Although *benshi* often specialized in only one type of *setsumei*—either foreign film *setsumei* or *kowairo setsumei*—they were not restricted to that *setsumei*. *Benshi* sometimes performed both types, thus learning different vocal techniques and skills. Still, *benshi* and critics habitually viewed *kowairo setsumei* as a lower form of the art. The Pure Film Movement directed its most vehement attacks against *kowairo benshi*, and, to many others, *kowairo setsumei* was a blemish that needed to be erased. Yoshizawa Shunmu ranked *benshi* who specialized in *kowairo setsumei* much lower on his *banzuke* than *benshi* who specialized in foreign film *setsumei*.

There are many reasons why *kowairo setsumei* disappeared, and most are related to the Pure Film Movement. For one, Japanese audiences started to turn away from theatrical movies. Exhibitors had added *kowairo* to make cinema a poor man's theater, but, as the internal structure of movies became less theatrical, the application of *kowairo* to them became increasingly anachronistic. To eliminate the necessity for *kowairo setsumei*, filmmakers began incorporating an increasing number of dialogue intertitles into their works: The use of dialogue intertitles made verbal dialogue less meaningful. Thus, as Japanese motion pictures "improved" and became more like foreign films, it seemed only natural to replace the "inferior" type of *setsumei* that accompanied Japanese movies with the more "advanced" form of *setsumei* that accompanied foreign films. There is also evidence indicating that audiences had grown tired of *kowairo setsumei* and were demanding that filmmakers make Japanese movies to which *benshi* could apply foreign-film-type *setsumei*.[10] Finally, one of the main reasons why exhibitors discontinued the custom of group *kowairo setsumei* was the cost. It did not make good business sense to continue hiring four or five *benshi* to provide *kowairo se-*

tsumei, when there was the viable alternative of hiring only one *benshi* to give foreign film *setsumei*. Some *kowairo benshi* did perform solo, but the majority performed in groups. Few people had the skill to *kowairo* an entire film successfully. Thus, as films improved and audiences' tastes changed, exhibitors willingly complied with the growing trends. Naturally, *kowairo benshi* resisted as best they could, but in the end they either adapted their skills, so that they could provide the new kind of *setsumei* that was developing, or they disappeared.

Unlike the elimination of *maesetsu*, which featured a definitive beginning, identifiable chain reaction, and fairly clear end, tracing the disappearance of *kowairo setsumei* is much more difficult. What is certain is that, by the time Emperor Taishō died, in 1926, *kowairo setsumei* had died as a popular means of entertainment in most cinema houses throughout Japan. One of the reasons for the murky view of how *kowairo setsumei* faded away is that *kowairo benshi* resisted the efforts to do away with their profession.

In 1917, the director Inoue Masao made and released *Taii no musumei* (*The Captain's Daughter*). It was a new kind of film, based on Pure Film Movement theories, and contained many scene changes and other Western film techniques. After seeing the film, one *benshi* claimed, "Because the film uses so many foreign film techniques, I believe it would be impossible to perform *kowairo setsumei* for it."[11] At least a few exhibitors and *benshi* agreed. One Asakusa exhibitor had Nishimura Rakuten provide foreign film *setsumei* for *The Captain's Daughter*, and this appears to be the first time foreign film *setsumei* was applied to a Japanese film since the Period of Experimentation had divided the art into two main streams.[12]

Nishimura Rakuten's *setsumei* for the film was the first step in doing away with *kowairo setsumei* as a separate branch. However, unlike Fujinami's and Musei's efforts to do away with *maesetsu*, it did not lead to early abandonment of *kowairo setsumei*. Over the next several years, foreign film *setsumei* was applied to only a few other Japanese films. Fiery protests from *kowairo benshi*, such as

Tsuchiya Shōtō, forced companies to revert to making more "traditional" films for which *kowairo benshi* could perform *kowairo setsumei*.

Despite *kowairo benshi* remonstrations, filmmakers, exhibitors, and critics continued to push for the elimination of *kowairo setsumei*. In 1921, the San'yūkan advertised its showing of the film *Uki shizumi* (*Floating Sinking*) with the byline, "Of course, there is no *kowairo*."[13] Nevertheless, even in 1921, Japanese films shown without *kowairo setsumei* appear to have been an anomaly.

The real turning point in the elimination of *kowairo setsumei* was the Great Kantō Earthquake that hit Tokyo at 11:58 A.M. on September 1, 1923. The shock waves that shook the city brought down buildings, bridges, and other structures throughout the capital; however, the fires that erupted afterward caused the most devastation. When the blazes finally died out and the dust settled, very little was left of the Tokyo film industry. Most theaters and studios lay in rubble, and for a brief time most film production shifted to Kyoto. The earthquake also opened the door for foreign film companies to move in.[14]

The quake killed several *benshi* and forced hundreds to seek work else-where while their theaters were rebuilt. Nikkatsu and Shōchiku both forced all of their *benshi* under contract to quit; they provided severance pay to only a handful of them. Some *benshi* applied their vocal skills to hawking wares; others traveled to the countryside, or up to Hokkaido, seeking employment as *benshi*. Two weeks after the earthquake, and fearing that it would take 5 years for the enter-tainment industry to revitalize itself, Tokugawa Musei began working for the Hōchi newspaper. Because the earthquake had destroyed the Hōchi presses, Musei traveled around the countryside, verbally reporting the news for free. Musei became an "oral newspaper."[15]

As people recovered from the quake, editorials appeared in trade journals calling for the quick rebuilding of Tokyo's entertainment districts. Reporters wrote that people needed to be entertained during this time of recovery and re-building.[16] One writer professed, "Just as man needs food to live, he also needs entertainment for the soul. Therefore, the Tokyo motion picture world must be rebuilt as fast as possible."[17] Two months after the quake hit, the Shinjuku Musa-shinokan and the Meguro theater reopened for business. They suffered only minor damage in the quake and had avoided the conflagration that destroyed an estimated 70% of Tokyo. The Musashinokan quickly hired Tokugawa Musei back from his job as a traveling vocal newspaper. Despite unbelievably high ticket prices of 2 to 3 yen for the best seats, people still flocked to the cinema during this time of ruin. Every day, those cinema houses that were opened were packed to record levels, earning theater workers "good-receipts bonuses" for weeks on end. There was, however, a change in audience demographics. After the quake, workers unprecedentedly began going to the theater by themselves, without their families.[18]

More than anything else, it was the Great Kantō Earthquake that elimi-nated the practice of *kowairo setsumei*. As theaters rebuilt and rehired *benshi*, many decided to employ only one foreign-film-style *benshi*, instead of four or five *kowairo benshi*. Unemployed, *kowairo benshi* had lost their bargaining power. They either had to learn how to give explanatory *setsumei* or find work elsewhere. The female *benshi* Ishikawa Mitsumaru recalls that, after the quake, she successfully made the transition from *kowairo setsumei* to foreign film *se-tsumei*. Unfortunately, many of her fellow *kowairo benshi*, especially female ones, were unable to make the shift and left the profession.[19]

Even so, the elimination of *kowairo setsumei* was a difficult process, as exemplified by its removal from the Fujikan. In March 1923, Miyake Iwao, the manager at the Fujikan, prohibited *kowairo setsumei* from being attached to his shows. Objections by both *benshi* and audiences, however, forced Miyake to re-tract his order, and, in May, *kowairo setsumei* returned. The earthquake hit in September, forcing the Fujikan to close until January 1924. In April, Miyake again attempted to eliminate *kowairo setsumei*, but this time, instead of a com-plete moratorium on *kowairo setsumei*, he did away with it slowly. For some Japanese films, he continued to use *kowairo setsumei*; for others, he used foreign-film-type *setsumei*. Gradually, a shift took place from *kowairo setsumei* to foreign film *setsumei*, as customers became more accustomed to the foreign-film-type *setsumei* for Japanese films. Miyake finally eradicated *kowairo setsumei* in October. He even showed Matsunosuke films—the most Japanese of Japanese movies—with foreign-film-type *setsumei*. In April 1925, however, under new management, the Fujikan temporarily revitalized *kowairo setsumei* for Matsunosuke films for nostalgic reasons. How long this revival lasted is unclear, but eventually *kowairo setsumei* disappeared completely from the Fujikan.[20]

Despite occasional revivals of *kowairo setsumei*, most writings of the era indicate that, by the end of 1925, *kowairo setsumei* had disappeared from almost all urban theaters. One could still hear it occasionally in the countryside or on the radio, but it was no longer the accepted form of *setsumei*. *Kowairo setsumei*, consisting solely of dialogue supplied from the shadows by a group of people or by a solo *benshi*, largely vanished, but the use of mimetic or impersonating voices to supply dialogue for a portion of a scene did not disappear: It was incorporated into foreign-film-style *setsumei*.

What took place during the Period of Unification was just that—unification. Disparate parts and branches were unified into a whole. *Benshi* no longer came out, introduced a film, then faded into the shadows, either to explain what was unfolding or to dub dialogue into the mouths of the projected characters. After the Period of Unification, films began without any introduction. Solo *benshi* sat in the shadows and provided *setsumei* that was part dialogue, part informative explanation, and part narrative. It was a mix of imitative voices and narrative recitation. Contained within this new form of *setsumei* was everything a spectator needed to know to enjoy a movie. When performed skillfully, *setsumei* would blend into the moving images, drawing audiences unnoticeably into the diegetic illusion. It required the entire Taishō period for *setsumei* to mature. By the time Hirohito officially assumed the throne, heralding in the Shōwa era (1926–1989), *setsumei* had attained its highest form. It was time for *benshi* to flaunt their talent during the Golden Age of *Setsumei*.

9

THE ART OF *SETSUMEI*

For Japanese movie fans, an era ended not with the death of the mentally ill and cloistered Emperor Taishō on Christmas day, 1926, but with the deaths several months earlier of Rudolph Valentino and Onoe Matsunosuke. The American film legend Rudolph Valentino died at the age of thirty-two, on August 23, 1926. Among Japanese cinephiles, Valentino was one the most popular and beloved foreign film stars. A prevalent expression among urban Japanese women at the time was, "That person is as dreamy as Valey,"[1] and, in an effort to garner for themselves some of the lustful adoration that Valentino generated among women, Japanese men often sported the "Valentino look."[2] For many women throughout the world, Valentino was the ultimate lover, and his untimely death even provoked a few distraught souls to take their own lives.[3] A few weeks after Valentino's death, on September 11, 1926, Onoe Matsunosuke, the king of Japanese period dramas, passed away one day shy of his fifty-second birthday. Having starred in close to 1,000 movies, Matsunosuke literally worked himself to death. His death marked the end of Matsunosuke-style period dramas. Henceforth, a more "realistic" form of swashbuckling, sword-play films would dominate Japanese cinema.

The deaths of the Taishō emperor, Rudolph Valentino, and Onoe Matsunosuke mark the passing of both a political and a cinematic era. They also coincide with the dawning of the Golden Age of *Benshi* and *Setsumei*, which began
in 1926 and lasted through 1931. During these 6 years, most critics stopped arguing over the necessity of *benshi* and accepted them as an integral part of the
cinematic performance. Audiences, meanwhile, continued to enjoy *benshi* as they
always had. The *setsumei* that *benshi* performed during these years were the fruition of nearly 30 years of experimentation, amalgamation, and refinement. In the
years preceding 1926 and following 1931, many *benshi* performed the model
form of *setsumei* that rang through Japanese cinema houses during the Golden
Age. Nevertheless, the period 1926–1931 is special, because it was a time when
almost all *benshi* performed *setsumei* at its highest level, without interference
from outside forces. The period marked by theoretical discussions over the importance of *benshi* had passed, and the challenge of the talkies had yet to arise. It
was a golden age not only in terms of quality, but also quantity. The best estimate
for the number of people working as *benshi* during any year of the Golden Age of
Benshi is between 6,000 and 7,000.[4]

By 1926, movies were the overwhelmingly dominant form of public entertainment in Japan. There were over 1,000 movie theaters, with more than 117
million spectators. With a population of about 60 million, that averages out to the
equivalent of every Japanese attending the cinema at least twice a year. The
number of movie theaters and the size of the audience continued to grow well into
the 1930s.[5] People from all walks of life attended the cinema. Stereotypically,
the high-brow intellectual type preferred foreign films; everyone else preferred
Japanese films. In 1927, about 70% of the movies shown in Japan were Japanese,
27% American, and 3% European.[6] Some theaters showed a mixed bill of Japanese and foreign films; others showed only one or the other. Japanese films became increasingly popular as the Shōwa era progressed. The most popular type of
Japanese film was the sword-fighting genre. The rising popularity of Japanese

films and the subsequent decline of foreign films coincided with the rise of xeno-phobic Japanese militarism and nationalism.

The number of *benshi* employed by a movie theater depended on the size and genre of the theater, but usually theaters employed around six to eight *benshi*. Customarily, there were a few head *benshi*, several associate *benshi*, perhaps a female *benshi*, and a few apprentices. The typical program of four or five movies was a mixed bill of news, comedy, drama, and action. Usually, an apprentice or junior *benshi* would open the show by providing *setsumei* for a newsreel or serial. That would be followed by one or two more short films, which in turn were fol-lowed by one or two features. As the show progressed, the better *benshi* emerged, with the best *benshi* typically closing the show.

During the first decade or so of motion pictures in Japan, because films were so short, a *benshi* could *setsumei* an entire film by himself. However, as films became longer, *benshi* began to share the duties, because providing *setsumei* was physically exhausting and incredibly hard on the voice. An examination of contemporary movie theater programs indicates that one *benshi* usually handled movies that were an hour or less, while two or three *benshi* handled the longer, two- to three-hour features. The change of narrative performer midway through a performance was not unique to cinema. It was also a common practice in *bun-raku* and *kabuki*. Since each *benshi* had his own style, every time the *benshi* changed, the *setsumei* changed as well. Thus, for the sake of continuity in the program it was important that not more than two or three *benshi* share the duties for one film.

If a *benshi* provided an outstanding *setsumei*, or an outstanding segment of *setsumei*, for a particular motion picture, he sometimes went on tour with that *se-tsumei* and would provide encore performances every couple of years. Somei Saburō, for example, performed his *Antony and Cleopatra setsumei*, with its in-famous "and" in it, throughout the silent era and even at post-World War II *benshi* recitals. The demand by fans to hear a highly regarded piece of *setsumei* meant that a *benshi* might perform one piece of *setsumei* hundreds of times in his life-time. *Benshi* showed off popular pieces of *setsumei* at a "*benshi* exhibition."

Benshi exhibitions were events at which a number of *benshi* would gather to perform. They also provided audiences with the opportunity to view and to compare some of the best *benshi* in one performance, and it gave *benshi* a chance to compare their *setsumei* with those of other *benshi*. Often, these exhibitions are referred to as, or entitled, "tournaments" or "competitions," but they were not really competitive tournaments as much as they were displays of the best *benshi*. These events were always sold out and took place in one day or over several days.

The first such exhibition was held on November 29, 1909, at the Ueno Kyōsokan. About one dozen Pathé *benshi* participated in this "*Setsumei tengu-kai*" (*setsumei* boaster gathering).[7] Six months later, on July 2–3, 1910, the movie magazine *Katsudō shashinkai*, in celebration of its first anniversary, sponsored an exhibition of six of the top *benshi* at the Hongōza. Somei Saburō, Nakagawa Keiji, and Ōyama Takayuki were among the participants. A full-page advertise-ment in the *Katsudō shashinkai* explained that one of the reasons the magazine was sponsoring this event was so that fans could evaluate the *benshi*. The fol-lowing issue of *Katsudō shashinkai* published several evaluations of the *benshi* who participated in the exhibition.[8] *Benshi* exhibitions were held almost yearly throughout the remainder of the silent era. They usually took place in the major cities of Tokyo and Osaka. At some events, over 50 *benshi* performed.[9] These displays of *benshi* oratorical skills served as a barometer for determining and judging the top *benshi* and *setsumei* in Japan and as a place to study the art and skill of *setsumei*.

Setsumei Outside the Cinema

Throughout their existence, motion pictures have had a profound effect on society. One of their greatest impacts has been the fabrication and popularization of an idealized cultural model of what is trendy, chic, and fashionable. In an ef-fort to emulate the stars projected onto the silver screen, people throughout the world—from average citizens to presidents of the United States—have smoked certain brands of cigarettes, worn particular clothes, walked in a stylized manner, and used expressions coined by cinematic icons. In short, motion pictures have engendered cultural trends and desires by amplifying archetypes of consumption, beauty, and dress. In post-World War I Japan, that often meant smoking Golden Bat cigarettes and wearing Harold Lloyd glasses.

For most viewers throughout the world, silent movies typically generated visual mimicry; that is, they usually popularized visible trends. The aural component of music only occasionally influenced the musical tastes of the masses. Most music that accompanied silent films was a compilation of mood music based on cue sheets, which generated a musical atmosphere to fit the scene. Although the compilation may have been original, the parts were generally stock segments of previously composed music that had been circulating for years and thus had little impact on popular music trends. In general, it was the purposely composed scores from big-budget films that made an impact on cultural trends. For most spectators, therefore, the visual images customarily determined what was culturally popular.

In Japan, however, where there existed the added aural element of the *benshi*, the popularization and creation of vernacular sayings were just as prevalent as the formulation of visual trends. *Benshi* often introduced and popularized expressions that had been prevalent only among a small group of school students. Ikoma Raiyū's skillful incorporation into his *setsumei* of the expression *heiki da heiki da* (no problemo) instead of *daijobu* (all right), for example, quickly popularized an expression that had hitherto been seldom used. Similarly, his use of the expression *sugoizott* (Aaawesome) brought the use of that word into vogue.[10] Over the years, moralists condemned *benshi* for coining "vulgar expressions" that children eagerly mimicked when they left the theater.[11] The tirades of the moralists, however, did not deter the *benshi* from continuing to incorporate trendy phrases into their *setsumei*. One contemporary asserted that, if an early Shōwa era Japanese wanted to stay hip, he "had to listen to *benshi*'s *setsumei*."[12]

Listening to *setsumei* only at movie theaters did not satiate many Japanese movie fans. They wanted to enjoy the euphony of *setsumei* at home as well. Consequently, sometime during the late Meiji or early Taishō period, record companies began issuing phonograph recordings of famous *setsumei*.[13] With the production of *setsumei* recordings, the narrative art of *setsumei* was literally separated from the cinema. *Setsumei* had gained its independence. Every record produced is a testament to the autonomy of *setsumei* as an art form. Just as people liked listening to *gidayū* and *nagauta*, they loved listening to *setsumei*.

Along with those people who just wanted to enjoy the pleasure of listening to *setsumei* in their homes, many people bought records of *setsumei*, so that they could practice along with the popular *benshi*. Throughout the silent era—and even to this day—but especially during the Golden Age of *Benshi*, imitating *benshi* was a popular pastime among cinephiles. Movie fans often performed famous *setsumei* for their friends, in a form of presentation that can best be described as "*setsumei karaoke*." Phonograph recordings of *setsumei* provided fans with a means to facilitate the process of imitation. With the purchase of an *eiga setsumei* record, a fan could practice and perform *setsumei* at home, by listening to a record of a master *benshi* over and over again.

If, for many Japanese, performing *setsumei* was a popular parlor trick, for others it was a means by which they could openly express discontent. After the March 15, 1928, and April 16, 1929, police arrests of Communists and Communist sympathizers throughout Japan, voicing opposition to the Japanese government became increasingly difficult. Because expressing dissatisfaction in the political arena was dangerous, many Japanese chose to voice their discontent at the cultural level. Following the Communist crackdown, one means used by some people to safely express their uneasiness with the government was to recite *setsumei*. Many liked performing the following *setsumei* from Itō Daisuke's *Samurai Nippon* (*The Japanese Samurai*), because of its metaphorical poignancy. The *setsumei* revolves around the assassination of Ii Naosuke, the Great Councilor (*tairō*) who strove for Tokugawa absolutism, and who ruthlessly attacked his critics and enemies in the Ansei Purge of 1858–1859.

> [Voiced *setsumei*]: March 3, 1860, in the midst of an untimely and heavy spring snow, the procession marched solemnly toward Edo castle, where eighteen masterless samurai from Mito and one from Satsuma were outside the snowy Sakurada gate, waiting to kill the Great Councilor, Ii Naosuke. At that time, Shinno Tsurushio, Ii's illegitimate son, knew that his father was in danger. When Himeigiku tried to stop him, he pushed her aside and went to Sakurada gate.

> [Singing *setsumei*]: Should I risk my life or should I stay with her? To live or to die? It is a toss-up. Like it or not, I am ready to draw my sword as the snow falls on Edo's Sakurada gate.

> [Voiced *setsumei*]: The battle continues, but Tsurushio's effort to save his father was in vain, as his father became a cold corpse. Tsurushio was called a traitor. Ah, where will he go now?[14]

Many of the citizens who repeated this *setsumei* hoped that those government officials who were responsible for the "Communist Purge" would meet the same cold and deadly fate that Ii—the leader of the Ansei Purge—had met.

For people who lived in the countryside, records of *setsumei* often served as surrogates for films. Only a limited number of movies circulated through the countryside, so the only information some people had about certain motion pictures came from magazines and records. "For those pictures that we could not view," recalled Furuta Tamotsu, "we would listen to *setsumei* records and imagine what the scenes must have looked like."[15] For many Japanese, the narrative richness of *setsumei* was all they needed to visualize what others saw projected inside the darkened theaters of the large cities.

Others bought records of *setsumei* to listen to the Western–Japanese musical accompaniment that was unique to motion pictures and that frequently appeared as a musical interlude on *setsumei* records. Conversely, records of popular film music often contained *setsumei*. A related genre of record that likewise sold well was ballad movies (*kouta eiga*). During the 1920s, *kouta eiga* was a popular movie genre in Japan. The presentation of a *kouta eiga* involved either the *benshi*, or, at the finer theaters, a professional singer, usually a female, singing the song or songs composed especially for the film. The songs were usually "Western-like" and appeared during the climatic scene. That *benshi* sometimes had to sing during their performance further attests to the broad range of skills that they had to possess. *Kouta eiga* are also significant because they delineate another means by which the Japanese added a vocal element to their silent cinema.

Besides phonograph records of *setsumei*, books of transcribed *setsumei* were popular among fans, especially schoolboys. These anthologies, called *setsumeishū*, generally contained *setsumei* from 10 to 15 films. Some *setsumeishū* contained anonymous *setsumei*; others offered attribution to a particular *benshi*. These anthologies usually focused on a specific movie genre or theme, such as modern dramas, period dramas, foreign films, or recent films.

Outside the cinema, radio was another medium that disseminated *setsumei* to the public. In experimental broadcasts that began on March 22, 1925, Tokyo Broadcasting Station aired Japan's first radio broadcasts. Regular broadcasting started later that year, on July 12. Entertainers of all types performed on the radio. *Kabuki* and *shimpa* actors appeared before a microphone and performed excerpts from their respective repertoires, as did *naniwabushi*, *rakugo*, and *kōdan* storytellers. Some of the most popular performers during the first decade of radio were *benshi*, and the Sunday afternoon show *Special Collection of Movie Setsumei* was a favorite of many.

Live broadcasts from inside movie theaters frequently took place, as did the more conventional studio broadcasts. The mature solo form of *setsumei*, prevalent at the time, was broadcast, and on occasion, *kowairo setsumei* was also heard. On special occasions, the actual actors from the film would supply their own dialogue, while a *benshi* acted as a narrator. The most common type of *setsumei* on the radio was an enriched form that *benshi* initially created specifically for radio, called *eiga monogatari* (movie story). Because radio was a medium based on hearing rather than vision, *benshi* augmented their traditional *setsumei* with details that would facilitate listening and improve the mental image of the story. *Setsumei* could be heard on Japanese radio as late as the 1950s.

Another approach that several top *benshi* took at that time, to connect with their fans outside the cinema, was to perform at variety shows called *Nayamashikai (The Pranksters)*. Tokugawa Musei and Yamano Ichirō's love of variety theater gave birth to those events. One reason they decided to stage the *Nayamashikai* was to give *benshi* a chance to show their faces to the audience. With the elimination of *maesetsu* in the early 1920s, *benshi* always performed in the dark. Audiences knew what *benshi* sounded like, but not how they looked. *Nayamashikai* was a forum in which *benshi* could show their faces to their fans. They also provided *benshi* with an opportunity to do something different. The shows seldom made money, but, for the participants involved, that did not matter. They put on the *Nayamashikai* for the sheer joy of doing something different and out of the ordinary. The first *Nayamashikai* was held on March 14, 1926, and, thereafter, they were held about once a year, until the last one in 1935.

The *Nayamashikai* was only the most famous of a number of variety shows that *benshi* staged. *Samayoikai (The Wanderers)* and *Akiretakai (The Amazed)* were two rival shows with a similar format. Although mostly *benshi* performed in these variety shows, *rakugo* storytellers, movie stars, and anyone else the producers could round up, also participated. *Nayamashikai* contained a few skits and other dramatic performances, but mostly consisted of narrative recitations. *Eiga monogatari*, reading aloud, *rakugo*, and *kōdan* were among the narrative arts performed.

At these *Nayamashikai*, *benshi* occasionally antagonized the police, just as they did when they performed *setsumei*. One *benshi*, Ōtsuji Shirō (?–1952), was arrested by the police for his seditious one-man skit. Ōtsuji was a very talented comedic *benshi*. Although his delivery was rather methodical, his phraseology was humorous. He was particularly renowned for his retorts to hecklers. At the third or fourth *Nayamashikai*, Ōtsuji put on a skit, which he wrote, entitled "The Triumphant Return of the Valiant Hero." Appearing on stage wrapped from head to toe in bandages, he gave the following soliloquy. "My Fellow Japanese. On a battlefield of raining bullets, for the glory of the emperor, I was full of heroism, and, under the shadows and sunshine of the regimental flag, I took one step forward and two steps back, three steps forward and four back. I continued in this way until I received an injury that would bring me honor." Immediately after the performance, the police arrested Ōtsuji. They did not find Ōtsuji's "nationalistic" speech amusing. After reprimanding Ōtsuji, the police let him go.[16]

An especially popular segment of *Nayamashikai* was the *mandan* performances. *Mandan* was a narrative art that *benshi* created. It was basically a 15- to 20-minute monologue of random thoughts. *Mandan* emerged from the power failures that frequently plagued the Tokyo Konparukan. Tokugawa Musei, Ōtsuji Shirō, Izumi Kōfu, and Iguchi Shizunami all worked at the Konparukan in the early 1920s. When the power went out, they would retire backstage and wait for its return. While they waited, they would "play vaudeville" (*yose gokko*). That is, they would impersonate *rakugo*, *kōdan*, and *naniwabushi* performances. This private backstage camaraderie eventually developed into *mandan*.[17]

Tokugawa Musei and Ōtsuji Shirō are the two *benshi* most responsible for *mandan*'s creation and dissemination.[18] Musei had thought about creating a more modern and up-to-date form of *rakugo* and *kōdan* for sometime. The private backstage performing and bantering that took place during the power failures at the Konparukan was the initial spark in the creative process. The new narrative art really began to take shape with Musei's "reading" of a chapter from Natsumei Sōseki's *Wagahai wa neko de aru* (*I am a Cat*) at the Kanda YMCA in 1923. This reading inspired Musei and Ōtsuji to push the envelope on what constituted a narrative performance.[19]

Following the Kantō earthquake, Ōtsuji Shirō found himself temporarily jobless. Occasionally, he found employment with the navy, which invited him on board battleships to entertain the troops. He delighted the troops with the new form of storytelling that he and Musei had been creating over the previous few years. At the time, however, this new art form did not yet have a name. What he was doing was similar to *rakugo*, but Ōtsuji realized that it was not *rakugo* and hence needed its own name. In talking with Tokugawa Musei, he said, "Since there are 'arbitrary drawings' (*manga*, i.e., comics), why not have 'arbitrary talk' (*mandan*)?"[20] In other words, he compared this new and free style of narration, which Musei and he had created, to the kind of unfettered expression found in comic books.

According to Ōtsuji, the three keys to *mandan* are that it must be a true story, must not cause harm, and must not have a plot. The true art of *mandan* is talking for 15 minutes without a thread to the conversation, and making it seem natural. In many ways, *mandan* is very similar to *rakugo*, but with four important differences. First, in *rakugo*, there has to be a punch line to the story—a last laugh. In *mandan*, there can be a last laugh, but there does not have to be one. Second, *rakugo* generally has a coherent plot, but *mandan* does not. Third, in *rakugo*, a storyteller must learn his stories from a master; in *mandan*, the storyteller (most of whom were *benshi*) created the story himself. Finally, in *rakugo*, one did not have to adapt to the times; in *mandan*, it was essential that one stay very topical and current.[21]

The creation of the new narrative art of *mandan* indicates the mastery of oratorical skills, techniques, and theories by *benshi*, or at least a select group of *benshi*. The fact that most *mandan* performers were former *benshi* is further testament to the skills of the *benshi*, because only a skilled orator could talk for 15 minutes about nothing, in a highly entertaining and satisfying manner. *Benshi* truly were talented vocal artists, and it was during the Golden Age of *Setsumei* that they turned their movie narration into a genuine narrative art.

The Art of *Setsumei*

"Is *setsumei* an art?" was a frequently asked question during the Pure Film Movement's assault on *setsumei*. Whether one considered *setsumei* to be a narrative art or not usually correlated to how one viewed *benshi*. Those who believed that *benshi* were a detriment to motion pictures, and a blemish to the Japanese empire, tended not to think of *setsumei* as a narrative art. For some of these antagonists, *benshi* were not artists, but rather "explainers" or "linguists."[22] On the other hand, those who enjoyed what a *benshi*'s oration added to the cinematic experience often argued that *setsumei* was an art and that *benshi* were narrative artists.

One point of contention within this debate was whether *setsumei* could stand on its own, free of the film, or not. *Benshi* foes believed that *setsumei* could not exist apart from the film; it was dependent on the film. Thus, because *setsumei* was not an independent art form, they reasoned, *benshi* were not artists.[23] *Benshi* advocates, on the other hand, argued that *setsumei* could stand alone, and that, consequently, it was a narrative art and *benshi* were narrative artists.[24]

The existence of hundreds of phonograph records of *setsumei* indicates that *setsumei* could exist on its own as an independent art. However, *benshi* often incorporated supplementary descriptions into their recorded *setsumei*, and they created a new form of embellished *setsumei* called *eiga monogatari* for phonograph records and radio broadcasts, which implies that *setsumei* was sometimes difficult to understand by itself. If a motion picture is still fresh in a spectator's mind, listening to a record of *setsumei* can vividly conjure up the images of the film. If one has not seen the movie, however, picturing what must have unfolded on the screen is difficult solely by listening to a record.

People should not disregard or ignore *setsumei* as an important narrative art simply because it is not complete without motion pictures. Although the *jōruri* chanting that accompanies puppet dramas and the *nagauta* that accompanies *kabuki* are sometimes performed as independent narrative arts, both are incomplete without the puppets and actors that they respectively accompany. Similarly, if one listens to *jōruri* or *nagauta* from a play that one is unfamiliar with, what the play is about is difficult to fully envision. Despite this, people embrace both *jōruri* and *nagauta* as narrative arts, without any qualms. *Setsumei* should now be viewed in a similar way.

The *setsumei* of the Golden Age was a combination of narrative explanation, fabricated dialogue, and verbalized intertitles. "Intertitles," according to
Somei Saburō, "must be at the heart of the motion picture *setsumei*."[25] Intertitles
guided a *benshi* through the performance, and it was important that a *benshi* pas-
sionately read the intertitles and remain faithful to them. The more passion a *benshi* put into his reading, the more exciting the performance. The power of the
benshi, however, resided in what he said between intertitles; that is, in the dialogue and narration that he created to accompany the moving images. The more
skilled the *benshi*, the better the mix of dialogue and explanation, and the better
the word choice and word flow.

Benshi usually narrated in the past tense and provided dialogue in the present tense. This is similar to the tense structure found in novels written in the
third person: Events are described in the past, but people talk in the present. What
was unusual about *setsumei*, however, was that *benshi* applied it to moving images unfolding in the present. Thus, as a movie unfolded, the dialogue *setsumei*
applied to the mouths of the characters was in the present, but the descriptions and
information about those characters and about what was taking place were presented as if the events had already taken place.

Throughout the Meiji and Taishō eras, the majority of *benshi* used a
scratchy voice (*dorakoe*) very similar to the one found in *naniwabushi*. Some
continued to use this voice during the Golden Age, but the majority switched to a
less scratchy and more natural voice. Most *benshi* provided *setsumei* using the
regional dialect of the area in which they performed. Lacking all amplification, a
benshi had to project his voice so that those in the back of the theater could hear.
He also had to enunciate and articulate clearly and in a pleasing tone. To become
one with the film, *benshi* used emotive voices that matched the emotions on the
screen. If a character was crying, for example, a *benshi* would use a sniveling or
weeping voice. In this way, a *benshi* used his voice to draw the audience into the
sphere of the movie's feelings. If a *benshi* could modulate his voice to coincide
with the emotional ups and downs of the movie, he could keep his audience on the

edge of their seats. Thus, for many spectators, the emotional expression of the *benshi*'s voice was more important than the words he spoke.

Most *benshi* worked with a handful of stock voices that indicated characters, rather than imitated them. *Benshi* narrated and provided voices for both male and female parts, while paying careful attention to the class-specific locutions for each character. Courtesans had their own vocabulary, as did samurai, merchants, artisans, townspeople, peasants, monks, and criminals. Each class, for example, had a different word for "you." To apply the wrong vocabulary to a character on the screen would destroy the diegetic illusion. Sometimes it was difficult to discern who was talking, the *benshi* or a character, but, if the *setsumei* was good, it did not matter.

During the early years of *setsumei*, some foreign film *benshi* would habitually call the female lead Mary, the hero Jack, and the villain Robert.[26] Others bestowed waggish names on characters for comical effect, such as calling the daughter of the pharmacist "Aspirin" or the son of the cook "Pork Cutlet" and the daughter "Curry Rice."[27] As *setsumei* matured, *benshi* began referring to characters by the names provided in the scripts. Throughout the silent era, many *benshi* stated in their *setsumei* who the actor was appearing on screen.

A *benshi* also had to empathize with the personalities of the characters in the film; he had to enter the film and become the characters. "If Rudolph Valentino appears on the screen," wrote the *benshi* Matsui Suisei, "then the *benshi* must become Valentino. If he does this, the female fans will become excited."[28] As Somei Saburō explained, "When I *setsumei*, I first pay such close attention that I completely enter into the picture. If I don't become one with the characters, in the end, my *setsumei* will lose its vitality and seem out of place."[29]

To satisfy an audience, a *benshi* had to put his heart into his performance. He had to be enthusiastic about what he was doing. Audiences picked up on the *benshi*'s attitude, and, if the *benshi* was not engrossed in his performance, the audience would not be either. Sometimes, *benshi* had to provide *setsumei* for the same film dozens of times per week, or, sometimes, even five or six times on the same day. After watching a film so many times, the hero no longer looked heroic and the beautiful heroine looked less beautiful. Nevertheless, a talented *benshi* was able to treat each performance as if it were his first, with the same degree of enthusiasm and with the same amount of fervor needed for a packed theater. By doing so, he could impart a feeling of satisfaction to the audience.

A *benshi* had to do all of this, and more, without consciously thinking about it. *Benshi* did not have time to look at the screen, think of what to say, then speak. Ideally, a *benshi* saw and spoke at the same time. He instantly transformed the visual images into spoken words. "Watching every scene and instantly saying something relevant," Tokugawa Musei claimed, "is only possible if one practices and works hard. *Benshi* must cram their heads with every expression that they might possibly need. What a *benshi* needs is not a great memory, but rather the ability to assimilate expressions unconsciously, so that they instantly fly into the forefront of his consciousness whenever something triggers them."[30]

Benshi also had to make sure that their tone and word choice fit the audience to whom they were giving *setsumei*. If children composed most of an audience, then the employment of vulgar or erudite phraseology was not apropos. Conversely, a theater full of intellectuals did not want to listen to childish babble. Since most audiences contained a mix of people, finding the perfect balance was challenging. Nevertheless, the *benshi*'s job was to figure out what kind of audience he had and to provide the appropriate *setsumei*.

Setsumei also had to harmonize with the movie. If a *benshi* provided *setsumei* for a comedy, then he had to give comedic *setsumei*; likewise, a love story required sentimental *setsumei*, historical films needed historical facts, detective stories needed clues pointed out, and foreign films needed Western customs explained. Educational films needed detailed *setsumei*; love stories needed light *setsumei*. In short, each genre of film demanded a matching *setsumei*. For certain genres and themes, especially sexual and political ones, commentators strongly expressed their opinion about what should or should not be contained within a *benshi*'s *setsumei*. When it came to sexual matters, most commentators wanted *benshi* to be fuzzy on the details; they urged *benshi* not to be too explicit. When it came to political topics, commentators wanted *benshi* to be patriotic. One commentator implored *benshi* providing *setsumei* for military films: "Do not say anything to make the audience hate the military just because of the cruelty of war, and do not give *setsumei* that might lead to the formation of antinational sentiment." The commentator backed up this statement by pointing out that, in the United States and Great Britain, movies were also censored so that they conformed to these same patriotic ideals.[31]

What often caused *setsumei* to diverge from the motion picture was the subjectivity of the *benshi*. Providing objective commentary, therefore, was one of the elements of good *setsumei*. As Ikoma Raiyū stated, "Our duty as *benshi* is to communicate the thought of the film and to explain what is going on. We should avoid subjective *setsumei*."[32] A *benshi*'s subjectivity hindered an audience's imagination and appreciation of a motion picture. Spectators had the right to their own subjective opinion about a film unfettered and uninfluenced by the *benshi*.

A good *benshi* was a faithful commentator; he did not exaggerate or mislead audiences with his *setsumei*. He let the audience enjoy the film, without his *setsumei* impinging upon them. He did not state the ridiculously obvious; rather, he clarified elements that the audience could not gather by watching alone. He became one with the film. Tokugawa Musei put it this way: "When I perform, I separate myself from my ego, and, from the hidden shadows of the picture, I speak as if I were actually the movie talking. In other words, I do not think that I am a *setsumeisha* giving *setsumei*."[33] To accomplish this feat, a *benshi* had to prepare, and, to ensure that what he wanted to say fit into the time allotted, he had to possess a firm understanding of the plot and themes of the movie, as well as of the details of the passing scenes. He had to understand thoroughly the mood and tempo of the film, so that his *setsumei* would blend into it. If the tempo of the *setsumei* were not in synchrony with the tempo of the film, *setsumei* became obtrusive. In short, he had to create *setsumei* that was a mixture of tension and relaxation, that had peaks of excitement, valleys of serenity, and a climax that paralleled that of the film.

Although the skills and techniques discussed above were all a part of the *setsumei* of the Golden Age, by emphasizing and implementing each skill and technique to varying degrees, each *benshi* fabricated an individual style of *setsumei*. Over the years, writers and *benshi* have used various methods to try to group *benshi* and *setsumei* into larger, more encompassing categories, none of which are completely satisfying.[34] *Setsumei* sounds like no other narrative art in Japan, and, upon hearing it, one can easily distinguish it from other oral arts; nevertheless, there was such variety among the *benshi* that trying to confine all of their *setsumei* styles into precise categories is near impossible. Realistically, there were thousands of *benshi* styles. Or, as Somei Saburō expressed it, "*Setsumei* styles are unique to each *setsumeisha*."[35]

There are two categorizations, however, that, when defined very broadly, do provided insight into the *setsumei* of the Golden Age. These are the Yamanote and Shitamachi styles. "Yamanote" and "Shitamachi" refer to areas within Tokyo, the political, economic, and cultural center of the Japanese empire. As the cultural capital, many of the styles and trends found there eventually spread to other parts of the nation. The Yamanote and Shitamachi styles of *setsumei* were two such trends. The hilly Yamanote area of Tokyo was located to the west of the Imperial Palace and was the area of "high society." It was the patrician section of the city. Shitamachi, on the other hand, is more difficult to define geographically, but was where the working-class Japanese lived. It was the plebeian section of the city. In his book about the evolution of these two areas of Tokyo, Edward Seidensticker called the Yamanote area "High City" and the Shitamachi area "Low City."[36]

The Yamanote style of *setsumei* strove for realism. The *benshi* of this style, such as Tokugawa Musei, Yamano Ichirō, Takemoto Shōko, and Ōtsuji Shirō, were not concerned about talking; rather, they wanted the audience to appreciate the film as if the *benshi* was not there. The Yamanote style was usually used for Occidental films and was popular with the intelligentsia. It was also known as the nonsinging (*utawanai*) style of *setsumei*. It was more conversational in tone, objective, focused on the text, and avoided strongly stated emotion.

One of the keys to the Yamanote style was knowing when to talk and when to remain silent. According to Yamanote *benshi*, if a *benshi* talked too much, his *setsumei* became an overpowering nuisance. *Benshi*, therefore, had to know when to support a scene with his *setsumei* and when to let the music fill the theater and allow the pictures to do the talking. In Somei Saburō's opinion, continual *setsumei* that did not allow the audience to rest could "kill the film."[37] Talented *benshi* knew exactly when and where to insert their silence (*ma*). Silence added life to the *setsumei* and the performance. Tokugawa Musei viewed silence as the vitamins of a story. "A story may have calories, but without vitamins it is not nutritious."[38] Thus, the skilled *benshi* of the Yamanote style was one who knew not only what to say, but when not to speak. The Yamanote style of *setsumei* was much more diegetically inclined than was the Shitamachi style. In the words of Tokugawa Musei, "The ideal *setsumei* was a work of art that the audience was not consciously aware of. . . . *Setsumei* should not become the least bit interfering. It must appear as if the sound is emanating from the screen or as if one were saying the words from the bottom of one's heart. That is the kind of feeling that needs to be perpetuated—one must be spellbound by the screen. . . . In these situations, the audience becomes completely captivated."[39] Thus, before the audience could enter the diegetic illusion, the *benshi* had to enter it, and it was from inside the film, so to speak, that the *benshi* conveyed the audience into the movie's diegetic world.

The Shitamachi, or singing (*utau*), style strove for poeticism. For the *benshi* of this style, such as Ikoma Raiyū, Nishimura Rakuten, Nishimura Korakuten, and Kunii Shikō, the film was there as a visual source for the poetry that they frequently delivered in the *shichigo* meter. This style focused on rhythmic tones and poetry, and was less concerned with the exact text. The Shitamachi style began to take shape during the mid-Taishō period, when Universal's melodramatic Bluebird films were popular.[40] Although this style was originally developed for foreign films, it was mostly used for Japanese films. In the countryside, where Japanese films dominated the market, the Shitamachi-shichigo style was widely used.

Shitamachi *benshi* often inserted highly poetic lines into their *setsumei* because they sounded great, yet they often had nothing to do with the film and thus made little sense. Although superfluous, when used judiciously, they added to the poetic beauty and flow of the *setsumei*. Kunii Shikō, for example, liked to interject the following lines into his *setsumei*: "In the forest of flowers, the spring moon, one bird goes, another returns: don't cross the floating bridge of dreams."[41] Usually, *benshi* saved their most poetic phrases for the end of the film.

Throughout the silent era, *benshi* frequently concluded their *setsumei* with a stock rhetorical ending. During the early years, *benshi* used unimaginative phrases such as, "All reels have been shown," or some variant of this idea. Over time, however, *benshi* began to fabricate more elaborate *setsumei* ending lines for themselves. Often, these lines were poetically beautiful, but meaningless and unrelated to the film. Still, according to at least one writer, "These lines ought to be accepted into the textbooks at women's schools as examples of Meiji and Taishō poetry."[42]

Hayashi Tempū (Hayashi Shigeru, c. 1881–1935)[43] created one of the most famous and beautiful *setsumei* ending lines for the Bluebird film *Southern Justice*, which Universal released in Japan on January 18, 1918. Hayashi Tempū was the son of a famous Meiji era lawyer. He had planned on following in his father's footsteps, but, after a falling out with his father, he had to drop out of Meiji University for financial reasons. He became a *benshi* in 1910 and quickly distinguished himself. One problem with his *setsumei* was that he was a little too subjective. Audiences could instantly tell whether he liked or disliked a movie by the tone of his *setsumei*.[44] When he created the following lines for *Southern Justice*, he was an up-and-coming *benshi*. This was a breakout piece for him.

Out of the misty darkness
Spring radiating
Throughout every village
Stars all scattered
Across a lavender sky
Blossoms blown like snow
Over the green earth.
Spring, ah, Spring. Youth, ah, youth. Spring:
Romance in the South.
[As the final scene fades out and "The End" appears]
The title of this film: *Southern Justice*. In five reels.[45]

Although Hayashi Tempū developed these poetic lines, Ikoma Raiyū quickly usurped them and made them famous. Ikoma's regular incorporation of these lines into his *setsumei* led people to think that he created them, but the truth is that Hayashi authored them. Several other *benshi* also used this *setsumei* fragment, and some even continued to use it after the *benshi* era. When Nishimura Kora-kuten worked as a television host in the 1950s, he incorporated these lines into his introductory remarks.[46]

The use of the same *setsumei* fragments by numerous *benshi* was a common practice. That *benshi* willingly and frequently used the same *setsumei* segments implies that, in some ways, the art was separate from the artist. That is, in some cases, the lines themselves, rather than the individual who spoke them, were famous. From this perspective, *setsumei* had become a narrative art form in its own right, separate from the individual *benshi*. People could, and did, appreciate the composition of *setsumei* in and of itself. They appreciated the lyrical beauty that was the narrative art of *setsumei*, rather than, or along with, the narrative artist.

10

THE TALKIE REVOLUTION AND
DEMISE OF THE *BENSHI*

Talkies

Several inventors of motion pictures never wanted movies to be silent. Simultaneously with the invention of motion pictures in the 1890s, they searched for ways to unite recorded sound with the moving images. In 1895, Thomas Edison came out with the Kinetophone, a contraption that was basically a phonograph attached to a movie projector. Over the next 30 years, dozens of other similar machines emerged that attempted to mechanically combine a phonograph with motion pictures. Most of these machines failed because they could not maintain the synchronization between the phonograph and moving images for long periods of time, and because the amplification of the phonograph was too weak, preventing audience members throughout the theater from hearing it.

By the middle of the second decade of the twentieth century, most film studios had lost interest in developing sound pictures because of the shortcomings and continual failures of the early machines. Many studio heads also came to believe that the transition to sound would be a costly gamble that could result in ruin for the entire industry. The conversion to sound would require enormous sums of capital, because every theater would have to be wired for the purpose and would need new projectors. In addition, costly sound stages would have to be built to keep outside noise from interfering with the soundtrack—gone would be the days of filming in open-air studios next to busy streets. Furthermore, there were concerns over how silent movie stars, who had never had to speak, would deliver spoken dialogue and how audiences would receive them. Studio executives in the United States also worried about how lucrative overseas markets would be effected by films that narratively relied on spoken English.

Nevertheless, a series of technological breakthroughs in the early 1920s, such as electrical (as opposed to mechanical) methods for recording and playing back sound, and the invention of the loudspeaker by corporate giants American Telephone and Telegraph (AT&T) and Radio Corporation of America (RCA), produced some of the essential technology needed to make clearly audible and synchronized sound movies. At first, the only movie studio to show interest in this new technology was Warner Brothers Pictures.

By most accounts, the first successful sound movie was *Don Juan*, which Warner debuted in August 1926. *Don Juan* used the Vitaphone sound-on-disk technology. Where others had failed, the Vitaphone system succeeded in synchronizing the audio and visual elements. In addition, its use of electrical amplification meant that audience members throughout the theater could clearly hear the recorded material. *Don Juan*, however, was still basically a silent film, because the sound that was in perfect synchronization with the film was simply a musical accompaniment that replaced an absent live orchestra. No words were voiced in the film.

The first words synchronously spoken by a performer in a compelling fictional narrative were "Wait a minute! Wait a minute! You ain't heard nothin' yet!" Al Jolsen uttered these prophetic words in *The Jazz Singer*, which Warner premiered in October 1927. Words had been spoken in a few nonnarrative films prior to *The Jazz Singer*, but it was Al Jolsen's words that convinced studio heads and audiences of the viability of talkies. Technically, *The Jazz Singer* was a "partial-talkie," since it contained only a limited amount of dialogue and utilized the pantomime acting prevalent in silent films. Another year would pass before full-length feature films, using dialogue as an integral part of the narrative performance, would appear in theaters. Nevertheless, the huge success of *The Jazz Singer* signaled the demise of silent cinema.

Despite the enormous expense involved, studios and theaters in the United States quickly converted to sound, and, as it turned out, the huge crowds that talkies attracted more than compensated for the expense. In fact, the conversion resulted in huge profits for many studios. By the end of 1930, all the major studios in the United States were producing only talkies, and, by 1932, almost every theater in the United States was showing only talkies.[1]

The rest of the world lagged several years behind. There were many reasons for this. Several European countries tried to prevent American domination of their markets by limiting the importation of American talkies and talkie technology. Another important factor delaying the conversion to talkies around the world was the Great Depression. It hindered the capital flow and attendance necessary for the conversion. The United States converted just before the effects of the depression hit.[2]

Studios around the world that wanted to export their movies to foreign countries faced one daunting problem: How do we export our films to countries whose people do not speak our language? American studios, whose market share of total releases in most countries ranged from 75 to 90%, were particularly troubled by this difficulty. Because about 25% of Hollywood's profits came from exports, overcoming the language barrier was a top priority for many studios.[3]

Silents were comparatively easier to export, because the language problem was more readily overcome. During the early 1910s, American film studios devised cinematic methods for narrating a film that lessened the need for either spoken or written words. Pantomime acting, combined with good editing, could express a great deal of narrative information without words. When films needed words to help advance the narrative, filmmakers sparingly used intertitles. To overcome the language problem posed by intertitles, studios usually simply translated them into the foreign language of the country to which it was being exported. With talkies, however, overcoming the language problem was more difficult.

Initially, film studios, particularly those in Hollywood, dealt with the language problem in several ways. For talkies that did not contain any song or dance, studios would remove the dialogue from the soundtrack, leaving only the music and sound effects. They would then insert dialogue intertitles into the film. If the film contained a mixture of dialogue scenes and song and dance scenes, they would leave the song and dance scenes as they were, while treating the dialogue scenes in the manner just mentioned. Some studios dealt with the language problem by reshooting movies with different-language-speaking casts. That is, they would first shoot the film using an English-speaking cast, then they would reshoot it using a French cast, then a German one, and so on. In 1930, Paramount established a studio just outside Paris, where they made foreign versions in five languages.[4] The most promising method for dealing with the language problem was dubbing, but, because of technological limitations, this method took several years to prove itself. In the European market, some studios even experimented with using native language narrators—*benshi*—but audiences did not take to them. In Japan, however, where audiences accepted *benshi* as an integral part of the cinematic experience, *benshi* temporarily—although not without controversy—solved the language problem for foreign (American) imports, by providing *setsumei* for them.

In a prescient article published in 1921, Yoshiyama Kyokukō noted, "If talkies become a reality, then of course *kowairo* and *setsumei* will no longer be necessary—for Japanese films, that is. For foreign films, however, a voice will still be needed to translate the foreign language and to explain foreign manners and customs." Yoshiyama also pondered how to eliminate the voice from the soundtrack of a talkie, so that *setsumei* could be added—in other words, how to dub *setsumei* onto a talkie. Yoshiyama wrote this 6 years before *The Jazz Singer* proved the viability of talkies and 8 years before the first genuine talkies played in Japan.[5]

The first bona fide talkies shown in Japan were Fox's one-reel film *Song and Dance of Hawaii* and three-reel film *Marching On.* They premiered as the fourth and fifth films on a five-film bill at the Musashinokan on May 9, 1929.[6] *Benshi* performed *setsumei* for the first three silent films of the show, but did not provide it for the talkies. Theater management felt that, since the films were in English and most Musashinokan customers were well-to-do people who had had at least a middle-school education in which they had studied English, there was no need to *setsumei* the talkies. Management was wrong. Most customers found the spoken English and the movies themselves difficult to understand. Audiences demanded that, in the future, *setsumei* be added to the talkies, so that they could follow what was unfolding. Consequently, Tokugawa Musei—the head *benshi* at the Musashinokan at that time—provided *setsumei* for the talkies during the remainder of their stay at the theater.[7] After this initial showing, several American companies, particularly Paramount, moved rapidly to convert their Japanese theater holdings to sound.

The first talkies shown in Japan attracted large crowds, but they did not attract the huge crowds that attended the first talkies in other places around the world. For Japanese audiences, who were accustomed to a voice being attached to cinema, "talking pictures" were nothing new. There was nothing exceptionally attractive about them. As the director Inagaki Hiroshi saw it, "As for us in Japan, the impact of the appearance of talkies was not as great as it was in other countries, because *katsuben* had always been a part of Japanese motion pictures. At silent movies, we entered the theater knowing that there would be a voice to go with the images on the screen. Therefore, one can say that there never really was a silent film era in Japan." [8]

When comparing *benshi* to talkies, many people felt that, because of the poor sound quality of the early talkies, "the feeling one gets with *benshi* is better."[9] Fans preferred to see a movie with their favorite *benshi* doing the talking. In 1931, a foreign reporter noted, "The Japanese refuse to take seriously the transition from silent films to those synchronized with sound. Since May 1929, nearly every American sound film worthy of notice has been pushed into Japan but without any great success."[10]

Nevertheless, for *benshi*, the arrival of genuine talkies in 1929 triggered alarm bells. They realized that talkies were a real threat to their livelihood. "The five years from 1929 to 1933 were the worst years of my life. . . because of the uncertainty of my future," recalled Tokugawa Musei. "They were worse than the war years, because they were so personal. In fact, I was nervous from about 1928 on, when word that talkies were coming started circulating."[11] One thing *benshi* had going for them, however, was that, by the time talkies arrived in Japan, they and their narrative art of *setsumei* had become a strong tradition—and changing or moving away from tradition is often very difficult.

Between May 1929 and July 1931, the only talkies shown in Japan came from America. One problem that American exhibitors faced in Japan, as they did elsewhere around the world, was the language barrier. As mentioned, Japanese audiences demanded that *setsumei* be added to foreign talkies, because they could not understand what was unfolding. The problem with this, however, was that, when the two sources of narrative information—*setsumei* and dialogue—were emitted simultaneously, they clashed with one another and became a jumble of noise. In other words, listening to one was difficult while the other was also in the air. This battle between man and machine was expressively summed up in a contemporary poem:

> The *benshi* bawls
> But the talkie squalls
> And it weareth the *benshi* down.[12]

Talkies wore the *benshi* down, because the *benshi* competed against them with unamplified voices. It never occurred to *benshi* to use microphones. They thought of them as expensive and uneconomical items. Not until 1934 did *benshi* begin to use microphones, but by that time the amplification of their voices was the least of their concerns.

Shouting over the talkies was hard on the *benshi* and the audience. One way that *benshi* tried to solve this audio problem was to leave the sound on for some scenes and turn it off during others. The *benshi* used a bell to signal the projectionist when to turn the sound on and off (or up and down). This *setsumei*, given while the projectionist adjusted the volume of the talkie, was called cut-in-*setsumei* (*kirisetsu*). Ideally, what the *benshi* wanted, and some received, was their own knob to control the volume. At other theaters, *benshi* demanded that the soundtrack be turned off during the entire performance, thus rendering talkies into silents. Besides adjusting the volume of talkies, *benshi* also attempted to adapt their art to the new medium: Instead of adjusting the volume of the talkie, they waited for breaks in the dialogue to insert their *setsumei*.

In the Golden Age of *Benshi* and *Setsumei*, most cinema fans wanted *benshi* attached to talkies. Critics and foreigners living in Japan, however, complained about the sound being turned off, and debates raged in the trade journals over whether or not *benshi* should provide *setsumei* for talkies. Critics argued that *benshi* were redundant and destroyed the cinematic experience of talkies, by being intrusive; they ruined the harmony of the talkies' visual and aural components. *Benshi* were skilled artisans, but they could never create an aural match as good as the one made specifically for the film. *Benshi* defended their actions by arguing that only those few people who knew English fluently could understand talkies without *benshi*. For the majority of people who did not know English, *benshi* were an indispensable aid. Moreover, the audiences themselves demanded that *benshi* be attached to talkies. As Tokugawa Musei astutely pointed out, most critics complained, "'*We* all understand talkies and hence do not need *benshi*,' when in fact what they actually meant, but never said, was, '*I* can understand talkies and think *setsumei* is unnecessary *for me*.'"[13]

A testament to the popularity of *benshi* being attached to talkies is the live radio airing of *benshi* performances accompanying foreign talkies. These broadcasts, called *Remote Broadcasts of Talkies* (*tōkī chūkei*), aired on NHK (Nippon Hōsō Kyōkai). Broadcast live from inside a theater would be the *benshi*'s *setsumei* in Japanese, heard over the foreign language soundtrack, which was turned down and played as background.[14]

The key to the debate over talkies versus *benshi* revolved around the problem of understanding the foreign language (English) spoken in the talkies. Although American studios did not like *benshi* destroying the audio–visual unity of their movies, they did appreciate the fact that *benshi* solved the language problem for them, and thus allowed them to export talkies to Japan. Nevertheless, if studios could devise a means for Japanese audiences to understand foreign talkies without *setsumei*, the totality of the motion picture would be preserved and theaters would no longer have to pay *benshi* for their services.

The search for a better means took several years and involved much experimentation. Several studios tried to dub films into Japanese, employing Japanese who lived in California to do the dubbing. Their Japanese, however, was rather old-fashioned, and their inability to synchronize their words with the actors moving lips produced nothing but box office disappointment for the American studios. One of the more unusual solutions suggested was to print programs for the films that contained a translated version of the dialogue spoken.[15] Some studios experimented with inserting translated intertitles into their talkies. Although it may not have been intentional, the insertion of intertitles into talkies provided *benshi* with a place in the film to perform their *setsumei* that did not conflict with the audio–visual unity of the film.

Another method attempted was the use of sidetitles, that is, Japanese translations were projected onto a screen set up next to the main screen upon which the movie was projected. Despite an initial warm response, sidetitles quickly proved impractical. Audiences began complaining that it was too difficult to look back and forth between the two screens. While they read the titles, they missed what was happening in the film. Moreover, the titles were often not in synchronization with the film. A few theaters tried to overcome the shortcomings of sidetitles by projecting the titles onto the same screen as the movie. This method also proved unpopular, however, because the projected titles were hard to read and they destroyed the visual clarity of the movie itself.[16] Nevertheless, the people who experimented with this technique were very close to the method that finally allowed studios to overcome the language barrier.

That system was superimposed subtitles. Instead of projecting the titles on top of the movie with a separate projector, the titles were burned into the film itself. Thus, they appeared rather clearly on the same screen as the movie. Paramount pictures devised this method as a cost-effective means of overcoming the language problem in exporting talkies throughout the world. In 1930, Paramount released movies with superimposed titles in Spain, Portugal, France, and Holland. The first film for which Paramount made Japanese superimposed subtitles was *Morocco*. It premiered on February 2, 1931, at the Tokyo San'yūkan and quickly became a huge hit (primarily because it was a good film, not because of the subtitles). Initially, all subtitling was done at Paramount's head office in New York. Paramount hired Tamura Yoshihiko to translate the dialogue and two other men, who could write beautiful Japanese calligraphy, to transcribe the translations.[17]

With *Morocco*, Paramount proved to itself and to Japanese audiences that it had developed a viable means for overcoming the language barrier. The titles and images were in synchronization and the titles were not intrusive. Several *benshi* visited Paramount's Tokyo office to protest the use of superimposed subtitles, but to no avail. Henceforth, Paramount would release only subtitled films into Japan. Metro, Fox, United Artists, Warner, and National quickly followed suit. After *Morocco*, first-tier theaters began in earnest to convert to sound, as newspaper articles proclaimed the demise of the *benshi*.[18]

Yet, even after the release of *Morocco*, many Japanese movie fans still favored *benshi*, and becoming a *benshi* was still a highly desirable job. While *Morocco* was playing in theaters, over 150 people applied for 10 *benshi* openings at three theaters. The theaters required that all the applicants take a special exam that required at least a middle-school education. Over 40% of the applicants had graduated from a university.[19] That same month, the Metropolitan Police reported an increase in the number of applicants taking the *benshi* licensing exam.[20] Thus, despite talkies, the lure to become a poet of the dark was still great, and, despite superimposed subtitles, *benshi* continued to turn the sound down in order to *setsumei* talkies. A testament to the popularity of *setsumei* at that time is the insertion of *setsumei* for *Morocco*, and *setsumei* from other talkies, into *setsumeishū* (books containing transcribed *setsumei*).[21] That *benshi* provided *setsumei* for talkies with superimposed subtitles, however, raised new debates within the trade journals.

Critics insisted that, with superimposed titles, spectators could easily understand and enjoy foreign talkies without *benshi*. Because talkie *setsumei* was merely translation, they argued, it served the same function as subtitles. *Benshi* countered by saying that they did more than translate. They helped convey the plot to the audience, and, what is more important, they entertained the audience. "Just because people may understand a film," claimed Tokugawa Musei, "does not mean that they find it entertaining."[22] As *benshi* saw it, they added to the entertainment value of the film. *Benshi* also maintained that subtitles frequently appeared so fast on the screen that the audience did not have time to read them. *Setsumei*, on the other hand, kept audiences fully abreast of what was going on.

This debate evolved into one about whether seeing or hearing was the better method for mentally processing narrative information. In other words, was it better for there to be visual confusion—the mixing of the picture and the superimposed subtitles—or aural confusion—the mixing of *setsumei* and the soundtrack? While reading subtitles, audience members missed what was happening in the picture; however, while listening to *setsumei*, they missed what was happening on the soundtrack. Some people felt that it was easier to listen to the *benshi*'s dialogue than to read the superimposed dialogue; others felt the opposite.

Confident that spectators preferred listening to *setsumei* to reading subtitles, *benshi* proposed that certain theaters be set aside as *setsumei*-less theaters. Thus, for those who thought *benshi* were bothersome and wanted to experience talkies without them, there would be a place to go. At first, the few theaters that showed *setsumei*-less films only showed them a few days a week. Gradually, however, the number of days per week increased, as did the number of theaters showing *setsumei*-less foreign films.

There were several reasons for this, most important of which was that theater owners preferred showing talkies with subtitles and without *benshi*, because it cut down on their expenditures—they no longer had to pay large *benshi* salaries. Although a few top *benshi* continued to possess a drawing power that more than compensated for their salary—that is, they attracted many more patrons to the theater than the film alone would have—many *benshi* did not. As audiences became accustomed to subtitles, foreign film theaters increasingly began to show movies without *benshi*. Many second-tier theaters, however, continued to use *benshi* to *setsumei* the numerous nonsubtitled foreign films that were still in circulation.

With the introduction of superimposed subtitles, *benshi*, particularly foreign film *benshi*, worried increasingly about the serious threat talkies posed to their profession. *Benshi* found especially ominous the rapidity with which several theaters dismissed their musicians after the arrival of talkies. All talkies that arrived in Japan had two aural components: foreign dialogue and music. Theaters needed *benshi* to interpret the foreign dialogue, but they did not need musicians, because talkies contained a musical soundtrack. Moreover, unlike *benshi*, virtually all musicians were anonymous and held no box office appeal. Consequently, soon after converting to sound, many foreign film theaters fired their orchestras.

Theater owners also discovered, at that time, that it was more economical to buy and use phonograph music than to employ a group of musicians. Thus, many theaters, particularly those in the countryside, which did not have the capital required to convert to talkies, but that wanted to present the aura of talkies, replaced their musicians with phonographs. Although a few musicians remained until the end of the silent era, most did not survive the initial onslaught of talkies. The dismissal of musicians, and the implementation of superimposed titles, frightened *benshi*, but the irrefutable shock to the profession was the appearance of Japanese talkies.

The first technologically successful full-talkie (as opposed to partial-talkie) feature film, domestically produced in Japan, was Shōchiku Studios' *Madamu to nyōbo* (*The Neighbor's Wife and Mine*) directed by Gosho Heinosuke. It premiered on July 29, 1931, at the Teikokugekijō, and utilized the Tsuchihashi sound-on-film technology. The film was a box office hit. For *benshi*, the perfection of a Japanese talkie was frightening, since Japanese films constituted over two-thirds of the domestic market.

In large part because of *benshi*, Japan took over 10 years to convert to sound. In 1931, only 6% of theaters in Japan were wired for sound. This increased to 23% in 1932, 52% in 1934, and 84% in 1936.[23] The changeover to producing talkies in Japan also took many years. In 1932, 93% of films made in Japan were silent, 75% in 1934, 25% in 1936, and 5% in 1938—9 years after talkies entered Japan.[24] Japan was making and showing silents long after most other countries had fully converted to sound and, by some accounts, continued to show silents until after the Second World War.[25] For a short time, the slow diffusion of sound in Japan created a two-tier situation, in which the largest and most profitable theaters converted to sound, while the far more numerous smaller theaters continued to show silents.

Although *benshi* played a significant role in slowing the Japanese conversion to sound, several other important factors also contributed to the sluggish pace of diffusion. Many companies lacked the capital necessary to convert to talkies. Exacerbating this circumstance was the policy of the government, which, in 1929, under the leadership of Prime Minister Hamaguchi Osachi, put Japan on the gold standard. Hamaguchi hoped that a stable yen would boost foreign trade. His timing could not have been worse. He put Japan on the gold standard just as the stock market crashed in the United States and sent the world into a great depression. Gold began pouring out of Japan, rapidly depleting Japan's reserves. In 1931, Prime Minister Inukai Tsuyoshi took Japan off the gold standard, but the damage was already done. The world depression, the outflow of gold, and a drop in exports brought about by a disadvantageous exchange rate, combined to create an economic crisis. With the economy almost in shambles, Japanese movie studios were reluctant to invest the large sums of capital needed to convert their studios and theaters to sound.

Another factor slowing the diffusion of sound movies in Japan was that the Japanese wanted to develop their own sound system. They did not want to have to pay royalties to use American or European equipment. Thus, Japanese studios waited for the indigenous invention of sound technology. Although most studios agreed to wait for such a system, they did not cooperate in creating that product. The failure of companies to work together and pool their resources further delayed Japan's conversion.[26]

As they waited for Japanese studios to develop and invest in real talkies, a few theaters that specialized in Japanese films tried to create their own talkies by bringing back group *kowairo*. Group *kowairo* had lain dormant for many years; now, however, confronted with foreign talkies, managers brought it back to life. To sell it to audiences, theaters did not advertise it as *kowairo setsumei*, but rather as human talkies (*yūman tōkī*).[27]

Some other minor factors delaying Japan's conversion to sound included a reluctance among audiences and filmmakers to embrace talkies. For over 30 years, Japanese audiences were accustomed to *benshi* providing *setsumei* for films. They expected and appreciated a form of cinema presentation in which the *benshi* supplied them much-wanted supplementary narrative information. Accepting talkies meant adapting to a new form of presentation, in which actors spoke and for which there was no ancillary narrative information. One had to rely solely on the text of the film itself and on one's own interpretation of that text. Critics complained about *benshi* altering the meaning of motion pictures, but *benshi* also played an important role in satisfying audiences, by providing a clear and unified reading. The *benshi*'s interpretation might not have been the one that the filmmaker or the government wanted, but audiences welcomed it, because it made the film understandable and entertaining. With the advent of talkies, audiences were on their own. If a film did not effectively employ clear audio–visual clues to carry an audience through the twists and turns of the plot, a majority of those in attendance would probably be lost and unsatisfied. Thus, for Japanese filmgoers, there was also a sense of insecurity in having to interpret a film on their own, without the help of *benshi*.

The reluctance of many Japanese filmmakers to convert to sound also slowed its diffusion. Ozu Yasujirō, one of Japan's finest directors, did not make his first talkie until 1936. Ozu and other Japanese directors felt that silent movies were on the verge of reaching a new artistic pinnacle, when sound suddenly came in and disrupted everything.[28]

Actors took time to acclimate themselves to talkies. Throughout the world, the transition to sound ruined the careers of many silent actors who had unpleasant-sounding voices. Audiences did not embrace actors whose voice or diction did not fit the voice that silent movies had conjured up in their minds. Japanese period dramas actors, especially, took time to figure out how to deliver their lines, because they came from different theatrical backgrounds that employed different styles of language and delivery. In his first talkie, Bandō Tsumasaburō, the king of Japanese period dramas at the time, used a *benshi*-like voice. Since he was unsure how to deliver his lines, he spoke as they did at the movies—he mimicked the *benshi*.[29] The problems that Tsumasaburō and other Japanese actors faced in deciding upon a standardized style of dialogue, especially for period dramas, delayed audience acceptance of talkies, and hence factored into the slowness of Japan's conversion to sound motion pictures.

Still, *benshi* played a significant role in delaying Japan's conversion to talkies. In part, this was because they offered a viable solution for theaters that lacked the money or the will to convert, because silent films with *benshi* continued for many years to attract enough customers that theaters could still compete and earn a profit without converting. More important was the *benshi*'s open animosity to talkies. The hostility that *benshi* showered upon talkies occurred as Japan's political scene was violently shifting away from liberalism and toward militarism.

Benshi Strike Back

During 1931 and 1932, a series of events took place, in and out of Japan, that heralded trouble for party politics and the beginning of military-dominated politics. Two of the most important events were the Manchurian Incident and the May 15 Incident. On September 18, 1931, a group of radical Kwantung Army officers in Manchuria blew up a section of the South Manchuria Railway line near Mukden. They accused the Chinese of planting the bomb and ordered troops in to secure the area. By the New Year, the Kwantung Army occupied almost all of eastern Manchuria. Without the permission or approval of the central government, the Kwantung Army had, by its own initiative, expanded the Japanese empire. This event is also significant because it marks the beginning of Japan's Fifteen-Year War with China.

Benshi helped their fellow Japanese stay abreast of what was happening at home and abroad, by providing current event movie *setsumei* (*jikyoku eiga setsumei*) for motion pictures that depicted contemporary events. The following *setsumei* by Hamaguchi Ryutarō, for the film *Manmo sensen shisatsu* (*An Inspection of the Manchurian–Mongolian Border*) recounts a battle that took place in Manchuria shortly after the Manchurian Incident.[30]

> The large group of soldiers continued to advance. It was unseasonable weather, as a wind peculiar to the border of Manchuria and Mongolia began to blow. It was thirty below zero that night on the battlefield.
>
> "Major Kurihara, it has begun to snow."
>
> "Yes, I see. Have the troops stay here and wait for daybreak. Have everyone sleep armed and ready."
>
> The freezing cold shot through the major's body. As he sat amidst the falling snow, his thoughts were of his mother in his far-

away homeland. His countrymen's voices, from when he left the homeland, still rang in his ears.

"Banzai!"

[*Kowairo* female voice]: "Well now, let's say goodbye here. When you go to Manchuria, whenever you serve your country, definitely do not show any cowardice. Please become an admirable man."

[*Kowairo* male voice]: "Goodbye. You have spoken well. Yes, I am an imperial soldier. I want to leave you with these words: For my motherland, I will definitely show great valor."

"Banzai!"

"To respond to the cheers of the veterans and youth groups, I must die a glorious death in battle. Ahh, it's snowing. Underneath this pure white snow hundreds of thousands of my fellow countrymen who fought before me are sleeping. Yes, let's fight! While I have been thinking, time has passed. . . ."

At three o'clock on the eighteenth, as the snowstorm raged on, our troops, led by the valiant leader Lieutenant General Tamon, attacked the tens of thousands of troops led by Ma Chan-shan. It was thirty below in the wilderness of northern Mongolia, where this desperate historical battle occurred. Our soldiers lay in ambush for three hours before implementing Tamon's strategy of cutting through the middle. In the end, our soldiers killed or wounded around eight thousand of the enemy's soldiers. While the snowy wilderness preserved the silence of death, with magnificent dignity, our troops, led by Tamon, took Qiqihar.

However, if we look back, we will become tearful about our imperial army. I think our imperial nation has invested one billion four hundred million yen into Manchuria and one million Japanese now live there, but peace does not yet exist. Days passed as we ninety million Japanese fretted in vain. Since the great riot at Tientsin, the situation became extremely dangerous, as the rebel leader commanded a general attack on our occupying army. The chief cabinet ministers hurried and visited the palace, and an emergency cabinet meeting issued orders for this division and that division of the army, as well as a fleet, to be sent.[31]

Another major political incident took place on May 15, 1932, as a group of junior naval and army officers attempted to bring about a "Shōwa Restoration," by a coordinated attack on several political and economic buildings and big business and government leaders. By the end of the day, they had ransacked several buildings and offices, assassinated Prime Minister Inukai, and wounded several other key government officials. The rebels also planned to assassinate Charlie Chaplin, whose arrival the day before, and welcome by thousands of adoring fans, was front-page news. Chaplin was at a sumo match with the prime minister's son when the prime minister was killed. Had Inukai's son not been with Chaplin, he probably would have been killed with his father. When Chaplin later learned that the rebels had planned on killing him to anger America, he quipped in his autobiography, "I can imagine the assassins having carried out their plan, then discovering that I was not an American but an Englishman—'Oh, so sorry!'"[32] The rebels failed to bring about a Shōwa Restoration; however, they did succeed in greatly reducing the scope of party politics in Japan.

Just as the Japanese government mustered together troops to defend and enlarge the Japanese empire, *benshi* rallied together to fight for their profession and livelihood. Despite a valiant effort, 1932 marked the beginning of the end for the institution of *benshi* and the art of *setsumei*. Although some *benshi* continued to provide *setsumei* for years to come, both the art of *setsumei* and the beauty of the performance were disappearing from theaters and from people's memories. By 1939—only 8 years after the Golden Age of *Benshi*—the situation had deteriorated to the point that, in the opening line of an article titled "There Used to Be *Benshi*," a writer sarcastically asked, "Do you know what a *benshi* is?"[33] Before *benshi* and *setsumei* disappeared from popular memory, however, the *benshi* engaged in a stalwart attempt to preserve their vocation.

Since at least 1913, *benshi* had organized themselves into friendship associations (*benyūkai*, *shinbokukai*, and *shinkōkai*), alliances (*dōmeikai*), associations (*kyōkai*), clubs (*kurabu*), and leagues (*renmei*). These organizations were almost always regional and usually formed along company lines. Membership ranged from a handful of *benshi* to several hundred members. Often, these groups pressured management for better wages and workers' rights. They also lobbied against anti-*benshi* discourse and what they perceived to be unfair legislation, such as the law requiring *benshi* to be tested every 3 years to be licensed.

Many organizations also acted as mutual aid associations. The Benyū Shinkōkai (Friends of the *Benshi* Friendship Association), for example, helped member *benshi* through trying times. If a constituent became sick, he would receive 5 yen from the association; if he died, his family would receive 10 yen; and if one of the *benshi*'s relatives died, the *benshi* would receive 5 yen.[34] Other *benshi* organizations held special "tournaments" to raise money for *benshi* who lost their jobs because of a recession.[35]

In August 1921, upon the recommendation of the Metropolitan Police and the Ministry of Education, 1,000 Tokyo *benshi* formed the Dai-Nippon Setsumeisha Kyōkai (Greater Japan *Setsumeisha* Association),[36] the largest *benshi* organization formed until that time. Shortly after its formation, however, membership decreased as rival organizations emerged. A great deal of animosity existed among the various organizations. Indeed, in 1923, one writer pleaded with the *benshi* to unite into a single group and to stop being so individualistic and narrow-minded. The author viewed the fighting among the various groups as counterproductive to the betterment of *benshi* as a whole. He believed that if the *benshi* could unite and work together, they could improve the wages and working conditions for all.[37] The *benshi* never heeded this advice.

Although various *benshi* organizations existed, not all *benshi* belonged to one. Immediately after the arrival of talkies in 1929, however, membership in *benshi* organizations increased dramatically, as did the emergence of new ones, some of which used for the first time the word union (*kumiai*) in their name. In this fight for survival, "clubs," "friendship associations," and "alliances" would not do. What the *benshi* needed were powerful associations and strong unions, to combat the studios and theater management.[38]

At that time, the *benshi* also began to unionize with other theater workers. Usually, they unionized along company lines. In 1932, the two strongest organizations in Tokyo were the Zen Kantō Eiga Teigyōin Kumiai (All Kantō Movie Workers Union), which was composed solely of Nikkatsu theater employees, and the Zenkoku Eiga Gekijō Teigyōin Kumiai (National Movie Theater Workers Union), which was a national organization of Shōchiku theater employees.

For *benshi*, the most confrontational year was 1932. *Benshi* had fought with management many times over the years, but nothing could compare with the scope, passion, and virulence that appeared in 1932. On April 8, the Shōchiku-Paramount Theater Company fired, without notice, the 10 *benshi* working at its Daishōkan and Denkikan theaters in Tokyo. Although *benshi* had been living in fear for several years, this action took them by surprise. In fact, one of the 10 *benshi* dismissed was in the middle of his *setsumei* when the theater manager suddenly called him backstage and fired him. For people in the audience, the abrupt stoppage of *setsumei* and disappearance of the *benshi* must have been rather perplexing.[39]

Management offered the fired *benshi* the remainder of their April salary and their May salary as severance pay. This offer was unacceptable to the *benshi*. They claimed that the theater was robbing them. This unexpected dismissal of 10 *benshi* led to a massive strike of all *benshi* working at Shōchiku-Paramount's 30 Tokyo theaters. The striking *benshi* quickly rallied the support of the other theater employees who were members of the same union. Together, they issued a declaration containing the following eight demands:

1. We oppose the dismissals.
2. We demand bonuses.
3. We demand that women be allotted days off for menstruation.
4. We oppose salary reductions.
5. We demand that the "good-receipt" bonus system be reinstated.
6. We demand shorter working hours.
7. We demand a minimum wage system.
8. We demand the establishment of a retirement system.

During the negotiations with the company, the *benshi* made two additional demands:

1. Reinstate the dismissed *benshi* for at least 6 months.
2. Pay each striker 10 yen per day that he was on strike.[40]

What is significant about these demands is their progressiveness. The strikers were concerned not just about saving the *benshi*'s jobs, but also about improving the quality of the working environment for all movie theater employees. The demand that women be given days off for menstruation, for example, was primarily aimed at improving the working conditions of the hundreds of female ushers, not the handful of female *benshi*. These demands reflect sentiments that workers in other industries were also expressing and demanding at the time.

Negotiations between the strikers and management lasted 10 days. The leader of the *benshi* was Suda Teimei (Kurosawa Heigo, 1905–1932), filmmaker Kurosawa Akira's older brother. On April 19, theater management succumbed to the demands of the strikers and reinstated all the *benshi*. It agreed to employ the *benshi* throughout the remainder of the year, although they would not have to *setsumei* talkies. In effect, the company agreed to pay the *benshi* the equivalent of 6 to 8 months in severance pay.[41]

After the Shōchiku-Paramount strike broke out, a general strike swept through the Asakusa movie theater district, affecting most cinema houses. A few theaters, however, continued to show movies. The Yūrakukan and Kawai Kinema hung placards outside their entranceways, stating: "Since the *benshi*, musicians, and management of this theater all work happily together, there will be no strike here." As only a few theaters remained open, they attracted huge crowds. With the resolution of the Shōchiku-Paramount strike, the clamor at the other Asakusa theaters died down. The situation did not stay quiet for long, however.[42]

On April 29, 1932, Nikkatsu Studios announced that it was going to hold an all-talkie program at one of its theaters. At the time, Nikkatsu had only wired about one-third of its theaters for sound and had not yet fired any *benshi*. Nevertheless, fearing for their livelihood, and well aware of how Shōchiku-Paramount treated its *benshi*, the Nikkatsu *benshi* and musicians, joined by the other theater employees, initiated a preemptive strike. Nikkō studio *benshi* also participated in this strike. On April 30, the day before they went on strike, the *benshi* issued two petitions, containing 15 demands in all. The demands dealt with their opposition to workers being dismissed and the need for the company to adequately compensate workers who might be dismissed in the future. They also dealt with wages, bonuses, working conditions, the need for more days off, and better dressing rooms. The strikers also insisted that no one be fired for participating in the strike and that all strikers be paid their full salaries for the time they were on strike.[43]

On May 1, a general strike broke out at the 23 theaters directly managed by Nikkatsu and Nikkō. The largest demonstrations took place at the Kanda Nikkatsukan and the Asakusa Fujikan. According to one newspaper report:

> At around 5:50 this morning, about 75 people connected to the All Kantō Movie Workers Union unexpectedly and forcefully attacked the Kanda Nikkatsukan. The night watchman, Kobayashi Shigeki (age 40), was pushed aside as they entered the night watchman's room, where Shinohara Minoru (age 28) and Katō Fukumatsu (age 24) were sleeping. They seized the master key to the theater and imprisoned the three watchmen. Later, they unloaded, from a truck they had prepared, over a hundred blankets and futons, rice, soy sauce, *miso*, green onions, and other provisions for a month-long siege. Through careful planning and forethought, they brought with them a portable gas stove, in case the gas was cut off. To terminate communication with the outside world, they cut the telephone lines and smashed the radio. They also destroyed the musical instruments in the music room.
> To defend against a police raid, other members of the group locked and secured all the doors with iron bars and chairs, and tied them up with rope.[44]

Clearly, the strikers meant business. Shortly after they took over the theater, the police arrived. In the confrontation between police and protesters that ensued, 22 people were hurt, and everyone who participated in seizing the theater was arrested. Across town, the police thwarted a similar effort by 82 *benshi*, musicians, and theater workers to take over the Fujikan. Fifteen people were arrested. Although violent confrontations subsided after the first day, emotions continued to run high, as both sides issued proposals and counterproposals. Finally, on May 10, the Metropolitan Police stepped in to mediate a settlement. Unlike most prewar strikes, in which the police sided with the companies and were in fact often viewed as capitalist tools who put pressure on the strikers, in this strike they negotiated a settlement that favored the strikers. In the mediated settlement, a fair compensation system for dismissed workers was developed. Dismissed workers would receive at least 3 months notice, and would receive a base 6-month salary bonus, plus a continuing-service compensation paid at the rate of 3 months for every year of service to the company. The company also agreed not to fire anyone because of the strike, to pay all unpaid wages incurred because of the strike, and to bear the burden for costs incurred because of the strike.[45] Both sides also agreed that the strikers would stop demonstrating on May 11; the 12th would be a day of rest, and work would resume on the 13th. Charlie Chaplin arrived on the 14th, and Prime Minister Inukai Tsuyoshi was assassinated on the 15th.

The Nikkatsu strike reveals that *benshi* recognized that the end was near, and they wanted to ensure that management compensated them for their years of dedicated work. If a theater was going to fire them, reasoned the *benshi*, then it had to give fair warning and just recompense. That management agreed to most of the strikers' demands indicates the power that *benshi* still held at the time, and the limited diffusion of sound. Theaters still needed *benshi*; hence, *benshi* had the upper hand, at least temporarily.

Following these two major strikes, many other strikes took place throughout the country. Most took place during the spring and summer of 1932. None, however, were as violent as the Nikkatsu–Nikkō strike. *Benshi* usually made demands similar to those made in the Shōchiku-Paramount and Nikkatsu–Nikkō strikes. Frequently, the strikes were preemptive; that is, the *benshi* struck when they still held power and before the theater could fire them. On June 5, 1932, for example, at the Musashinokan (Japan's crown jewel cinema palace), the *benshi*, in partnership with the other theater employees, waited for the sold-out crowd of

2,500 to take their seats, before launching their strike. With the audience in their seats, the *benshi* projected onto the screen a sign that read, "The thirty workers of this theater are now going on strike. We kindly request your cooperation in this matter." They then walked out, leaving the manager the unpleasant task of dealing with the hostile crowd.[46]

One person who did not like cooperating with his enraged employees was Ōkura Mitsugi—the king of obscene *setsumei*. By 1932, Ōkura was no longer performing on stage, because he was too busy running the 30 movie theaters that he owned. For over a year, his employees protested his conversion to sound. When Ōkura's fellow *benshi* called him a traitor and a capitalist pig, Ōkura replied that the conversion to talkies was "the inevitable result of the evolution of mechanical civilization. Isn't your opposition the same thing as opposing the evolution from stagecoaches to taxis?"[47] Gradually, most *benshi* came to realize that Ōkura was right: They were becoming as anachronistic as stagecoaches. Although the *benshi* did all they could to ensure that they would be financially secure while they looked for new jobs, they could not stop the inevitable. Like the stagecoach, *benshi* and *setsumei* were becoming symbols of a bygone era.

Starting in 1932, their ranks began to thin, as theaters converted to sound and fired their *benshi*. Although some people still wanted to become *benshi*, the allure was fading. In 1933, the Metropolitan Police reduced the number of times it administered the *benshi* licensing exam from nine to six per year, with more reductions soon thereafter.[48] In April 1936, the Metropolitan Police officially terminated the *benshi* testing and licensing system, because of waning demand.[49]

First-run theaters were the first to wire for sound. Consequently, it was the top *benshi* at the best theaters who lost their jobs first, while the vast number who lingered on worked at second- and third-run theaters. Fans who loved *benshi* and Japanese silent films had to go to dilapidated theaters. Periodically, first-run theaters showed silent movies with "top-class" *benshi*. These special showings nostalgically tried to recreate the glamour of the silent era, by showing highly regarded silent films with the best *benshi* of the silent era, such as Tokugawa Musei and Ikoma Raiyū, providing *setsumei*. These mini-revivals, however, could not negate the fact that the art of *setsumei* was fading away.

Some *benshi* were able to continue working years after the arrival of talkies, because of Daito Films, which continued to make silent films until 1938. In 1933, Kawai Movie Company incorporated into Daito Film Studios. This studio emerged after other Japanese studios had started to make talkies. Daito continued to make silents at a time when most other studios were making talkies, because there was a demand in rural areas and at contracted theaters. Most Daito films were low-budget period dramas that glorified the samurai spirit. Daito only began to make talkies in 1937.

In addition to providing live *setsumei* for silents, some *benshi* ventured into making *setsumei* talkies (*setsumei tōkī*). These were silent films for which a *benshi* would record a *setsumei* soundtrack. These films were also known as *afureko* (after recording), because the *benshi* added the soundtrack after the film had been shot. Studios paid a *benshi* about 500 yen to record *setsumei* for one of these films.[50] This format allowed theaters to show "*setsumei* movies" without having to pay the daily cost of a *benshi*. To capitalize on this trend, studios rereleased their most popular silent films, with *benshi* soundtracks.

Benshi lost their jobs at a time when it was difficult to find employment in Japan. Although a few studios helped *benshi* find new jobs elsewhere in the company, others did not. Some *benshi* worked within the film industry as actors, theater managers, technicians, film distributors, movie critics, and even studio executives. Others used their storytelling talents in vaudeville, performing *mandan*, *manzai*, *rakugo*, or *kōdan*. Many roamed the streets as *kamishibai* (paper play) performers. Several became professional masters of ceremonies; a few of the most popular *benshi*, such as Tokugawa Musei and Nishimura Korakuten, became radio and eventually television announcers and hosts. At least one—Suzuki Kōtarō (Suzuki Senhachi)—became a member of the Diet, and others went on to become reporters. The majority of *benshi*, however, became office workers, traveling salesmen, shop keepers, day laborers, or rickshaw drivers. Undoubtedly, there were also several *benshi* like Kurosawa Heigo—the leader of the April 8, 1932, Shōchiku-Paramount strike, and brother of Kurosawa Akira—who killed themselves out of despair.

11

FORGOTTEN BUT NOT DEAD

By the beginning of the Pacific War with the United States in 1941, the institution of *benshi* had been completely dismantled. Over the ensuing years, most Japanese forgot about *benshi* and *setsumei*, as a lengthy and tumultuous period of war and reconstruction embroiled the nation. Thanks to a handful of *benshi* and silent film fans, however, *setsumei* never completely died out.

During World War II, *setsumei* frequently served as a means of entertainment for soldiers. Matsuda Shunsui (1925–1987) was one of several *benshi* who performed *setsumei* for his comrades-in-arms throughout the war. "Even as a soldier, I was a *benshi*! I was a Japanese soldier during the war. I sometimes narrated films for soldiers in the barracks. We had some silent versions of talking pictures. It was such versions that I narrated in those days. When we were taken prisoner by the Soviet army, I narrated for the other prisoners of war in jail in the USSR. The soldiers had to imagine the scenes that I narrated, since there were no projectors or films." Matsuda used his *setsumei* as a way to acquire cash, so that he could buy food or cigarettes in the POW camp. He always stopped in the middle of his *setsumei* to collect payment from his comrades, because, if he waited until the end, they would run off without paying.[1]

Another person who provided *setsumei* entertainment for his fellow soldiers was a Corporal Gekkan.[2] Gekkan was the eldest son of Tokyo furniture makers. In his youth, he loved *setsumei*, and he avidly bought *setsumeishū* and committed them to memory. As a soldier in the Japanese Imperial Army, Corporal Gekkan was committed to the Japanese war effort and thought only of Japan's victory. He frequently entertained his fellow soldiers by reciting *setsumei*.

Corporal Gekkan was on the island of Rabaul the day Japan unconditionally surrendered, and it was there that he gave his last performance. Because there were no films, the soldiers had to visualize the images that Gekkan described. The following *setsumei* is from a movie entitled *Shinpan—Ōoka seidan: Suzukawa Genjūrō no maki* (*The Judgments of Magistrate Ōoka—New Edition: Suzukawa Genjūrō reel*). In brief, the film was about a sword-collecting *daimyō* who orders his retainer, Tange Sazen, to steal a set of two magical swords—one a short sword, the other a long sword—for his collection. Tange Sazen manages to steal the long sword. When one sword is separated from its mate, however, the magical qualities of the sword possess the wielder to kill. Thus, Sazen goes on a rampage that elicits the attention of the authorities. In the end, the *daimyō* sells out Tange Sazen to protect himself from the authorities. For the final scene, in which Tange Sazen is talking to himself, Corporal Gekkan provided the following *setsumei*.

> You, my fallen comrades, whom did you work for? Whom did you die for? We were completely betrayed and disposed of by our lord, who, because of his ardent wish for territorial peace and a desire to protect himself, weighed our efforts against his sixty thousand *koku* territory. Our loyalty was dragged through the mud, and our honor is not even worth dust. I was so stupid, believing in the lord and obeying his orders. I, who was going to sacrifice my life for him, am truly stupid.[3]

Corporal Gekkan's *setsumei* deeply moved all the soldiers. Like Tange Sazen, they may all have wondered why they had been so willing to sacrifice their lives for the emperor.

During the American occupation of Japan, theaters occasionally held special *benshi* tournaments that lasted from one night to several weeks. Top *benshi*, such as Tokugawa Musei, Somei Saburō, and Kunii Shikō, appeared at these events. *Benshi* usually performed one of their classic *setsumei*. Somei Saburō, for example, would provide his *Antony and Cleopatra setsumei*. One of the reasons for holding these tournaments was to introduce young people to *benshi* and *setsumei*. To help audiences contextualize the movies and to teach people about *benshi* and the art of *setsumei*, *maesetsu* (introductory remarks) returned and was a part of all postwar shows. Curiously, not all the movies shown in the immediate postwar years were silents. Sometimes they were recent films with their sound turned off.[4]

Sometime in 1953 or 1954, Nishimura Korakuten, Kunii Shikō, Kumaoka Tendō, and several other *benshi*, came up with the idea of erecting a stone to commemorate the *benshi*. They wanted to build an enduring monument that symbolized the importance of *benshi* and that would forever remind people of the fact that *benshi* "added to the splendor of [Japan's] cultural development."[5] One problem, however, was that they lacked the money to build it. Thus, they asked Ōkura Mitsugi, whose motion picture company was doing very well at the time, to finance the project. Ōkura agreed to pay for the memorial, but on the condition that it contain only the names of those *benshi* he liked; it would not contain the names of *benshi* he hated.[6] The commemorative granite slabs initially contained the names of 55 *benshi*. An additional 50 names were added to a separate section of the monument in 1964. In a special ceremony in August 1959, attended by dozens of former *benshi*, the granite wall was unveiled in the Asakusa Sensōji Temple precinct, where it still stands as a tribute to the *benshi*.

Starting in the late 1950s, various silent film and *benshi* appreciation associations appeared. The *Musei eiga kanshōkai* (Silent Movie Appreciation Association) became the most prominent organization and is the only one that still exists today. This association began holding monthly *benshi* performances in July 1959, and continues to do so. Matsuda Shunsui, a *benshi* and film collector, founded the association. Over his lifetime, Matsuda amassed a movie collection of about 1,000 titles. As a way to show his collection and the art of *setsumei*, he began holding monthly performances. In the beginning, various *benshi* provided *setsumei* at these showings, with different *benshi* performing each month. This allowed fans to listen to their favorite *benshi*. Gradually, however, as *benshi* started to pass away, Matsuda and his apprentices became the only performers. Usually, recorded music accompanied these shows, but on special occasions, there were live bands.

Initially, some *benshi* resented Matsuda. They called him a "fake *benshi*," because he had only performed as a child during the silent era. They did not consider him a genuine *benshi*. In one *benshi*'s opinion, only those people who had taken the *benshi* licensing exam and passed should call themselves *benshi*; those people who only apprenticed as *benshi*, but who never took the test, should not.[7] Gradually, however, most *benshi* came to respect Matsuda and what he was doing for the profession. By collecting movies and holding monthly recitals, Matsuda played a significant role in saving *benshi* and the art of *setsumei* from oblivion. He kept the art alive. Matsuda also preserved the art by appearing as a *benshi* in several movies and television shows set in the silent era.

Today, there are several people who professionally continue the tradition, and there are a handful of others who study *setsumei* as a hobby. The most prominent *benshi* today are Waka Kōji (Nakazawa Kunio, b. 1923), Inoue Yōichi (b. 1938), and Sawato Midori (Sawato Kuniko).[8] In 1931, at the age of nine, Waka Kōji became Tokugawa Musei's apprentice. After a 2-year apprenticeship, he began providing *setsumei*. He became a *benshi* during the twilight years of the profession. Throughout most of the postwar era, he has earned a living by performing various odd jobs in the film and entertainment industry. Waka performs *setsumei* about three or four times a year, mostly in the Nagoya area.[9]

In Kansai, Inoue Yōichi is the most eminent *benshi*. He takes the stage once or twice a month at various venues throughout the Kansai region. In 1970, at the age of thirty-two, he became an apprentice of Hama Seiha. When Inoue first asked Hama if he could become his apprentice, Hama refused, because he did not want any added competition. Eventually, however, Hama consented to Inoue's becoming his apprentice. If Inoue can touch an audience with his performance, he feels that he has done his job well.[10]

Ironically, given the male dominance of the profession during the silent era, today the most celebrated *benshi* is a woman: Sawato Midori. In October 1972, shortly after graduating from Hōsei University, Sawato saw Matsuda Shunsui provide *setsumei* for Mizoguchi Kenji's *Taki no shiraito* (*White Threads of the Cascades*) at one of the Silent Movie Appreciation Association's monthly shows. Matsuda's *setsumei* deeply moved her. After the show, she talked with Matsuda. During their conversation, Matsuda suggested that she become a *benshi*, and she did. In January 1973, just over 2 months after seeing her first *benshi* performance, Sawato Midori debuted. She provided *setsumei* for Charlie Chaplin's *The Rink*.

At first, many people thought that a female *benshi* was unusual. They did not realize that female *benshi* had existed in the past. Some people complained that, as a woman, she did not know how to provide proper male dialogue. Nevertheless, today most silent movie fans have come to appreciate her as a true master of the art of *setsumei*. According to Sawato, "It does not matter if you are male or female, it only matters if you are good or bad. If you are good, people will accept you."[11]

At first, in addition to being a *benshi*, she also earned a living as a female television announcer. However, for the last 15 to 20 years she has worked solely as a *benshi*, now the only person in Japan who still earns a living in this field. She is currently the headline performer at the Silent Movie Appreciation Association's monthly shows. In addition to these shows, she performs between 3 and 15 times per month at other venues throughout Japan and around the world, from San Paulo to New York, Sydney to Antwerp.

When asked what the most important role of *benshi* is today, she replied, "Communicating the spirit of the films made in the past to today's audience."[12]

In discussing the survival of *benshi* and the art of *setsumei*, Sawato had this to say: "In order for silent movies and *katsuben* to survive, not merely as an exercise in nostalgia, but as one form of entertainment among many entertainments, it is important to perceive the modern world logically and to contemplate future trends. I am trying my best to increase the number of *katsuben* fans. I feel that a good way to increase the number of people who like silent movies and *katsuben* is to survive as a *benshi*."[13]

In addition to the modern-day *benshi* who keep *setsumei* alive, the art also lives—unbeknownst to most Japanese—on radio, on television, and in the movies. By becoming some of the first performers on radio, *benshi* influenced and helped shape Japanese radio delivery. Over the years, *benshi* vocal techniques were absorbed into a more standard form of delivery; there is no denying the influence that *benshi*, especially men like Tokugawa Musei, had on the early sound of Japanese radio. Newsreel commentators and educational film narrators also rely heavily on *benshi* vocal techniques. Today, many Japanese television dramas have a ubiquitous narrator who reminds viewers of what has happened in the past and sets the stage for what is going to happen in the future. By emphasizing the emotional high points of the program and by guiding the spectator through the show, these narrators function as modern-day *benshi*. The abundance of voice-over narration in Japan today is a vestige of the influence that *benshi* and the art of *setsumei* had on Japanese culture during the silent era.

From late Meiji through early Showa, *benshi* occupied a central position in Japan's cultural realm. Consequently, *benshi* serve as an invaluable window from which one can explore early twentieth century Japanese history. From the beginning, *benshi* were an integral part of motion pictures, and, as such, they reveal how Western ideas and inventions were adapted to fit Japanese needs. The westernization that took place during the Meiji period was not a blind acceptance of Western ideas and goods, but rather an adaptive process in which foreign items were tailored to Japanese needs, then assimilated into the culture. The introduction of motion pictures illustrates the race among Meiji entrepreneurs to be the first to introduce the latest Western inventions and the ways in which they went about marketing their product. Some entrepreneurs employed men skilled in traditional narrative arts, to attract people to their shows; others used men skilled at pitching products. These men were the founding *benshi*, who introduced the Japanese public to motion pictures and who played a prominent role in popularizing cinema.

From the first exhibitions, *benshi* established themselves as an indispensable element of Japanese silent cinema, thus fashioning a cinematic model on which Japanese audiences came to insist. Film lecturers existed in other countries, but they were an oddity and were never considered an essential part of the cinematic experience. In Japan, on the other hand, *benshi* and their *setsumei* were regarded as fundamental ingredients, and, as such, it was impossible to eliminate them, although people tried. By being an essential component of exhibitions from the very beginning, *benshi* transformed cinema presentation from the Western norm into a Japanese form; in essence, the addition of *benshi* and *setsumei* to motion pictures "Japanized" cinema. Moving pictures were no longer a mass-produced commodity presented to everyone in the exact same way; rather, they were an individually forged theatrical experience.

One reason why Japanese audiences readily accepted the *benshi* was because they were accustomed to commingled theater, that is, theater in which the aural and visual elements were separate, but united together in one performance. The main reason why they welcomed the *benshi*, however, was because the *benshi* made the show more enjoyable, by being both entertaining and informative. The poetic *setsumei* that *benshi* performed guided audiences through the plot, accentuated the emotional atmosphere of the scenes, imparted knowledge about what appeared on the screen, and transported spectators into the diegetic world of the film, all in a highly engaging fashion.

The fundamental aim of entertainment is to give the audience pleasure: *Setsumei* was extremely pleasurable. *Setsumei* enriched motion pictures by helping audiences enter the diegetic world of the film. A talented *benshi* was able to

226

possess the audience, and, under his magic spell, the images projected onto the screen were no longer mere photographs: they became real life. As the *benshi* Matsuki Kyōrō put it, "Compared with the light that is projected on the screen, *setsumeisha* breathe life into the projected images."[14] The greater the skill of the *benshi*, the more the audience was absorbed into the fantasy world of the picture: They became one with the film. Simply watching with one's eyes did not have the same effect as watching and listening. The aural element of *setsumei* enhanced the emotional impact of the projected visual images, and the totality of both made Japanese cinema diegetically rich.

Jōruri, kōdan, rakugo, naniwabushi, manzai, mandan, and *gidayū* are just a few of the narrative arts mentioned when one talks about the art of storytelling (*wajutsu*) in Japan. *Setsumei* is never mentioned. This is a shame, for *setsumei* was one of the most dynamic narrative arts to emerge in Japan during the twentieth century, and, during the 1910s and 1920s, it was the most popular. *Setsumei* is like *kōdan*, in that it is story-like; it is similar to *rakugo*, in that it is theater-like; it employs a voice that is scratchy and rough, like the one used by *naniwabushi* storytellers; and it is identical to *jōruri*, in that it supplies a vocal element to a visual performance. Although *setsumei* borrowed from Japan's narrative tradition and contains elements from various vocal arts, it has its own unique sound and structure. During the course of the silent era, *setsumei* evolved, from lecturing about the film to experimenting with various theatrical means of vocal additives; to a split in the art, as Japanese film *benshi* performed *kowairo setsumei*, and foreign film *benshi* provided explanatory *setsumei*; to a unification, as Japanese film *setsumei* and foreign film *setsumei* merged into one. The history of the *benshi* and their *setsumei* was one of change and adaptation.

Just as *setsumei* is a narrative art deserving of recognition, it is time to acknowledge *benshi* as masterful narrative artists. Other narrative artists could take years to perfect a piece, performing and refining it over time, but *benshi* had to perfect a piece within a couple of days, because motion pictures changed weekly. Moreover, *benshi* were the only narrative artists who had to deploy their art within a strict time constraint. They had to describe a scene before it changed. Sometimes, a *benshi* could provide 20 words of *setsumei*; other times, he only had time for 5 words. The ability to create poetic rhetoric that perfectly coalesced with the moving images is a testament to the skill and artistry of *benshi*.

As intermediaries between the screen and the spectator, *benshi* influenced how audiences perceived what was projected onto the screen. Given that cinema has been one of the most influential media of the twentieth century, the position that *benshi* held within Japanese culture during the first 30 years of the twentieth century was significant. Motion pictures were not just the most popular form of mass entertainment, they were also a means of propaganda and a tool for social education. Because of the power that *benshi* wielded over the moving images, many people viewed them as social educators who could mold public thought, and there is no denying that they did. If a movie about the American Civil War was playing, it was the *benshi*'s job to teach the audience about the war and its significance in American history. Sometimes, *benshi* accurately informed audiences with their *setsumei*, and sometimes they misinformed them. *Benshi* could both reinforce political dogma or undermine it. A *benshi* with socialist leanings could turn a Chaplin comedy into a socialist diatribe, by emphasizing that the occupants of the large houses that appeared in the movie were the exploiting bourgeoisie, and those living in the dilapidated row houses were the victimized proletariat. On the other hand, an anti-American film, combined with jingoistic *setsumei*, could quickly fuel anti-American sentiment throughout the empire. The direction that *setsumei* took, and its entertainment value, depended on the skill and mood of the *benshi*. Over the years, *benshi* opponents denounced the *benshi* in an effort to curtail their influence. Yet, regardless of how virulent the assault, the *benshi* stood strong. At times, *benshi* had to adapt and fortify their art of *setsumei*, but they still survived, primarily because they had secured for themselves a pivotal position that audiences cherished within Japanese silent cinema.

Benshi situated themselves next to the screen, in part because of a cultural tradition of positioning a narrator next to the mode of entertainment. In other words, *benshi* emerged out of traditional Japanese culture. Their place in late Meiji through early Showa, however, was completely countercultural. *Benshi* represented a bohemian lifestyle that often challenged the status quo. They challenged authority and cultural norms, as they lived life on the edge—the edge of propriety, the edge of moral decency, and often the edge of society. From their subversive readings of films, to being a haven for progressive and discordant elements of society, through their backgrounds and outlooks as socialists, labor radicals, hedonists, people with disabilities, and others, these were people who often tapped into some of the darker and shadowy elements of Japanese culture. These were poets of the dark, not only in the sense that they gave poetic readings in the dark, but also in the sense that they represented the darker side of Japanese culture. Newspapers, magazines, and government officials frequently reprimanded *benshi* for taking the virginity of fawning nubile fans, for performing drunk, for having affairs with married women, for swindling women out of money, and for giving lewd and lascivious *setsumei*. The government and others tried hard to control this dark side and its perceived effect on society. Yet, the laws and means the government used to control the *benshi* never completely reined them in, because *benshi* frequently and openly ignored them. *Benshi* reveal that early twentieth century Japan was not all about politics and war: It was also about challenging moral propriety, living life to its hedonistic fullest, and having fun.

NOTES

1: SETTING THE STAGE

1. Names such as Nakagawa Keiji, Somei Saburō, Tsuchiya Shōtō, Ōtsuji Shirō, Kunii Shikō, Nishimura Rakuten, Nishimura Korakuten, Matsui Suisei, Yamano Ichirō, Hayashi Tempū, Hanai Hideo, Ōkura Mitsugi, Ikoma Raiyū, and Tokugawa Musei.
2. M, "Benshi gettan," *Katsudō shashinkai* 4 (January 25, 1910): 8.
3. Musō Byōe, *Eiga setsumei no kenkyū* (Tokyo: Chōyōsha, 1922): 63–64.
4. When translating from Japanese to English, however, I use the signifier found in the original source. In other words, if a source uses the word *setsumeisha*, I use *setsumeisha* in my translation. Since well over 90% of all *benshi* were male, I use male pronouns throughout, except, of course, when specifically discussing female *benshi*.
5. "'*Katsuben*' hai subekika," *Dōtonbori* 9 (November 1, 1919): 20.
6. Charles Musser, "Archaeology of the Cinema: 8," *Framework* 22/23 (autumn 1983): 4–11; Charles Musser and Carol Nelson, *High-Class Moving Pictures: Lyman H. Howe and the Forgotten Era of Traveling Exhibition 1880–1920* (Princeton: Princeton University Press, 1991): 86–88.
7. "Pictures at the Columbia," *Cincinnati Commercial Tribune* (May 31, 1908): 21.
8. "Diluted Vaudeville To-day's Show Menu," *New York Times* (December 27, 1908): pt. 1, p. 1.
9. The only European country where scholars have been unable to find any evidence for silent film lecturers is Italy. André Gaudreault and Germain Lacasse, "Editorial," translated by Deborah Glassman, *Iris* 22 (autumn 1996): 12, 16 n. 4.

230

10. W. Stephen Bush, "The Picture and the Voice," *The Moving Picture World* 14, no. 5 (November 2, 1912): 429.

11. "Facts and Comments," *The Moving Picture World* 11, no. 11 (March 16, 1912): 940.

12. The main reason scholars have spent so much time searching for *benshi* outside of Japan is to show how they influenced the creation of this narrative cinema.

13. Tom Gunning, *D. W. Griffith and the Origins of American Narrative Film: The Early Years at Biograph*, the entire book is about the development of narrative cinema; Miriam Hansen, *Babel & Babylon*, 95–98; Musser, "Archaeology of the Cinema: 8," 4–11; Musser and Nelson, *High-Class Moving Pictures*, 184–92.

14. One of the more famous American movie lecturers was President Theodore Roosevelt. In December 1914, he expounded on *The Exploration of a Great River* at the Museum of Natural History in Manhattan and at the Brooklyn Institute. Musser and Nelson, *High-Class Moving Pictures*, 234.

15. The existence of narrators in America was rescued from historical oblivion only in 1975 by Charles M. Berg, who relied on Bush's articles for his research. "The Human Voice and the Silent Cinema," *Journal of Popular Film* 4, no. 2 (1975): 165–79.

16. The only possible times when a *benshi* might not have been attached to a show were a few early exhibitions about which the sources are unclear.

17. I write this with one additional proviso. Silent film narrators also appear to have been a fixture of Thai cinema throughout the silent era and beyond. Satō Tadao believes that "*benshi*" emerged in Thailand because the first movies shown in Thailand were those of a Japanese touring cinema show that utilized *benshi*. Because of a lack of scholarly research into Thai cinema, however, very little is known about how widespread Thai *benshi* were, who became *benshi*, what effect they had on Thai cinema, and a myriad of other questions. Satō Tadao, *Nihon eigashi* (Tokyo: Iwanami Shōten, 1995), vol. 1: 5, 9, 100.

18. "Ajia musei eiga gannen: Nikkan *benshi* taidan Shin Churu, Sawato Midori, Poku Wanmo," *Asia Center News* 3 (Fall 1996): 15–18; "Korean 'Benshi' Performers," in Ishizaki Kenji, ed., *Japan Foundation Asia Center Asian Classical Cinema Series No. 2: Korean Silent Film and 'Benshi' Performer* (Tokyo: The Japan Foundation Asian Center, 1996): 2–3.

19. Victor N. Kobayashi, "Benshi in Hawaii," in *When Strangers Meet—Cross-Cultural Perspectives from the Humanities: Viewers Guide* (Honolulu: Hawaii International Film Festival, 1984): 82–83; Junko Ogihara, "The Exhibition of Films for Japanese Americans in Los Angeles During the Silent Film Era," *Film History* 4 (1990): 81–87; Tats Yoshiyama, "The Benshi," *Film Comment* 2, no. 2 (Spring 1964): 34–35.

  The Picture Bride (1995), about Japanese emigrants in Hawaii, contains a scene in which a traveling cinema show holds an outside performance for the migrant Japanese sugarcane workers. The renowned actor Mifune Toshiro portrays the *benshi*. Mifune was a great actor in his prime, but he is not a very good *benshi*.

20. Katano Akeji, "Setsumeisha sompai ron no kōsatsu," *Katsudō gahō* 6, no. 2 (February 1922): 38.

21. Barbara Ruch, "Medieval Jongleurs and the Making of a National Literature," in *Japan in the Muromachi Age*, edited by John Whitney Hall and Toyoda Takeshi (Berkeley: University of California Press, 1977): 288.

22. Frank Hoff, "Killing the Self: How the Narrator Acts," *Asian Theatre Journal* 2, no. 1 (Spring 1985): 7; Roland Barthes, *Empire of Signs*, translated by Richard Howard (New York: Hill and Wang, 1982): 55.

23. *Gentō* is also known as *utsushie*. Technically, *gentō* and *utsushie* used different types of slides and catered to different clientele: *gentō* was for the elite, *utsushie* for the masses; nevertheless, for all intents and purposes, they were basically the same. That is, they were both magic lanterns.

Prior to the introduction of magic lanterns, shadow puppetry (*kage-e*)—using paper cutouts, one's hands, or even one's body—was a popular form of entertainment. For more information on *kage-e*, see Yamamoto Keiichi, *Edō no kage-e asobi* (Tokyo: Sōshisha, 1988).

24. Iwamoto Kenji, "Hikaku gentōshi kangae," *Nihon no bigaku*, no. 20 (1993): 190.

25. Tsurubuchi & Co., advertisement, *Kinema record* 4, no. 31 (January 10, 1916): 39.

26. Yoshida Chieo, *Mōhitotsu no eigashi: katsuben no Jidai* (Tokyo: Jiji Tsūshinsha, 1978): 3.

27. Nickelodeons sat between 60 and 500 people, with an average between 100 and 200. In 1922, 26.88% of American movie theaters sat between 0 and 250, 36.91% had a seating capacity of 251–500, 27.44% sat 501–1,000, and only 8.77% had a capacity over 1000. By contrast, in 1918, only 12% of Japanese movie theaters had a seating capacity of less than 500, 49% sat 501–1,000, and 38% had a seating capacity over 1,000. Richard Koszarski, *History of the American Cinema*, vol. 3, *An Evening's Entertainment: The Age of the Silent Feature Picture, 1915-1928* (Berkeley: University of California Press, 1990): 15; "Zenkoku katsudō shashin jōsetsukan ikkanpyō," *Katsudō no sekai* 3, no. 8 (August 1918): 75–89.

28. Komatsu Hiroshi and Charles Musser, "Benshi Search," *Wide Angle* 9 (1987): 86.

29. As for why narrators did not become popular in European nations with a more heterogeneous movie audience, more research needs to be done.

30. Joseph L. Anderson, "Spoken Silents in the Japanese Cinema; or, Talking to Pictures: Essaying the *Katsuben*, Contextualizing the Texts," in *Reframing Japanese Cinema: Authorship, Genre, History*, edited by Arthur Nolletti Jr. and David Desser (Bloomington: Indiana University Press, 1992): 277.

232

31. Toge Jinto, "Eiga '*Morokko*' kara Mori-shi no setsumeisha-ron sonohoka," *Kinema shūhō* 50 (February 27, 1931): 35.
32. "Iyoiyo honkenchikuki mo chikazuite shihonka no jukukō o unagasu," *Katsudō zasshi* 12, no. 11 (November 1926): 40.
33. Tanaka Jun'ichirō, *Nihon eiga hattatsushi*, vol. 1 (Tokyo: Chūō Kōronsha, 1957): 169.
34. Komatsu Hiroshi, "Some Characteristics of Japanese Cinema before World War I," translated by Linda C. Ehrlich and Yuko Okutsu, in *Reframing Japanese Cinema: Authorship, Genre, History*, edited by Arthur Nolletti Jr. and David Desser (Bloomington: Indiana University Press, 1992): 257.
35. Aaron A. Gerow, *Writing a Pure Cinema: Articulations of Early Japanese Film* (Ph.D. diss., University of Iowa, 1996): 209–210.
36. "Nihon eiga o tsukutta hitobito: kantoku kara kyakuhonka, haiyū, gijutsusha, gyōkaijin made, Nihon eiga o ugokashita hitobito no shōzō," *Kinema junpō* 208 (July 1, 1958): 50–71.
37. Noël Burch, *To the Distant Observer: Form and Meaning in the Japanese Cinema* (Berkeley: University of California Press, 1979): 85.
38. Anderson, "Spoken Silents," 259–311; Appendix A: "Second and Third Thoughts about the Japanese film," in Joseph L. Anderson and Donald Richie, *The Japanese Film*, expanded edition (Princeton: Princeton University Press, 1982): 439–456.
39. Don Kirihara, "A Reconsideration of the Institution of Benshi," *Film Reader* 6 (1985): 41–53.
40. Gerow, *Writing a Pure Cinema*, 213. The sections on *benshi* are based upon an article Gerow published in 1994: Aaron A. Gerow, "The Benshi's New Face: Defining Cinema in Taishō Japan," *Iconics* 3 (1994): 69–86.
41. Yoshida Chieo, *Mōhitotsu no eigashi*; Misono Kyōhei, *Katsuben jidai* (Tokyo: Iwanami Shoten, 1990). *Mōhitotsu no eigashi* is based upon a series of articles Yoshida published a few years earlier: "Katsuben no rekishi," *Eigashi kenkyū*, nos. 1–10; 12–14 (1973–78). *Katsuben jidai* is basically a republication of an earlier work that had limited circulation: *Aa, katsudō daishashin* (Tokyo: Katsudō Shiryō Kenkyūkai, 1966).
42. Mizuno Eizaburo, *Nagoya katsuben ichidai: shomin ga mita mōhitotsu no gendaishi* (Nagoya: Fūbasha, 1995); Waka Kōji, *Katsudō daishashin shimatsu ki* (Tokyo: Sairyūsha, 1998).
43. Mizuno, *Nagoya katsuben ichidai*, 8.

2: INTRODUCTION OF MOTION PICTURES INTO JAPAN
AND THE BIRTH OF *BENSHI*

1. Tsukada Yoshinobu, *Nihon eigashi no kenkyū: katsudō shashin torai zengo no jijō* (Tokyo: Gendai Shokan, 1980): 62–76.
2. Inabata Katsutarō, "Shinematogurafu o yunyūshita zengo," no. 7 of "Nippon eigashi sokō," *Kinema junpō* 558 (November 11, 1935): 71.
3. It is unclear exactly how many machines Inabata Katsutarō imported into Japan. Some sources say two, others, three. As Tsukada Yoshinobu points out, however, given the dates and places of exhibition, he must have imported at least four, if not five, machines. Tsukada, *Nihon eigashi no kenkyū*, 124–41. Mitsuda Yuri asserts that Inabata imported two machines and François Girel one. Mitsuda Yuri, "Seikimatsu Nippon o otozureta futari no eiga gishi," in *Eiga denrai: Shinematogurafu to Meiji no Nihon*, edited by Yoshida Yoshishige, Yamaguchi Masao, and Kinoshita Naoyuki (Tokyo: Iwanami Shoten, 1995): 47.
4. *Osaka mainichi shinbun* (February 16, 1897): 6. According to several statements made by Inabata Katsutarō, a preview showing was held in the garden of a Kyoto electric company sometime between February 11 and 14, 1897. Inabata states that the show was so popular that the crowds destroyed the vegetable store next door. Inabata, "Shinematogurafu," 71; Inabata Katsutarō, "Massaki ni katsudō shashin o yunyūshita watakushi," *Nippon eiga jigyō sōran*, edited by Ishii Bunsaku (Tokyo: Kokusai Eiga Tsushinsha, 1926): 438–439. Despite the popularity of the apparatus, Inabata soon left the entertainment business and returned to the world of textiles, where he invented a method for dyeing khaki. Later, he became a member of the House of Peers. Takanashi Kōji, ed., *Inabata Katsutarōkun den* (Osaka: Inabata Katsutarō Okina Kijukinen Denki Henshūkai, 1938): 331.
5. Yokota had planned to open on March 5, but, because of apparent mechanical problems, the debut of the Cinématographe was delayed until March 8. *Miyako shinbun* (March 3, 1897); *Miyako shinbun* (March 4–7, 1897); *Tokyo nichi nichi shinbun* (March 7, 1897).
6. Tsukada, *Nihon eigashi no kenkyū*, 247–70.
7. "Katsudō shashin ga umareta koro no hanashi," *Katsudō zasshi* 8, no. 10 (1922): 83; Araki Waichi, "Vitasukōpu o yunyūshita zengo," no. 8 of "Nippon eigashi sokō," *Kinema junpō* 559 (November 21, 1935): 85–86. Although Araki clearly purchased and exhibited a Vitascope, the photograph of a contract between him and Edison published in Kinema junpō indicates that he bought a "Standard Edison kineto scobe" for $100. *Kinema junpō* 221 (December 25, 1958): 7.
8. Robert C. Allen, "Vitascope/Cinématographe: Initial Patterns of American Film Industrial Practice," in *Film Before Griffith*, ed. John L. Fell (Berkeley: University of California Press, 1983): 148.

234

9. *Yomiuri shinbun* (March 3, 1897). There is proof that the machine was imported by an employee of the Arai company and that Shibata Chūjirō imported the Vitascope. No direct evidence, however, links Shibata to Arai.

10. Araki Waichi, quoted in "Kyōiku kikan toshite no katsudō shashin (1)," *Osaka Asahi shinbun* (June 29, 1922); "Katsudō shashin ga umareta koro no hanashi," *Katsudō zasshi* 8, no. 10 (1922): 82–83. There were also electrical problems with exhibiting the Vitascope in the United States. "All the early Vitascopes were made to work only on direct current, and in 1896, municipal lighting systems were a hodge-podge of incompatible currents and voltages." Robert C. Allen, "Vitascope/Cinématographe," 149.

11. Several advertisements state that it was supplied by "Jūmonji Shinsuke." See Kanda Kinkikan theater advertisement, *Tōkyō nichi nichi shinbun* (March 3, 1897); Kanda Kinkikan theater advertisement, *Miyako shinbun* (March 5, 1897). A few, however, simply say that it was supplied by "the Jūmonji Company." See "Katsudō daishashin kōkoku," *Hōchi shinbun* (February 28, 1897).

12. Shinmachi Enbujō theater advertisement, *Asahi shinbun* (Osaka), (February 22, 1897); Tsukada, *Nihon eigashi no kenkyū*, 183–94.

13. Nakagawa Keiji, "Katsudō shashin konjaku monogatari (1)," *Katsudō kurabu* 4, no. 9 (September 1921): 35; Mizuno Hifumi, "Kansai eiga ochibo shū (2)," *Eiga shiryō* 9 (May 15, 1963): 3.

14. Mitsuda Yuri, "Seikimatsu Nippon," 44–59. Mitsuda's analysis of the length of Girel's stay is based on the latter's diary. Foreign Ministry records indicate that the work permit issued Girel was valid only from February 21 to March 30, 1897. Foreign Ministry Record 3.9.4.130, February 1897.

15. Peter B. High, "The Dawn of Cinema in Japan," *Journal of Contemporary History* 19 (1984): 24.

16. Girel did not limit himself to filming in the major cities, but traveled throughout Japan, including Hokkaido, where he took pictures of Ainu. He developed the movies in Japan and sent them back to France to be exhibited throughout Europe and the United States. Throughout much of the silent era, films of oriental exoticism were popular in the West. Several of the films shot by Girel and others during the late 1890s and early 1900s still survive. They provide a rare look into Japanese society at the turn of the century. Almost none of the motion pictures that Girel shot in Japan were ever shown domestically. Komatsu Hiroshi, "The Lumière Cinématographe and the Production of the Cinema in Japan in the Earliest Period," trans. Ben Brewster, *Film History* 8 (1996): 435–38. For still photographs from these films, see Yoshida et al., *Eiga denrai*.

17. Inabata, "Shinematogurafu," 72.

18. "Sufu-shi shittō ni arazaruka," *Kōbe yūshin nippō*, (November 19, 1896).

19. See, for example, "Chogen," *Kōbe yūshin nippō*; (November 25, 1896); Nanchi Enbujō theater advertisement, *Mainichi shinbun* (Osaka) (December 4, 1896).

235

20. Shūkan Asahi, ed., *Nedan no fūzokushi: Meiji, Taishō, Shōwa* (Tokyo: Shūkan Asahi sha, 1982), vol. 1: 45, 80; vol. 2: 225; vol. 3: 119.
21. According to Takahashi Shinshichi, the son of Takahashi Shinji, the fee was 30 sen in Kobe and 20 sen in Osaka. Takahashi Shinshichi, "Kinetosukōpu no kōgyō wazuka hantoshi no seimei," no. 5 of "Nippon eigashi sokō," *Kinema junpō* 555 (October 11, 1935): 71
22. "Katsudō daishashin kōkoku," *Hōchi shinbun* (February 28, 1897); Asakusa Kōen Shinematoguramukan advertisement, *Miyako shinbun* (March 4, 1897); Kanda Kinkikan advertisement, *Miyako shinbun* (March 5, 1897); Kabukiza advertisement, *Miyako shinbun* (July 13, 1899); Kanda Kinkikan advertisement, *Tōkyō nichinichi shinbun* (March 3, 1897).
23. Raidai Kamezo, "Shichimatogurafu o miru," *Shōnen kurabu* (May 1897); Nakagawa Keiji, "Konjaku monogatari (1)," *Katsudō shashinkai* 18 (March 1, 1911): 16.
24. Nakagawa, "Konjaku monogatari (1)," 16; Nakagawa Keiji, "Konjaku monogatari (2)," *Katsudō shashinkai* 19 (April 1, 1911): 14; Nakagawa, "Katsudō shashin konjaku monogatari (1)," 34–35; "Katsudō shashin (2)," *Mainichi shinbun* (Osaka), (April 15, 1912); Anderson Richie, *The Japanese Film*, 22.
25. The practice of watering down the screen appears to have begun when the pictures were projected from behind the screen. It continued, however, for several years, even after it became customary to project the Cinématographe from the front of the screen. Uehara Rorō remembers the screen being watered down when motion pictures were first exhibited in Nagano in 1903. Uehara Rorō, "Katsudō shashin e no kaisō," *Eiga shiryō* 6 (July 15, 1962): 7. This practice may have only been employed for the Cinématographe.
26. According to an article about Japanese cinema published in the British film magazine *Kinetograph and Lantern Weekly*, sometime before 1914, "five or six people were 'working' in the projection room, though most were playing." Therefore, at least at some theaters, the practice of employing several projectionists appears to have continued for some time. Given the cost of employing so many unnecessary workers, however, I doubt that this custom was widespread. J. C. A. "Sekai shijō ni taisuru Nippon katsudōkai: gaijin wa ikani sono ketten o shitekiseruka," *Kinema record* 2, no. 12 (1914): 4-5.
27. Mizuno, "Kansai eiga ochibo shū (2)," 3.
28. Eisha Dōji, "Katsudō benshi no ganso: Ueda Hoteiken," *Shinengei* 1, no. 3 (1916): 151–52.
29. It is unclear if he provided *setsumei* only on February 15, for part of the February 15–28 booking, or for the entire booking.
30. Eisha, 151–52.
31. Ibid., 149–50.
32. Ueda Hoteiken's name is the one most often associated with providing *setsumei* for the Kinetoscope exhibitions in Osaka that began on January 29, 1897. The repeated assertions found in secondary sources that he supplied

setsumei for the Kinetoscope, however, remain problematic and can be traced back to a series of articles appearing in *Mainichi shinbun* April 16–28, 1912. In one of these the author declares, "I heard Ueda Hoteiken was the *benshi* for the Kinetoscope when it was shown in Osaka." "Katsudō shashin (3)," *Mainichi shinbun* (Osaka) (April 16, 1912). As a result of this and other statements in the series, subsequent histories of the first *benshi* have consistently identified Ueda as the founding father. Possibly Hoteiken was the *benshi* for the Kinetoscope, but the 1916 article "Katsudō *benshi* no ganso," which appeared in the periodical *Shin engei*, raises doubts. Although published under the name Eisha Dōji, the article is basically a transcribed conversation by Ueda. In the article, Ueda goes into great detail about the importation of the Vitascope and Cinématographe, but completely ignores the Kinetoscope. He variously states that Takahashi Senkichi, who performed *setsumei* for the first public showing of the Cinématographe when it opened in Osaka on February 15, 1897, and Ueda himself, who provided *setsumei* for the Vitascope when it opened in Osaka on February 22, 1897, were the first *benshi*. If Ueda had really done *setsumei* for the Kinetoscope several months prior to the Vitascope and Cinématographe showings, he could have easily claimed the honor for himself alone. Since he does not, it is logical to assume that he was not the man who provided *setsumei* for the Kinetoscope. See Eisha, 150–52.

33. *Keisatsumei dai 15 gō: Misemonoba torishimari kisoku*, 1891, Chapter 3, Article 19.
34. Mizuno Hifumi, "Kansai eiga ochibo shū (4)," *Eiga shiryō* 11 (January 15, 1964): 3–4.
35. "Katsudō shashin (4)," *Mainichi shinbun* (Osaka) (April 17, 1912).
36. Eisha, 151–52.
37. Kobayashi Isamu writes that "a certain Honda" also appears to have provided *setsumei* at the Minatoza. I have not been able to find any other information about Honda. Kobayashi Isamu, *Eiga no tōei* (Tokyo: Itō Shobō, 1933): 2–3.
38. Nakagawa Keiji, "Katsudō shashin konjaku monogatari (2)," *Katsudō kurabu* 4, no. 10 (1921): 36.
39. Nakagawa, "Katsudō shashin konjaku monogatari (1)," 35; Nakagawa, "Konjaku monogatari (1)."
40. Nakagawa, "Katsudō shashin konjaku monogatari (2)," 36.
41. "Katsudō shashin meiyo no setsumeisha," *Katsudō shashinkai* 2 (October 20, 1909): 9–10.
42. Tokugawa Musei, *Musei Jiden*, vol. 1 (Tokyo: Kodansha Bunko, 1978): 129.
43. Yoshida Chieo, "Katsuben no rekishi (1)," *Eigashi kenkyū* 1 (Spring 1973): 22–23.
44. Ōnoda Tadashi, ed., *Jūmonji Daigen den: Bungaku hakushi bungen* (Jūmonji Daigen fu Kihen Sankai, 1926): 159.
45. Inabata, "Shinematogurafu," 71.

46. Nomura Hōtei, "Inabatasan no katsudō shashin," in *Nippon eiga jigyō sōran*, ed. Ishii Bunsaku (Kokusai Eiga Tsushinsha, 1926): 440. Very little is known about Sakata, including the correct pronunciation of his name: "Chikuma" or "Senkyoku." Chikuma is written as both 千曲 and 千駒.

47. Mizuno Hifumi, "Kansai eiga ochibo shū (3)," *Eiga shiryō* 10 (September 15, 1963): 3. As the film scholar Yoshida Chieo suggests, it was only to be expected that a peddler would become flustered in the presence of such a great person as Napoleon. Yoshida, *Mōhitotsu no eigashi*, 24.

48. Kobayashi, *Eiga no toei*, 3–4.

49. Komada Kōyō, "Eiga jūgonen hashirigaki," *Kinema junpō* 516 (September 1, 1934): 52–53.

50. The first *benshi* for the Cinématographe in Tokyo, Nakagawa Keiji, writes that, several months after he became a *benshi* he fell ill and could not perform. Because there were no substitute *benshi*, others had to fill in. Nakagawa asserts that, at first, Akita Ryūkichi, the owner of Hiromeya and the man hired by Arai Saburō to advertise the Vitascope, tried his hand, but failed. Komada Kōyō, a band director at the Hiromeya, then took a turn and did *setsumei* in Nakagawa's place for 3 days. Nakagawa Keiji, "Katsudō shashin konjaku monogatari (4)," *Katsudō kurabu* 4, no. 12 (1921): 69. Unfortunately, Nakagawa's account of these events is the only one available. No other primary sources indicate that Komada or the Hiromeya were connected with the Cinématographe. If Nakagawa's statements are correct, Jūmonji Daigen presumably worked as *benshi* for the Vitascope for several weeks, and Arai Saburō headhunted the Hiromeya Advertising Company and Komada Kōyō away from the Cinématographe. However, Nakagawa may have fabricated this story in order to convince people that he became a *benshi* long before Komada did. Nakagawa disliked his rival, Komada, who was sometimes said to be the first *benshi*. "One thing I [Nakagawa] want you to remember is that Komada Kōyō made exaggerated advertisements and [falsely] asserted that he was the founder of motion pictures." Nakagawa, "Katsudō shashin konjaku monogatari (3)," 51.

51. *Katsudō shashin setsumeisho* (n.p., c. 1897 or 1898): 18–19.

52. His full nickname was "Above and Below Heaven, the Self-righteous, Very, Very Great Professor."

53. See, for example, Kabukiza advertisement, *Miyako shinbun* (July 13, 1899); Naniwaza advertisement, *Asahi shinbun* (Osaka) (April 2, 1902); Kokkaza advertisement, *Miyako shinbun* (January 29, 1906).

54. Kobayashi, *Eiga no toei*, 130.

55. Mizuno Hifumi, "Kansai hōmen no kōkai: Meiji yonjūnendai," no. 45 of "Nippon eigashi sokō," *Kinema junpō* 619 (August 11, 1937): 71.

56. See, for example, Kabukiza advertisement, *Chūō shinbun* (March 26,1898); Kabukiza advertisement, *Chūō shinbun* (March 27, 1898); Kabukiza advertisement, *Miyako shinbun* (March 26,1897).

57. "Katsudō daishashin kōkoku," *Hōchi shinbun* (February 28, 1897).

238

3: LAYING THE FOUNDATION

1. Noël Burch, *To the Distant Observer*, 58.
2. Rachael Low, *The History of the British Film, 1896–1918*, vol. 2 (London: George Allen & Unwin, 1949): 15.
3. Robert Sklar, *Movie-Made America: A Cultural History of American Movies*, 1974, revised and updated (New York: Vintage Books, 1994): 45.
4. Tokugawa Musei, "Eiga setsumeishi," *Kinema Kōza 2* (Tokyo: Shigensha, 1927): 8.
5. There are several contradictions in Somei Saburō's own accounts of when he actually became a *benshi*, but it appears fairly certain that he first began working as a *benshi* in 1903. Somei Saburō, "Shashin o ikasu kushin," *Katsudō no sekai* 1, no. 3 (March 1916): 40–44;"Kyōmi aru mondai ni taisuru toka benshi shōkun no kaitō happyō," *Katsudō gahō* 2, no. 5 (May 1918): 133; Somei Saburō, Unpublished notebook (n.p., c. 1931–1934): 9–10; "Eigakai mukashi monogatari zadankai," *Nippon eiga* 4, no. 10 (October 1939): 185. Many authoritative sources, however, claim that Somei began working at the Denkikan in 1906. Yoshida Chieo states that "according to Somei's recollections he first took the stage as a *benshi* at the Asakusa Denkikan in 1906." Unfortunately, it is unclear what Yoshida means by "recollections," Yoshida, *Mōhitotsu*, 136. Because Yoshida's book is treated as the authoritative history of *benshi*, most subsequent historians have tended to rely on it. This perpetuates the assertion that Somei became a benshi in 1906.
6. Tanizaki Jun'ichirō, "Katsudō shashin no genzai to shōrai," *Shinshōsetsu* 22, no. 9 (September 1917): 41.
7. "Eiga-kai mukashi monogatari zadankai," 185.
8. Muromachi Kyōji, *Katsudō haiyū mi no ue banashi* (Tokyo: Sankōsha, 1920): 80–81.
9. *Kōjōii* was used as both a verb and a noun.
10. Somei, Unpublished notebook, 9.
11. Ibid., 10–11.
12. *Osaka Asahi shinbun* (July 16, 1903): 11.
13. Anderson and Richie, *The Japanese Film*, 24.
14. Kobayashi, *Eiga no toei*, 6.
15. Tōji, "Katsudō Mango," *Katsudō shashinkai* 14 (November 1, 1910): 7; Tokoshi, "Hyōbanki," *Katsudō shashinkai* 11 (July 25, 1910): 13–14.
16. Raidai, "Shishimatogurapu."
17. Matsui Suisei, *Suisei on Parade* (Tokyo: Ōraisha, 1931): 114.
18. Y., "Watashi ga chāmu sareta benshi," *Katsudō zasshi* 6, no. 8 (August 1920): 174.
19. Shūhō, "Katsudō shashin no *benshi*," *Bungei kurabu* 16, no. 8 (August 1910): 206–7.
20. Somei Saburō, "Benshi toshite no kushin," *Katsudō shashin zasshi* 3, no. 1

239

(January 1917): 50.

21. Somei Saburō, "Eiga no setsumei ga akunin o hansei saseta jitsurei," *Katsudō gahō* 6, no. 2 (February 1922): 41.
22. Itō Naoki, *Nipponohon onpumonku zenshu* (Tokyo: Ekisei Kankatsu Banbu, 1917): 486–87.
23. Nishimura Korakuten, "Waga seishun no katsuben jidai," *Geijutsu seikatsu,* no. 307 (March 1975): 111. Kobayashi Isamu also commented that Somei's "And" reflected the feeling of the age. Kobayashi, *Eiga no toei,* 31.
24. Sōgetsu, "Katsudō shashin hinpyōkai sunpyō," *Katsudō shashinkai* 11 (July 25, 1910): 16.
25. Sasaki, "Setsumeisha no hinpyō," *Katsudō shashinkai* 11 (July 25, 1910): 18.
26. Kobayashi, *Eiga no toei,* 123–24.
27. Komatsu, "Some Characteristics of Japanese Cinema," 239.
28. Yaji, "Daikokuza no katsudō shashin o miru," *Kobe shinbun* (April 15, 1905): 7.
29. "Aikokushin no kanshaku," *Kobe shinbun* (September 28, 1908): 7.
30. Hanai Hideo, "Shōki no eiga setsumeisha to Asakusa," *Nippon eiga jigyō soran* (Tokyo: Kokusai Eiga Tsushinsha, 1936): 459–62; Kobayashi, *Eiga no toei,* 144–48.
31. Kaun, "Katsudō Shashin," *Kobe shinbun* (June 19, 1905): 5.
32. Takamatsu Toyojirō conversation in "Pakku katsudō shashin seisakusha Takamatsu Toyojirō shi dan," no. 32 of "Nippon eigashi sokō," *Kinema junpō* 590 (October 11, 1936): 76; Okabe Ryū, ed., *Nihon eigashi sokō, 9: Takamatsu Toyojirō to Osagawara Meiho no gyōato* (Tokyo: Film Library Kyōgikai, 1974): 3–12.
33. Kobayashi, *Eiga no toei,* 170.
34. "Pakku katsudō," 76; Okabe, *Takamatsu,* 8.
35. Okabe, *Takamatsu,* 9–10.
36. "Kinkikan no kifu katsudō shashin," *Miyako shinbun* (February 13, 1908).
37. "Kinkikan no shinga," *Miyako shinbun* (February 16, 1908).
38. The first theater built in Osaka was the Bunmeikan, which opened sometime slightly prior to July, 1907. The Osaka Denkikan opened on July 6, 1907. No. 35 "Nippon eigashi sokō," *Kinema junpō* 597 (January 1, 1937): 219–20; no. 46 "Nippon eigashi sokō," *Kinema junpō* 622 (September 11, 1937): 72.
39. Shibata Masaru, "Tōkyō no katsudō shashin (eiga) jōsetsukan no hensen (1–4)," *Eiga shiryō* 8–11 (March 15, 1963–January 15, 1964).
40. Yamano Ichirō, *Ninjō eiga baka* (Tokyo: Nippon Shūhōsha, 1960): 54.
41. "Zenkoku katsudō shashin jōsetsukan ikkanpyō," *Katsudō no sekai* 3, no. 8 (August 1918): 75–89.
42. United States Bureau of Foreign and Domestic Commerce, "Motion Pictures in Japan, Philippine Islands, Netherland East Indies, Siam, British Malaya, and French Indo-China," *Trade Information Bulletin,* no. 634 (Washington, D.C.: Government Printing Office, 1929): 6.
43. Miyoshi Masahisa, "Katsuben tsuresure kusa," *Eiga shiryō* 16 (1968): 18.

44. *Keishichō meirei jūgo gō: kōgyōjō mata kōgyō torishimari kisoku*, 1921: Article 62, Paragraph 1.
45. Nojigiku Bunko, ed., *Kōbe shinkaichi monogatari* (Kobe: Nojigiku Bunko, 1973): 31.
46. Edwin T. Layton, with Roger Pineau and John Costello, *"And I was There"*: *Pearl Harbor and Midway—Breaking the Secrets* (New York: William Morrow, 1985): 40.
47. Anderson and Richie, *Japanese Film*, 456; A. C. Pinder, "Japan," *1977 International Motion Picture Almanac* (New York: Quigley Publishing, 1978): 692–93; David Bordwell, "Our Dream Cinema: Western Historiography and the Japanese Film," *Film Reader* 4 (1979): 48.
48. Akiyama Sokkitei, "Yoki jidai no katsuben fūfu: Takemoto Shōkosan to Takemoto Suzume-san," *Bungei Asahi* 4, no. 7 (July 1965): 87.
49. Anderson and Richie, *Japanese Film*, 439.
50. Tachibana Takashirō, *Katsudōkyo no techō* (Tokyo: Kōbunsha, 1924): insert between pages 92 and 93.
51. Mikuni Ichirō, "Katsuben no Wagei," in *Musei eiga no tanjō*, edited by Imamura Shōhei et al., *Kōza Nihon eiga*, vol. 1 (Tokyo: Iwanami Shōten, 1985): 300.
52. Nishimura Korakuten, "Katsuben ōrai," 423; Mizutani Hironari, "Watashi no ashiato: ginmaku 45 nen," *Eiga shiryō* 12 (July 15, 1964): 11.
53. "Jōsetsukan uchi no kangengaku hensei ni kan suru risō to jissai," *Kinema junpō* 27 (April 11, 1920): 9.
54. "Hagaki Kurabu," *Kinema Record* 2, no. 12 (June 3, 1914): 39; Kobayashi, *Eiga no toei*, 17.
55. Hugo Munsterberg, *The Photoplay: A Psychological Study* (New York: D. Appleton, 1916): 204–5.
56. Fujinami Mumei, "Eiga no setsumei to ongaku," *Miyako shinbun* (December 8, 1924).

4: THE PERIOD OF EXPERIMENTATION, 1908–1914

1. Gunning, *D. W. Griffith*. The entire book is about this transformation. This analysis and what follows summarizes Gunning's work, with additional information assimilated from the following sources: Eileen Bowser, *History of the American Cinema*, vol. 2, *The Transformation of Cinema, 1907–1915* (Berkeley: University of California Press, 1990); Hansen, *Babel & Babylon*; Fell, *Film Before Griffith*.
2. Kinkikan advertisement, *Miyako shinbun* (May 7, 1908): 4.
3. Fujikan advertisement, *Miyako shinbun* (August 29, 1908): 4.
4. *Kowairo* was also called *kakeai* (dialogue) and *mono mane* (mimicry).

5. No primary source exists stating that Hanai came up with the idea. All accounts with this claim are secondary. Kobayashi, *Eiga no toei*, 132–33; Yoshida, "Katsuben no rekishi," nos. 8–9; Yoshida, *Mōhitotsu*, 47–49; Tanaka, *Nippon eiga*, vol. 1, 167; Satō, *Nihon eigashi*, vol. 1, 102; Komatsu Hiroshi and Charles Musser, "Benshi Search," *Wide Angle* 9 (1987): 71–90.

6. Daishōkan advertisement, *Miyako shinbun* (September 30, 1908): 6. The exact same advertisement ran regularly over the next few weeks.

7. Uchida Tsukibito, "Katsudō shashin no konjaku," *Katsudō shashin zasshi* 1, no. 6 (November 1915): 16–17.

8. San'yūkan advertisement, *Miyako shinbun* (November 9, 1908): 4.

9. Where they were positioned is unclear. The primary sources do not say; the secondary sources contradict each other. Given the conflicting statements about where *kowairo benshi* were situated, their position probably varied, depending on the architecture of the theater.

10. Tsuchiya Shōtō, "Benshi toshite no kushin," *Katsudō shashin zasshi* 3, no. 1, (January 1917): 48.

11. Tsuchiya Shōtō, "Watashi ga seiyomono o setsumei shita toki," *Katsudō zasshi* 8, no. 5, (May 1922): 140–41; "Katsudō benshi ichinenshi," *Katsudō shashin zasshi* 4, no. 1 (January 1918): 70.

12. Yamano, *Ninjō eiga baka*, 45–47.

13. Itō, *Nipponohon onpumonku zenshu*, 793–94.

14. Somei Saburō, "Biwa ōyō no setsumei," *Katsudō shashin zasshi* 2, no. 10 (October 1916): 128.

15. Daishōkan advertisement, *Miyako shinbun* (April 2, 1909): 4.

16. This data is based on an analytical reading of movie theater advertisements that appeared in the *Miyako shinbun* from 1908 to 1914. Theater advertisements that sporadically appeared in other newspapers confirm the trend delineated in the *Miyako shinbun*.

17. Tanaka Jun'ichirō, "Uta shigure," *Kinema junpō* (Special Edition, October 1966): 29. I have used the translation by Linda C. Ehrlich and Yuko Okutsu found in "Some Characteristics of Japanese Cinema Before World War I," by Komatsu Hiroshi in *Reframing Japanese Cinema*, 248.

18. *Keishichō meirei jūni gō: katsudō shashin kōgyō torishimari kisoku*, 1917. There is no single article that proscribes *rensageki* within this law. Rather the explicit stipulations about where, when, and how motion pictures could be exhibited hindered *rensageki*.

19. Shibata Katsuo, *Jitsuen to eiga: Rensageki no kiroku* (Tokyo: n.p., 1982).

5: THE *BENSHI* THEMSELVES

1. Yoshida Chieo, "Katsuben no rekishi (3)," 32–33.

242

2. Hitotsuya Kōseki, "'Benshi no onryō' ni tsuite," Katsudō gahō 6, no. 12 (December 1922): 135.

3. Misono Kyōhei, Aa, katsudō daishashin (Tokyo: Katsudō Shiryō Kenkyūkai, 1966): 61; Misono Kyōhei, Katsuben jidai (Tokyo: Iwanami Shoten, 1990): 39.

4. According to Ōkubo Tenrai, a graduate of the school, 30 students were accepted into the program. Kobayashi Isamu also writes that 30 students enrolled. It is unclear, however, how many students actually applied. Kobayashi states that "around two hundred people applied." Subsequent historians such as Yoshida Chieo and Misono Kyōhei also state that 200 people applied, but they appear to be basing their assertions on Kobayashi's work. I am troubled by Kobayashi's figures, however, for two reasons. First, in a later part of the monograph, when writing about another benshi training school that opened in 1907, Kobayashi states that "around two hundred people applied." Is it purely coincidental that the same number of people applied to both schools or did Kobayashi confuse his facts? Second, according to Nikkatsu's own company history—Nikkatsu yonjūnenshi (A forty year history of Nikkatsu)—the company accepted only one in 15 applicants. If this is true, and if the school actually accepted 30 students, then around 450 people applied. Ōkubo Tenrai, "Shi Hayashi Tempū o omou: Soshite tsunagaru iroiro no omoide," Eiga shiryō 16 (1968): 16; Kobayashi, Eiga no tōei, 74; Yoshida, Mōhitotsu, 77; Misono, Aa, katsudō daishashin, 61; Misono, Katsuben jidai, 39; Nikkatsu yonjūnenshi (Tokyo: Nikkatsu Kabushiki Gaisha, 1952): 83.

5. Ōkubo, "Shi Hayashi Tempū," 16.

6. Seigankō, "Katsudō shashin no benshi," Katsudō shashinkai 19 (April 1, 1911): 1–2.

7. Tokugawa Musei, Musei jiden, vol. 1, 278–80.

8. Yoshida, Eigashi kenkyū 3 (1974): 34.

9. Anderson and Richie, The Japanese Film, 28.

10. High, "The Dawn of Cinema in Japan," 40. In 1912, Umeya came up with the idea of amalgamating Japan's four major film companies into Nikkatsu. Shortly after incorporation, he left the company and went on to other enterprises.

11. Kobayashi, Eiga no tōei, 129.

12. Yoshida, Eigashi kenkyū 2 (1973): 5–6; Yoshida, Mōhitotsu, 67.

13. "Taishō jūnen no eigakai," Katsudō zasshi 7, no. 1 (January 1921): 85.

14. Matsuki et al., Setsumeisha ni naru chikamichi, 14–16.

15. Ibid., 14–16.

16. Tamaki Kōsui, "Hatsu butai no omoide," Kurashiku eiga nyūsu 201 (April 1, 1975): 12.

17. Sapporo Hidematsu, "Benshi tonatta boku," Katsudō shashin zasshi 2, no. 4 (April 1916): 60.

18. Nishimura Rakuten, "Benshi setsumei furi no hensen," Katsudō gahō 1, no. 3

(March 1917): 154–55; Shiuhō, "Katsudō Shashin no Benshi," *Bungei kurabu* 16, no. 8 (August 1910): 203; M, "Benshi gettan," 8.

19. Nishimura, "Benshi setsumei furi no hensen," 155–56.
20. Tsuda Yoshinto, "Benshi setsumei furi no kaibō: Nishimura Rakuten," *Katsudō gahō* 1, no. 4 (April 1917): 157.
21. Nishimura, "Katsuben ōrai," 422.
22. *Keisatsu kōshūjo gakuyūkai*, vol. 1, (Tokyo: Keisatsu Kōshūjo Gakuyūkai, 1919): 9.
23. Naimushō (Home Ministry), *Katsudō shashin (fuirumu) ken'etsu nempō, 1936* (Tokyo: Naimushō Keihōkyoku, 1937): 62–63. See also Ishikawa Sai, ed., *Nippon eiga jigyō sōran: 1928/29 nen han* (Tokyo: Kokusai Eiga Tsushinsha, 1928): 72–73.
24. Matsuki et al., *Setsumeisha ni naru chikamichi*, 45–59.
25. "Setsumeisha shizen tōta jidai kuru," *Katsudō zasshi* 9, no. 8 (August 1923): 70.
26. Yoshida Chieo, "Katsuben no rekishi (13)," *Eigashi kenkyū* 14 (1979): 72–73.
27. *Keisatsu kōshūjo gakuyūkai*, 9; Ishikawa, 72–73; Naimushō, 62–63.
28. Kobayashi, *Eiga no tōei*, 57–58.
29. Katsura Ni, "Kagezerifu no onna monogatari," *Katsudō shashin zasshi* 3, no. 6 (June 1917): 188.
30. Tokugawa Musei, *Musei jiden*, vol. 1, 310–11.
31. Akiyama, "Yoki jidai no katsuben fūfu," 82.
32. Ishikawa Mitsumaru, "Katsuben monogatari," nos. 191–202, *Kurashiku eiga nyūsu* 393–404 (4/1991–4/1992); "Ume no go taimen," *Katsukichi* 63 (January 1, 1991): 1.
33. Heinz Morioka and Miyoko Sasaki, "The Blue-Eyed Storyteller: Henry Black and His *Rakugo* Career," *Monumenta Nipponica* 38, no. 2 (1983): 133–62; Heinz Morioka and Miyoko Sasaki, *Rakugo, the Popular Narrative Art of Japan* (Cambridge: Harvard University Press, 1990): 250–58. Advertisements for Black working at the Pathekan first appeared in the *Miyako shinbun* on January 30, 1912, and they appeared regularly over the next several months.

    Katsudo zasshi reported that, on January 15, 1922, "an English-speaking foreigner provided *setsumei* for a Pathe film in English and the audience loved him." Who this "foreign *benshi*" was, and why he performed, is unclear. "Setsumeisha fuhitsuyō no koe ha naze okoruka," *Katsudō zasshi* 8, no. 3 (March 1922): 122.
34. Komatsu Hiroshi and Charles Musser, "*Benshi* Search," *Wide Angle* 9 (1987): 78.
35. Nishimura Korakuten, *Watashi wa Shōwa no katari shokunin* (Tokyo: April Music, 1978): 40.
36. According to one 1920 survey of entertainers in Tokyo, 24.7% of all entertainers were *benshi*. The only group with more members were comedic ac-

244

tors, with 26.4%. Most other groups constituted a far smaller percentage: *gidayū* performers accounted for 11.6%; *rakugoka*, 4.5%; and *kōdanshi*, 2.2%. Gonda Yasunosuke, *Gorakugyōsha no mure* (Tokyo: Jōgyō no Hihonsha, 1923): 63–65.

37. Musashinokan advertisement, *Kinema junpō* 186 (February 25, 1925): 38; Konparukan advertisement, *Kinema junpō* 16 (December 11, 1919): 6.

38. Shūhō, "Katsudō shashin no benshi," 204.

39. Miyoshi Masahisa, "Natsukashi setsumeisha tachi," *Eiga shiryō* 8 (March 15, 1963): 9.

40. Shūkan Asahi, ed., *Nedan no fūzokushi*, vol. 3, 235; vol. 2, 19; vol. 3, 69.

41. Izumi Tenryō, "Uite shizunde," *Eiga shiryō* 14 (June 15, 1965): 10; Izumi Tenryō, "Zoku uite shizunde," *Eiga shiryō* 15 (January 15, 1966): 10.

42. Chikushi Jirō, "Kowairo seikatsu," *Katsudō no sekai* 2, no. 3 (March 1917): 64–65.

43. Tadayoshi, "Osaka katsudōkai kikiroku," *Katsudō gahō* 2, no. 7 (July 1918): 148.

44. Miyoshi Masahisa, "Katsuben tsuresurekusa," *Eiga shiryō* 16 (January 15, 1968): 20.

45. Kusamori Junnosuke, "Eiga fudōchō," *Katsudō kurabu* 10, no. 1 (January 1927): 48–49.

46. Izumi Sōichirō, "Preface," in Matsuki et al., *Setsumeisha ni naru chikamichi*, 11–13.

47. Misono, *Aa, katsudō daishashin*, 56–57; Misono, *Katsuben jidai*, 84.

48. Kobayashi, *Eiga no tōei*, 97; Matsuki et al., *Setsumeisha ni naru chikamichi*, 49; Mizutani Hironari, "Watashi no ashiato: ginmaku 45 nen," *Eiga shiryō* 14 (1965): 9; Takahashi Kakudō, "Katsuben no nenmatsu," *Benyū* 7 (January 1967): 7

49. Kunii Shikō, *Dadakko jinsei* (Tokyo: Myōgi Shuppan, 1956): 200–201. Kobayashi Isamu also writes about Hokkaido theaters paying enormous salaries. What is unclear is from where the money to pay such large sums to the benshi came. It is hard to imagine that the box office receipts in Hokkaido were so good that Hokkaido theaters could afford to pay benshi some of the highest salaries in the business. Kobayashi, *Eiga no tōei*, 179–80.

50. "Ikoma Raiyū kun ga nisen yen seikyū," *Kinema shūhō* 41 (December 12, 1930): 20.

51. "Nikkatsu, Nikkō setsumeisha gakushi no han tōkī sōgi keika tenmatsu," *Kinema junpō* 435 (May 11, 1932): 82.

52. "Han tōkī sōgi kaiketsu," *Kinema junpō* 436 (May 21, 1932): 9.

53. Shisetsu, "Katsuben eisei shiken," *Katsudō shashin zasshi* 2, suppl. ed. (May 1916): 59–60.

54. See, for example, Fuji Sen'yū, "Katsudō shashin to kenkō," *Katsudō no sekai* 2, no. 12 (December 1917): 6–7; Tōyama Tsubayoshi, "Jōsetsukan ni okeru eiseiteki setsubi," *Katsudō no sekai* 3, no. 8 (August 1918): 15–18.

55. "Kyōmi aru mondai ni taisuru toka benshi shokun no kaitō happyō," *Katsudō*

gahō 2, no. 5 (May 1918): 132.

56. Imano Kenzō, "Setsumeisha jidai monogatari," *Engeki eiga* 1, no. 8 (August 1926): 48.
57. Shisetsu, "Katsuben eisei shiken," 59–60.
58. Fujikawa Chisui, *Kumamoto shinema kōdan* (Kumamoto: Kumamoto Insatsu Senta, 1978): 138–51.
59. Ōkura, *Waga gei*, 78.
60. Kunii, *Dadakko jinsei*, 9.
61. Takemoto Shōko, "Kaigō no tanoshimi," *Benyū* 1 (1963): 5.
62. Nojigiku, *Kōbe shinkaichi monogatari*, 131.
63. Fujikawa, *Kumamoto shinema kōdan*, 121.
64. Taishō Chōnin, "Benshi no gakuya ochi," *Katsudō shashin zasshi* 3, no. 12 (December 1917): 202.
65. Tokugawa, *Kuragari nijūnen* (Tokyo: Aoi Shobōban, 1934): 28–39; Tokugawa, *Musei jiden*, vol. 1, 101–103, 190–266, 292–335; Mikuni Ichirō, *Tokugawa Musei no sekai* (Tokyo: Seiabo, 1979): 41–78.
66. Haniya Yūkō and Maruyama Masao, "Taidan: bungaku to gakumon," *Eureka* 10, no. 3 (1978): 87.
67. Tokugawa Musei, *Anata mo sake ga yamerareru* (Tokyo: Bungei Shunjū Shinsha, 1959): 1–17, 77–94; Tokugawa, *Kuragari nijūnen*, 104–59; Tokugawa, *Musei jiden*, vol. 1, 330–419.
68. Ichikawa Mugō, "Katsudō benshi rōmansu," *Katsudō gahō* 3, no. 1 (January 1919): 139
69. Yamano, *Ninjō eiga baka*, 91–94.
70. "Shikima benshi yo kyōran no onna yo," *Katsudō gahō* 3, no. 11 (November 1919): 64.
71. "Onna gakusei to benshi: shakai no akufūchō," *Katsudō gahō* 3, no. 6 (June 1919): 152.
72. Tokugawa Musei, *Oya baka jūnen* (Tokyo: Sōgensha, 1950): 118–19; Yamano, *Ninjō eiga baka*, 49.
73. "Nippon eiga dokutōkū no eiga setsumeisha hyōban roku," *Katsudō zasshi* 11, no. 9 (September 1925): 90.
74. Nagai Kafū, *A Strange Tale from East of the River and Other Stories*, translated by Edward Seidensticker (Tokyo: Charles E. Tuttle, 1972): 102; Nagai Kafū, *Kafū Zenshū* (Tokyo: Chūō Kōron, 1949): 35.
75. Dazai Osamu, *Kirigirisu* (Shinchō Bunko, 1974): 139.
76. See, for example, Matsuki et al., *Setsumeisha ni naru chikamichi*, 63–66.
77. Maruyama Kō, "Setsumeisha e no gosōdan," *Katsudō kurabu* 3, no. 8 (August 1920): 65.
78. Aaron A. Gerow, "The Benshi's New Face: Defining Cinema in Taishō Japan," *Iconics* 3 (1994): 75.
79. Kobayashi, *Eiga no tōei*, 125.
80. Kinugasa Teinosuke, *Waga eiga no seishun* (Tokyo: Chūō Kōron sha, 1977): 17.

81. For a discussion of the development of the Japanese screenplay, see, Joanne Bernardi, *The Early Development of the Gendaigeki Screenplay: Kaeriyama Norimasa, Kurihara Tōmas, Tanizaki Jun'ichirō and the Pure Film Movement*, Ph.D. diss., Columbia University, 1992.

82. Kobayashi, *Eiga no tōei*, 126–29.

83. Gukyōshi, "Jimaku kenkyū," *Kinema junpō* 285 (February 1, 1928): 49.

84. Satō Shitsumei, "Hon'yaku no kanata e (5)," *Sakkaku* 2, no. 1 (January 1926): 34.

85. Matsui Suisei, "Taitoru to setsumeisha," *Sakkaku* 1, no. 1 (June 1925): 32.

86. Matsui, "Taitoru to setsumeisha," 32.

87. Ibid., 33.

88. Tamura Yukihiko, "Chikagoro zakkan," *Kinema junpō* 173 (October 1, 1924): 31.

89. "Eiga setsumei buri gappyō," *Katsudō gahō* 7, no. 3 (March 1923): 71.

90. "Arashi no koji gappyō" *Katsudō gahō* 7, no. 8 (August 1923): 107.

91. Somei Saburō, "Jimaku to setsumei," *Katsudō no sekai* 2, no. 6 (June 1917): 62.

92. Unpublished *benshi* script from the film *The World and Its Women* (1919).

93. Shomogawara Kinpei, "*Setsumeisha* no hansei o unagasu: daihon no rōdoku o haishiseyo," *Katsudō gahō* 7, no. 1 (January 1923): 123.

94. Satomi Yoshirō, *Tsubaki Hime* (*Camellia Princess*), Tombo Records, 15516.

95. Satomi Yoshirō, *Tsubaki Hime* (*Camellia Princess*), Orient Records 3431.

96. Satomi Yoshirō, *Tsubaki Hime* (*Camellia Princess*), Nitto Records 5174.

97. Tokugawa, *Kuragari nijūnen*, 143–44.

98. Tokugawa, *Oya baka jūnen*, 128–29.

99. S. T. "Ishoku no hito," *Benyū* 4 (July 1965): 4.

100. Musō, *Eiga setsumei no kenkyū*, 70–71.

6: GOVERNMENTAL ATTEMPTS TO CONTROL THE *BENSHI*

1. This is a good example of how *benshi* diverged from the text to make a joke. Although the movie is set in Paris, Yamano's inserts the name of a busy Tokyo train station—Shinbashi—to amuse the audience and to give the film a local flavor.

2. Yamano, *Ninjō eiga baka*, 35–37.

3. The series of editorials begin with: "Jigoma (1)" (*Zigomar* [1]), *Tokyo Asahi shinbun*, (October 5, 1912): 5. For a lengthy analysis of the affects of the *Zigomar* debate on Japanese cinema, see Aaron Gerow, *Writing a Pure Cinema*, 57–71.

4. In Tokyo, the two most important regulations were the 1891 *Keisatsu meidai 15 gō: misemonoba torishimari kisoku* and the 1900 *Keisatsu meidai 41 gō: engeki kōgyō torishimari kisoku*.

5. "Katsudō shashin no shin torishimari hō," *Hōchi shinbun* (December 15, 1916): 3.

6. "Katsudō shashin setsumeisha kōshūkai o shōyōsu," *Katsudō kurabu* 4, no. 5 (May 1921): 65.

7. Terakawa Makoto, *Eiga oyobi eigageki* (Osaka: Osaka Mainichi Shimbun-sha, 1925): 230–33.

8. *Keishichō meirei 12 gō: katsudō shashin kōgyōjō torishimari kisoku*, 1917: Article 35, Paragraph 6; Article 35, Paragraph 2; Article 40.

9. Ibid., Article 35, Paragraph 1.

10. Ibid., Article 14 and Article 27.

11. According to Kobayashi Isamu, in 1912, Saga prefecture "apparently" instituted the first benshi licensing system. Kobayashi, *Eiga no tōei*, 55.

12. *Keishichō meirei 12 gō*, Article 20.

13. "Katsudō benshi ninka," *Miyako shinbun* (August 11, 1917): 3.

14. Adachi Kinnosuke, "Censorship Under the Cherry Blossoms," *Motion Picture Magazine* 22, no. 8 (September, 1921): 92.

15. *Keishichō meirei 12 gō*, Article 26.

16. Hiroshima Prefecture, "Katsudō shashin setsumeisha menkyōshō," no. 185, issued in 1921 to Hasegawa Shōichi.

17. "Hōtei ni minshū geijutsu o toku benshi," *Katsudō kurabu* 6, no. 2 (February 1923): 103

18. Itoko and Mitsuko, "Ran kiku no en," *Katsudō kurabu* 3, no. 11 (November 1, 1920): 51.

19. "Naichi eigakai kinji," *Katsudō gahō* 4, no. 10 (October 1920): 53.

20. Misono, *Katsuben jidai*, 40–41.

21. Matsui, *Suisei on Parade*, 13–16.

22. "*Jukenki*," *Kinema junpō* 41 (September 11, 1920): 11.

23. Ibid., 10–11.

24. Iwatō Shisetsu, "Setsumeisha no shiken," *Katsudō gahō* 4, no. 10 (October 1920): 54.

25. "Benshi no ninka seidō chikaku haishi," *Kinema junpō* 472 (April 11, 1936): 11.

26. "Setsumeisha shiken shinseidō saiyō," *Kinema junpō* 380 (October 11, 1930): 15

27. "Shitsugyōsha o dasu koto o fusegu," *Kinema junpō* 384 (November 21, 1931): 14.

28. "Setsumeisha shiken seidō henkō," *Kinema junpō* 402 (June 1, 1931): 8.

29. Matsui, *Suisei on Parade*, 17–18.

30. *Aichiken meidai 60 go: katsudō shashin torishimari kisoku*, July 12, 1918.

31. Monbushō Futsū Gakumukyoku, *Zenkoku ni okeru katsudō shashin jōkyō chōsa* (Tokyo: Monbushō, 1921): 20.

32. "Eiga setsumeisha o zenkoku kyōtsū no menkyō seidō ni," *Kinema junpō* 224 (April 11, 1926): 24.

33. "Zenkoku eiga setsumeisha o ninkashō no yōhi," *Kinema junpō* 424 (January 21, 1932): 7.

34. Iwatō, "Setsumeisha no shiken," *Katsudō gahō* 4, no. 10 (October 1920): 53; "Benshi no shikatsu mondai," *Katsudō zasshi* 6, no. 10 (October 1920): 85.

35. "Ōsaka benshi no kōshūkai," *Katsudō zasshi* 7, no. 6 (June 1921): 110–11.

36. Matsui, *Suisei on Parade*, 12.

37. Nakagawa, "Setsumeisha kentei shiken o teppai seyo," *Katsudō zasshi* 9, no. 12 (July 1923): 139.

38. *Keishichō meidai 15 gō: kōgyōjō oyobi kōgyō torishimari kisoku*, 1921: Article 76.

39. This appears to be the first written articulation of the notion that *benshi* were social educators. Eda Fu, "Katsudō shashin no setsumeisha," *Katsudō shashinkai* 2 (October 20, 1909): 8.

40. Kishi Akio, "Benshi no shakaiteki kachi," *Kinema Record* 5, no. 49 (July 15, 1917): 324.

41. "Setsumeisha yo danseiteki ninare," *Katsudō zasshi* 9, no. 5 (May 1923): 70.

42. Subsequent symposia were held in later years, but were much less significant.

43. Takaoka Kurume, ed., *Dai ikkai setsumeisha kōshūkai koshūroku* (Tokyo: Dai Nihon Setsumeisha Kyōkai, 1921).

44. Hoshino Tatsuo, "Katsudō shashin no gijutsuteki kōsatsu," in Takaoka, *Dai ikkai setsumeisha kōshūkai*, 61.

45. Norisugi Kazu, "Shakai kyōiku to katsudō shashin," in Takaoka, *Dai ikkai setsumeisha kōshūkai*, 112–13.

46. Tachibana Takahirō, "Katsudō shashin no torishimari nitsuite," in Takaoka, *Dai ikkai setsumeisha kōshūkai*, 135–62.

47. "Kono katate ochi o dō kaisetsu suruka," *Katsudō zasshi* 6, no. 11 (November 1920): 162–63.

48. Gonda Yasunosuke, "Minshū goraku toshite no katsudō shashin," *Katsudō gahō* 5, no. 12 (December 1921): 36; Gonda Yasunosuke, *Minshū goraku ron*, vol. 2, *Gonda Yasunosuke chōsakushū* (Tokyo: Bunwa Shobō, 1974): 340

49. Siegfried F. Lindstrom, "The Cinema in Cinema-Minded Japan," *Asia* 31, no. 12 (1931): 769.

50. *Keisatsu meidai 15 gō: Misemonojō torishimari kisoku*, 1891: Article 19.

51. Ibid., Article 26.

52. Tokugawa, *Musei jiden*, vol. 1, 321; Nishimura, "Katsuben ōrai," 422.

53. T., "Kissu no ken'etsu," *Katsudō shashin zasshi* 3, no. 2 (February 1917): 152.

54. *Katsuben monogatari*, screenplay (1957): 12–13. Several sources relate this anecdote as fact. However, the lack of primary sources confirming this episode, and the fact that all of the sources that recount this story post-date the

film, gives rise to questions about its validity. In his version of the story, Matsuda Shunsui claims that a head *benshi* provided the *setsumei*; Yamano Ichirō insists that it was an apprentice. Matsuda Shunsui, "Tanoshikikana katsuben," *Shinario* 27, no. 5 (1971): 58; Komatsu and Musser, "Benshi Search," 79; Yamano, *Ninjō eiga baka*, 128.

Even if the story is fiction, however, it still accurately depicts the atmosphere of the era. Censorship of this sort did occur. Kobayashi Isamu, who published his work during the silent era, reports that Ōkura Tadataka had his license revoked after he provided the following *setsumei*: "The glory of the assassin's role required a hero." Without being prompted by any intertitles, Tadataka talked about the glory and honor of an assassin, and, to the officer sitting in the theater that day, that was inappropriate *setsumei*. Kobayashi, *Eiga no tōei*, 172.

55. "Profile of 'Benshi' performer Shin Chul," in Ishizaki Kenji, ed., *Japan Foundation Asia Center Asian Classical Cinema Series No. 2: Korean Silent Film and 'Benshi' Performer* (Tokyo: The Japan Foundation Asian Center, 1996): 4; "Ajia musei eiga gannen," *Asia Center News* 3 (Fall 1996): 16; conversation with author, July 14, 1996.

Anti-Japanese *setsumei* for this film appears to have been fairly common. See, for example, James Wade, "The Cinema in Korea," in *Korean Dance, Theater and Cinema*, edited by the Korean National Commission for UNESCO (Arch Cape, OR: Pace International Research, 1983): 176–77.

Im Kwon-taek's 1990 film, *The General's Son*, contains a scene with a Korean *benshi* providing setsumei for a fictitious film titled *National Border*. One will notice in the film that two *kenpetai* are stationed in the theater to keep an eye on the audience and the *benshi*.

56. Shin's first performance was a huge success, perhaps because of the nationalistic sentiment of his closing line. He continued to perform *setsumei* until the 1960s, at which point a loss of public interest in silent films forced him to retire. He held various odd jobs over the years, including working as a taxi driver. In 1991, when asked to perform at the founding ceremony of the Korean Film Society, he resuscitated the lost art of Korean *setsumei*. On occasion, he still performs. The rhythm and tone of Shin Chul's *setsumei* is more energetic and melodic than Japanese *setsumei*, taking on an evangelical feeling.

57. A number of other *benshi*, among them Kusui Shikō, Sugiura Ichirō, and Gota Chapurin, were also known as "The Chaplin *Benshi*," because they performed dressed as Charlie Chaplin. Japanese film companies even made imitation Chaplin films that starred actors such as Nakajima Kōyō, who were billed as "Japan's very own Charlie Chaplin."

58. Several other *benshi* also managed and/or owned theaters. A few succeeded, but most failed.

59. Ōkura Mitsugi, *Waga gei to kane to koi* (Tokyo: Tokyo Shobō, 1959).

60. Jōhei Nakio, "Eiga gekijō o mawaru seiteki kōsatsu," *Hentai shiryō* 3, no. 4

(April, 1928): 88.

61. Ōkura, *Waga gei to kane to koi*, 119.
62. Jōhei, "Eiga gekijō o mawaru seiteki kōsatsu," 88.
63. Nishimura, *Watashi wa Shōwa no katari shokunin*, 125–26.

7: THE PURE FILM MOVEMENT'S ATTACK ON THE *BENSHI*

1. See, for example, "Shinshun no kyōkō o abite," *Katsudō kurabu* 4, no. 1 (January 1921): 32; "Jinbutsu gantan," *Kinema junpō* 87 (January 1, 1922): 22.
2. Toshio, "Gujin no gugo ka aruiwa Nihon eiga no ketten ka," *Kinema Record* 4, no. 39 (September 10, 1916): 379; no. 40 (October 10, 1916): 427.
3. Earle Ernst, *The Kabuki Theater* (Oxford: Oxford University Press, 1956. Reprint. Honolulu: University of Hawaii Press, 1974): 10.
4. "Eiga ni joyū o shiyōseyo," *Katsudō shashin zasshi* 4, no. 1 (January 1918): 10.
5. Takeda Kōkatau, "Daben bokumetsu ron: ue," *Katsudō gahō* 6, no. 5 (May 1922): 133.
6. Tokugawa Musei, *Musei Mandan* (Tokyo: Shueikaku, 1927): 3.
7. Kaeriyama Norimasa, "Jun'eigageki to benshi tono kankei," *Katsudō kurabu* 4, no. 2 (February 1921): 19.
8. Commenting in 1929, Suzuki Shigesaburō announced that he was surprised to find that, in theaters throughout the countryside, motion pictures were usually subordinate to the *benshi*, and that even country *benshi* had a great deal of power over films. "Kaidanza," *Kinema junpō* 352 (January 1, 1930): 152.
9. Ōi, "Eiga no mitsu no mondai ni tsuite," *Kinema junpō* 173 (October 1, 1924): 37.
10. Kobayashi, *Eiga no toei*, 162–63.
11. Tanaka Eizō, "Mukojima jidai no omoide," *Kinema junpō* 641 (April 1, 1938): 141.
12. Kobayashi, *Eiga no toei*, 138; Komatsu Hiroshi, "Tennenshoku kara jun eiga e: Nippon eigashi ni okeru Tenkatsu no igi," *Geijutsugaku kenkyū* 5 (1995): 27–28.
13. The director Nomura Hōtei once told Nishimura Korakuten that he composed the first half of *Haha* (*Mother*, 1929) so that it would be easy for Korakuten to *setsumei*, and that he designed the second half of the film to bring out the eloquence of Shizuta Kinpa's *setsumei*. Nishimura, "Katsuben ōrai," in *Nihon eiga terebi purodūsa kyōkai*, 423.
14. Kaeriyama, "Jun'eigageki to benshi tono kankei," 19.
15. Takeda Akira, "Manju shage (sono hachi)," *Kinema junpō* 211 (November 11, 1925): 33.

16. Munsterberg, *The Photoplay: A Psychological Study* (New York: D. Appleton and Company, 1916).
17. Koszarski, *History of the American Cinema*, 209.
18. Munsterberg, *The Photoplay*, 78–79, 200–205.
19. Ibid., 202–203.
20. Takeda Kōkatsu, "Daben bokumetsu ron: shita," *Katsudō gahō* 6, no. 6 (June 1922): 122.
21. Matsuki et al., *Setsumeisha ni naru chikamichi*, 57.
22. Gerow, *Writing a Pure Cinema*, 234–35.
23. Mikuni, "Katsuben no Wagei," 307.
24. Matsuki et al., *Setsumeisha ni naru chikamichi*, 41.
25. Musser, "Archaeology of the Cinema: 8," 8.
26. Satō Tadao, *Nihon eigashi*, vol. 1 (Tokyo: Iwanami Shōten, 1995): 7. When explanatory titles first appeared in a Japanese production is unclear.
27. Saitō Kazuo, "Sōshun yoiwa," *Kinema junpō* 222 (March 21, 1926): 61.
28. Arai Saburō, "Setsumei haishi ronsha ni teisu," *Katsudō gahō* 5, no. 5 (May 1921): 98.
29. Gerow, *Writing a Pure Cinema*, 229–37.
30. Kaeriyama Norimasa, "Jimaku no eiga kōsei kachi," *Katsudō gahō* 3, no. 10 (October 1919): 24.
31. Kaeriyama Norimasa, *Katsudō shashin no sōsaku to satsuehō* (Tokyo: Hikōsha, 1917): 8–9, addendum 18–19.
32. Okamura Shihō, "Setsumei hō kaizen no kyūmu," *Katsudō shashin zasshi* 4, no. 7 (May 1918): 3.
33. In 1917, by one estimate, 96 foreign films were shown in 1 month, compared with only 24 Japanese films. More precisely, 419,000 feet of foreign film were exhibited, and only 145,800 feet of Japanese film were shown. Over the next several years, production of Japanese motion pictures rapidly increased. In 1920, 4,588 reels of American films, 231 reels of European films, and 1,914 reels of Japanese films played in Japan. Five years later, Japanese films overtook their American and European competitors, in terms of number of reels exhibited. In 1925, 9,679 reels were Japanese, 8,873 were American, and 1,023 were European. "Kakusha no ikkagetsukan no eiga seizōtaka oyobi yūnyūdaka," *Katsudō no sekai* 2, no. 9 (September 1917): 56–57; Ishimaki Yoshio, "Honpō eiga kōgyō gaikan," in Ishii Bunsaku, ed., *Nippon eiga jigyō sōran 1926*: 46.
34. "Nippon eiga kaizan no kihon mondai," *Katsudō no sekai* 4, no. 2 (February 1919): 7–9.
35. "Jun'eigageki hattatsushi," *Katsudō zasshi* 9, no. 5 (May 1923): 96.
36. "Junkatsudō shashin geki no seisaku," *Katsudō shashin zasshi* 4, no. 10 (August 1918): 47.
37. Bernardi, *The Early Development of the Gendaigeki Screenplay*, 51.
38. Kaeriyama Norimasa, "Eigageki to shimpa higeki," *Katsudō gahō* 5, no. 9 (September 1921): 42–43.

39. Kaeriyama Norimasa, "Jūnen mae no hanashi (2)," *Eiga jidai* 5, no. 5 (November 1928): 85.
40. Kinugasa, *Waga eiga no seishun*, 20–22.
41. "'*Katsuben*' haisubekika," *Dōtonbori* 9 (November 1, 1919): 20.
42. Furukawa Roppa, "Setsumeisha no kenkyū," *Katsudō gahō* 5, no. 9 (September 1921): 93.
43. Takeda Kōkatsu, "Setsumeisha no shimei," *Katsudō kurabu* 4, no. 12 (December 1921): 96; Takeda Kōkatsu, "Daben bokumetsu ron: shita," *Katsudō gahō* 6, no. 6 (June 1922): 122.
44. Koji, "Jimaku to setsumei oyobi ongaku," *Katsudō gahō* 5, no. 9 (September 1921): 96.
45. Musser and Komatsu, "Benshi Search," 86; Gerow, *Writing a Pure Cinema*, 251.
46. "Nippon katsudō shashinkai no gendai," *Katsudō no sekai* 2, no. 9 (September 1917): 55; Kinugasa, *Waga eiga no seishun*, 77–78; Mikuni, "Katsuben no Wagei," in *Musei eiga no tanjō*, 307; Katano Akeji, "Setsumeisha sompai ron no kōsatsu," *Katsudō gahō* 6, no. 2 (February 1922): 39; Takeda Akira, *Eiga junikō* (Tokyo: Shirōtosha, 1925): 240; Matsuki et al., *Setsumeisha ni naru chikamichi*, 56; Toyoda Bisei, "Kinkan futatsu," *Kinema junpō* 270 (August 11, 1927): 65; "Nippon katsudō shashinkai no gendai," *Katsudō no sekai* 2, no. 9 (September 1917): 55; Kinugasa, *Waga eiga no seishun*, 77–78.
47. Mikuni, "Katsuben no Wagei," in *Musei eiga no tanjō*, 307.
48. "Jun'eiga geki hattatsushi," *Katsudō zasshi* 9, no. 5 (May 1923): 96; Muso Byōe, *Eiga setsumei no kenkyū*, 3.
49. Konparukan advertisement, *Katsudō gahō* 2, no. 3 (March 1918). The advertisement also ran in July 1918, June–August 1919, and April 1920.

8: PERIOD OF UNIFICATION, 1917–1925

1. Yamano, *Ninjō eiga baka*, 35–36; Misono, *Katsuben jidai*, 34–35.
2. Kobayashi, *Eiga no tōei*, 13–14.
3. Midorikage, "Katsudō henpen," *Katsudō shashin zasshi* 2, no. 1 (January 1916): 122.
4. Amarō, "Maesetsu haishi an," *Katsudō gahō* 2, no. 11 (November 1918): 178.
5. Tokugawa, *Kuragari nijūnen*, 66–76. Several sources credit Takaoka Kurome with being the first to eliminate *maesetsu* in Yokohama, but it is unclear when he did so. Gonda Yasunosuke, *Eiga setsumei no shinka to setsumei geijutsu no tanjō* (Tokyo: Ōshima Hideo, 1923): 9–10; Kobayashi, *Eiga no tōei*, 21–23; Misono, *Katsuben jidai*, 82.

253

6. Tokugawa, *Kuragari nijūnen*, 68–69; Tokugawa, *Musei jiden*, vol. 1, 359–360.
7. "Dokusha kara," *Osaka Asahi shinbun*, night edition (August 9, 1920): 1; "Maesetsumei wa jidai ni tekiō sezu," *Katsudō gahō* 4, no. 10 (October 1920): 65; Kobayashi, *Eiga no tōei*, 101.
8. Shimogawa Kinpei, "Setsumeisha no hansei o unagasu," *Katsudō gahō* 7, no. 1 (January 1923): 123; Gonda, *Eiga setsumei*, 8.
9. Tokugawa, *Anata mo sake ga yamerareru*, 8.
10. Deguchi Kisō, *Eiga kyakuhon no kakikata* (Tokyo: Masakōsha, 1922): 51–52.
11. "Genzai no Nippon eiga," *Katsudō no sekai* 2, no. 8 (August 1917): 18.
12. Tsuda Yoshinto, "Benshi setsumei furi no kaibō," *Katsudō gahō* 1, no. 4 (April 1917): 154.
13. Misono, *Aa, katsudō*, 69.
14. For a discussion of some of the changes wrought by the earthquake, see Peter B. High, "Japanese Film and the Great Kantō Earthquake," *Chūbū University: Kokusai kankei gakubū kiyō* 1, no. 3 (1985): 71–84; Komatsu Hiroshi, "The Fundamental Change: Japanese Cinema Before and After the Earthquake of 1923," *Griffithiana* 38/39 (1990): 186–96.
15. Tokugawa, *Kuragari nijūnen*, 164–72.
16. See for example: "Fukkatsu no Asakusa eigagaiyo," *Katsudō zasshi* 10, no. 2 (February 1924): 34–39.
17. "Teito fukkatsuka eiga fukkatsuka," *Kinema junpō* 146 (December 11, 1923): 8.
18. Tokugawa, *Kuragari nijūnen*, 174–78; Miriam Silverberg, "Constructing the Japanese Ethnography of Modernity," *Journal of Asian Studies* 51, no. 1 (February 1992): 47.
19. Ishikawa Mitsumaru, "Katsuben monogatari (199)," *Kurashiku eiga nyūsu* 401 (December 11, 1991): 11.
20. Kobayashi, *Eiga no tōei*, 136–39; "Taishō jūsan nendo no waga eiga kai," *Katsudō zasshi* 11, no. 2 (January 1925): 73; "Nakamura Yonegorō," *Katsudō zasshi* 11, no. 5 (May 1925): 108; Misono, *Aa, katsudō*, 70.

9: THE ART OF *SETSUMEI*

1. Takei Hidesuke, "Daikon? Meiyū?," *Benyū* 10 (August 1968): 7.
2. Tokugawa, *Kuragari nijūnen*, 140–42.
3. Hansen, *Babel & Babylon*, 294.
4. Dai Nippon Katsudō Shashin Kyōkai, ed., *Saikin jūkkanenkan no Nippon eiga kai shōshi* (Tokyo: Dai Nippon Katsudō Shashin Kyōkai, 1934): three-page insert after page 43; "Sakunenchū no kanransha," *Kinema junpō* 303

254

(August 1, 1928): 20; "Katsuben," *Japan Today and Tomorrow*, no. 2 (December, 1928): 93; Matsui, *Suisei on Parade*, 15; Kobayashi, *Eiga no tōei*, 194.

5. Tadasi Iizima, Akira Iwasaki, and Kisao Uchida, eds., *Cinema Year Book of Japan, 1936–1937* (Tokyo: Sanseido Co., 1937): 114–16.

6. "The Movie," *Present Day Japan, 1928*, 80.

7. "Setsumei tengukai," *Miyako shinbun* (November 28, 1909): 3.

8. Advertisement for the exhibition, *Katsudō shashinkai* 10 (June 25, 1910): 21. *Katsudō shashinkai* published several articles in the next issues, critiquing the exhibition.

9. The June 11, 1926, *Kinema junpō* lists 58 benshi who performed in the Sanyūkan's "Setsumeisha Taikai." "Sanyūkan no setsumeisha taikai," *Kinema junpō* 230 (June 11, 1926): 32.

10. Morita Sōhei, "Ryūkōgo to eiga benshi," *Sakkaku* 2, no. 1 (January 1926): 14–15.

11. See, for example, Kakei Sanjin, "Jidō to katsudō shashin," *Katsudō shashinkai* 21 (June 1, 1911): 18; Mizuno Hafuna, "Otsushu shashin ni tsuite," *Katsudō zasshi* 5, no. 8 (August 1919): 60.

12. Morita Sōhei, "Ryūkōgo to eiga benshi," *Sakkaku* 2, no. 1 (January 1926): 16.

13. The first audio recordings made in Japan were recorded in 1903. Itō Naoki's 1917 collection of lyric sheets, *Nipponohon onpumonku zenshu*, indicates that records of *setsumei* existed prior to 1917. It is unclear, however, when, between 1903 and 1916, motion picture *setsumei* was first recorded. Kobayashi Isamu asserts that Hanai Hideo made the first *setsumei* record. It contained *Nogi Shogun no itako mawari* (*General Nogi's Coming Around the Tide*) on Side A and *Asakusa no konjaku* (*Asakusa's Past and Present*) on Side B. Kobayashi does not state when this occurred. Kobayashi, *Eiga no tōei*, 150.

14. Kata Kōji, "Taishū geijūtsu no nagare," in Tsurumi Shunsuke and Kata Kōji, eds., *Nihon no taishū geijutsu* (Tokyo: Shakai Shisōsha, 1962): 343–44.

15. Furuta Tamotsu, *Waga katsudō daishashin* (Tokyo: Seiwadō Shobō, 1972): 122.

16. Yamano, *Ninjō eiga baka*, 213.

17. Tokugawa, *Kuragari nijūnen*, 114; Yamano, *Ninjō eiga baka*, 108–115.

18. Kobayashi Isamu offers that perhaps the true father of *mandan* was neither Tokugawa Musei nor Ōtsuji Shirō, but rather Takamatsu Toyojirō (a *benshi* discussed in Chapter 3), because the types of stories that Takamatsu told were very *mandan*-like. Kobayashi, *Eiga no tōei*, 167.

19. Tokugawa Musei, *Wajutsu*, 3rd ed. (Tokyo: Hakuyōsha, 1990): 178.

20. Ibid., 179–180.

21. Kobayashi, *Eiga no tōei*, 107–108; Tokugawa, *Wajutsu*, 181–186.

22. Katano Akeji, "*Setsumeisha sonpairon no kōsatsu*," *Katsudō gahō* 6, no. 2 (February 1922): 39; Takeda Kōkatau, "Daben bokumetsu ron: ue," *Katsudō*

gahō 6, no. 6 (June 1922): 122.

23. Fukumen Inshi, "Benshi hyōron," *Katsudō no sekai* 3, no. 9 (September 1918): 37–38.

24. Tachibana Takahirō, "Katsudō shashin no torishimari ni tsuite," in Takaoka, *Dai ikkai setsumeisha kōshūkai*, 161–62.

25. Somei Saburō, "Jimaku to setsumei," *Katsudō no sekai* 2, no. 6 (June 1917): 62.

26. Utagawa Seika, "Chinmyō setsumei sandaikai," *Sakkaku* 1, no. 1 (June 1, 1925): 42–43; Furukawa Roppa, "Benshi toiu mono ga atta," *Esuesu* 4, no. 11 (Nov. 1939): 219. Joseph Anderson and Donald Richie state that the three names were Mary, Robert, and *Jim*. Anderson and Richie, *The Japanese Film*, 25.

27. Yamano, *Ninjō eiga baka*, 69; "Dokusharan," *Kinema record* 5, no. 27 (September 10, 1915): 32.

28. Matsui, *Suisei on Parade*, 133–34.

29. Somei Saburō, "Shashin o ikasu kushin," *Katsudō no sekai* 1, no. 3 (March 1916): 41.

30. Mikuni, "Katsuben no Wagei," 308.

31. Okamura Shihō, "Setsumei hō kaizen no kyūmu," *Katsudō shashin zasshi* 4, no. 7 (May 1918): 6.

32. "Eiga setsumei buri gappyō," *Katsudō gahō* 7, no. 4 (April 1923): 100.

33. "Eiga setsumei buri gappyō," *Katsudō gahō* 7, no. 3 (March 1923): 68.

34. See, for example, Musō, *Eiga setsumei no kenkyū*, 83–88, 182–183; Anderson and Richie, *The Japanese Film*, 442; Tachibana Takahiro, *Kage e no kuni: kinema zuihitsushū* (Tokyo: Shuhōkaku, 1925): 72; Somei, Unpublished notebook, 18-21; Somei Saburō, "Benshi toshite no kushin," *Katsudō shashin zasshi* 3, no. 1 (January 1917): 50; Kurofukumen, "Kantō Kansai eiga setsumei no soi," *Katsudō zasshi* 10, no. 6 (June 1924): 64–65; Ike Toshiyuki, "Zoku katsuben monogatari (20)," *Kurashikku eiga nyūsu* 220 (November 1, 1976): 4; Ike Toshiyuji, ed., *Katsudō shashin meiserifu shū* (Tokyo: Mei Shobō, 1985): 249–51.

35. Somei, Unpublished notebook, 23.

36. Edward Seidensticker, *Low City, High City* (Rutland, VT: Charles E. Tuttle, 1983).

37. "Nippon eiga dokuto no eiga setsumeisha hyōban roku," *Katsudō zasshi* 11, no. 9 (September 1925): 86.

38. Tokugawa, *Wajutsu*, 38–39.

39. Mikuni, "Katsuben no Wagei," 306.

40. Bluebird was a subsidiary of Universal Pictures. It was founded in 1916 and continued to make motion pictures until 1920. Bluebird films were extremely sentimental and melodramatic, with storylines that often revolved around the happiness of young couples. They were much more popular in Japan than they were in the United States. In fact, between 1916 and 1925, Bluebird films were the most highly regarded foreign films in Japan. Top

256

benshi performed the *setsumei* for them, and intellectuals flocked to them.
41. Kobayashi, *Eiga no tōei*, 37.
42. Utagawa Seika, "Chinmyō setsumei sandaikai," *Sakkaku* 1, no. 1 (June 1, 1925): 45–46.
43. Yoshida Chieo states that he was born in 1881, but Ōkubo Tenrai writes that he was born in 1884. Yoshida, "Katsuben no rekishi (5)," 40; Yoshida, *Mōhitotsu*, 144; Ōkubo Tenrai, "Shi Hayashi Tempū o omou: Soshite tsunagaru iroiro no omoide," *Eiga shiryō* 16 (1968): 19.
44. Chikushi Jirō, "Kowairo seikatsu," *Katsudō no sekai* 2, no. 3 (March 1917): 68.
45. Anderson, "Spoken Silents," 286. Since I feel that I cannot improve on Anderson's wonderful translation, I have used his.
46. Nishimura, "Waga seishun," 111.

10: THE TALKIE REVOLUTION AND DEMISE OF THE *BENSHI*

1. Sklar, *Movie-Made America*, 157; Douglas Gomery, "The Coming of Sound: Technological Change in the American Film Industry," in *The American Film Industry*, edited by Tino Balio (Madison: University of Wisconsin Press, 1985): 249–50.
2. Douglas Gomery, "Economic Struggle and Hollywood Imperialism: Europe Converts to Sound," *Yale French Review*, no. 60 (1980): 80–93.
3. Sklar, *Movie-Made America*, 217; Takeyama Masanobu, "Ōru tōkī no gaikokuban no mondai," *Kinema junpō* 360 (March 21, 1930): 31.
4. Gomery, "Economic Struggle and Hollywood Imperialism," 83–84.
5. Yoshiyama Kyokukō, "Hassei shashin no shorai ikani," *Katsudō zasshi* 7, no. 6 (June 1921): 115.
6. Despite its huge success in the United States, *The Jazz Singer* was not released in Japan until 1930.
7. Tokugawa Musei, *Musei jiden*, vol. 2, 51–56.
8. Yoshida, *Mōhitotsu*, 4.
9. Shinba Akihiko, *Eigakyō jidai* (Shizuoka: Shinba Akihiko, 1978): 7.
10. Lindstrom, "Cinema-Minded Japan," 807.
11. Tokugawa Musei, "Han tākī sutoraiki," *Bungei shunju* 33, no. 16 (August 1955): 117.
12. Tachibana Takashiro, "The Cinema in Japan," *Contemporary Japan* 1, no. 1 (June 1932): 123.
13. Tokugawa Musei, Yamano Ichirō, and Matsui Suisei, "Tookī to setsumeisha," *Kinema junpō* 352 (January 1, 1930): 299.
14. Nihon Hōsō Kyōkai Hōsō Shi Henshūshitsu, *Nihon hōsō shi* (Tokyo: Nihon Hōsō Shuppan Kyōkai, 1965): vol. 1, 209, 220–21.

15. Tokugawa Musei states that Paramount made translated scripts for films and that he once found one in a bookstore. He was unsure, however, if Paramount actually distributed them or not. Tokugawa Musei et al., "Tookī to setsumeisha," 299; "Tōkī kenkyū: zatsudankai zoku kiroku," *Kinema junpō* 341 (September 1, 1929): 108.

16. "Drama and Cinema in Japan: Legitimate Plays and Other Entertainments Overshadowed by the Movies," *Present Day Japan, 1932*, 30.

17. Tamura Yoshihiko, "America nikki (2)," *Kinema junpō* 390 (February 1, 1931): 57.

18. See for example: "Shin eiga hyō: Tomu Sōyā no bōken," *Asahi shinbun* (February 25, 1931): 7.

19. "Koko wa tōkī kenkyūkai," *Jiji shinpō* (February 20, 1931): night edition, p. 7.

20. "Tōkī jidai ni setsumeisha zōka," *Kinema junpō* 394 (March 11, 1931): 10.

21. Inoue Kentrō, *Gendai eiga setsumeishū* (Osaka: n.p., 1931): 96–107.

22. Tokugawa Musei, "Koubasisu Ben," *Kinema junpō* 422 (January 1, 1932): 79.

23. Tadasi et al., eds., *Cinema Year Book of Japan, 1936–1937*, 114.

24. "Theaters Are Becoming More International," *The Japan Advertiser Annual Review of Finance, Industry and Commerce, 1933–1934* (Tokyo: Japan Advertiser, 1934): 35; Kokusai Bunka Shinkōkai, ed., *Cinema Yearbook of Japan, 1939* (Tokyo: Kokusai Bunka Shinkōkai, 1939): 22.

25. Mizuno Eizaburo, *Nagoya katsuben ichidai: shomin ga mita mōhitotsu no gendaishi* (Nagoya: Fūbasha, 1995): 114.

26. Donald Kirihara, "A Reconsideration of the Institution of Benshi," *Film Reader* 6 (1985): 41–45.

27. "Kowairo narimonoiri eiga ga umareru," *Kinema shūhō* 25 (August 7, 1930): 7.

28. Anderson and Richie, *The Japanese Film*, 72.

29. Adachi Ken'ichi, *Taishū geijutsu no fukuryū* (Tokyo: Rironsha, 1967): 102.

30. For a description of the actual events portrayed in this *setsumei*, and to contextualize them in terms of Japanese aggression in Manchuria, see Alvin D. Coox, *Nomohan: Japanese Against Russia, 1939* (Stanford: Stanford University Press, 1985): 40–43.

31. Hamaguchi Ryutarō, *Manmo sensen shisatsu (An Inspection of the Manchurian–Mongolian Border)*, Jikyoku eiga setsumei, Tsuru Record, Asahi Chikuonki Co., 6142.

32. Charles Chaplin, *Charles Chaplin: My Autobiography* (Bodley Head, 1964. Reprint. New York: Plume/Penguin Books, 1992): 362–71, 380; *Asahi shinbun*, May 14–15, 1932.

33. Furukawa, "Benshi toiu mono ga atta," 218–22.

34. "Setsumeisha yo danseiteki ni nare," *Katsudō zasshi* 9, no. 5 (May 1923): 68.

35. "Sore wa taihen to benshigawa mo danketsu," *Katsudō zasshi* 11, no. 9

258

(September 1925): 82.
36. "Dai Nippon Setsumeisha Kyōkai naru," *Katsudō gahō* 5, no. 8 (August 1921): 105; "Katsudō benshi kyōkai hatsukaishiki," *Katsudō zasshi* 7, no. 9 (September 1921): 170.
37. "Setsumeisha yo danseiteki ni nare," *Katsudō zasshi* 9, no. 5 (May 1923): 66–71.
38. "Setsumeisha no rōdō kumiai," *Kinema junpō* 382 (November 1, 1930): 10; "Osaka eiga kaisetsusha kumiai soshiki," *Kinema shūhō* 62 (May 21, 1931): 26.
39. Mikuni, *Tokugawa Musei no sekai*, 258.
40. "Daishōkan, Denkikan ryōkan no setsumeisha sōgi," *Kinema junpō* 433 (April 21, 1932): 8.
41. "SP sōgi kyūten kaiketsu," *Kinema junpō* 434 (May 1, 1932): 10.
42. Mizutani Hironari, "Watashi no ashiato: ginmaku 45 nen," *Eiga shiryō* 16 (1968):13; "SP sōgi kyūten kaiketsu," *Kinema junpō* 434 (May 1, 1932): 10.
43. "Nikkatsu, Nikkō setsumeisha gakushi no han tōkī sōgi keika tenmatsu," *Kinema junpō* 435 (May 11, 1932): 82.
44. NHK "Documentary Shōwa" Research Group, eds., *Dokyumento Shōwa*, vol. 4, *Tōkī wa sekai o mezasu* (Tokyo: Kadokawa Shoten, 1986): 37–39. On page 38 of that work is a photostatic copy of this newspaper article. The caption reads "*Tokyo Asahi Shinbun*, May 2, 1932." I could not locate this article anywhere on the May 1932 reel of *Tokyo Asahi shinbun* microfilm.
45. "Keishichō no chōtei de ayumi yori han tōkī sōgi kaiketsu," *Kinema junpō* 436 (May 21, 1932): 9.
46. "SP e miuri no chokuzen Musashinokan toshite higyō," *Kinema junpō* 438 (June 11, 1932): 18.
47. Ōkura, *Waga gei to kane to koi*, 122–26.
48. "Eiga setsumeisha no kibōsha gekigen," *Kinema junpō* 460 (February 1, 1933): 10.
49. In 1936, there were 5,151 *benshi* registered to work in Japan. That number decreased to 3,726 in 1937, and, by 1939, there were only 1,302 *benshi* left. "Benshi no ninka seidō chikaku haishi," *Kinema junpō* 472 (April 11, 1936): 11; Naimushō, *Katsudō shashin (fuirumu) ken'etsu nenpō, 1936*, 62–63; Iwamoto Kenji and Makino Mamoru, eds., *Eiga nenkan, 1941* (Tokyo: Nihon Tosho Sentā, 1994): 42–43.
50. Nishimura, "Katsuben ōrai," in *Nihon eiga terebi purodūsa kyōkai*, 424.

11: FORGOTTEN BUT NOT DEAD

1. Komatsu and Musser, "*Benshi* Search," 80.
2. The source does not indicate his given name. Kata, "Taishū geijūtsu no na-

gare," 344–47.

3. Ibid., 344–47.

4. Joseph L. Anderson saw his first *benshi* performance in 1950, when he was nineteen years old. He remembers the experience quite well: "The bill was excerpts of foreign and domestic movies. The technical quality, continuity, and mise en scène were absolutely contemporary I concluded that the Japanese were producing silent movies with a mastery of American techniques before the Americans mastered them. Remarkable for a silent movie there were not intertitles. Several years later I figured out that this movie was a recent release. They simply turned off the sound track so that the *benshi* would have a silent text." Linda C. Ehrlich, "Talking About Pictures: The Art of the *Benshi*," *Cinemaya* 27 (1995): 36.

5. Part of the inscription appearing on the monument.

6. Nishimura, *Watashi wa Shōwa no katari shokunin*, 119–23.

7. Fujimura Rokurō, *Eiga hyakunen: kao no nai senshitachi* (Tokyo: Kioi Shobō, 1988): 22.

8. Sawato is always coy about her age. Suffice it to say that she became a *benshi* in 1972, shortly after graduating from Hosei University.

9. Waka Kōji, interview with author, May 2, 1997.

10. Inoue Yōichi, interview with author, October 22, 1996.

11. Sawato Midori, interview with author, May 4, 1997.

12. Ibid.

13. Ehrlich, "Talking About Pictures," *Cinemaya* 27 (1995): 40.

14. Matsuki et al., *Setsumeisha ni naru chikamichi*, 27.

SELECTED BIBLIOGRAPHY

Japanese Language Newpapers and Periodicals

Asahi shinbun (Osaka and Tokyo editions, selected dates)

Benyū (1963–1974)

Dōtonbori (1919–1921)

Eiga jidai (1917–1923)

Hōchi shinbun (Selected dates)

Katsudō hyōron/Katsudō kurabu (1918–1924)

Katsudō no sekai/Katsudō sekai (1916–1922)

Katsudō shashinkai (1909–1911)

Katsudō shashin zasshi/Katsudō zasshi (1915–1927)

Katsukichi (1965–1997)

Kinema junpō (1919–1940 and selected dates thereafter)

Kinema shūhō (1930–1931)

Kinema Record (1913–1917)

Kurashikku eiga nyūsu (1960–1997)

Mainichi shinbun/Tokyo nichinichi shinbun (Selected dates)

Miyako shinbun (1897–1920)

Sakkaku (1925–1926)

262

Japanese Language Books and Articles

Adachi Ken'ichi. *Taishū geijutsu no fukuryū*. Tokyo: Rironsha, 1967.

"Ajia musei eiga gannen: Nikkan *benshi* taidan Shin Churu, Sawato Midori, Poku Wanmo" *Asia Center News* 3 (Fall 1996): 15–18.

Akiyama Sokkitei. "Yoki jidai no katsuben fūfu: Takemoto Shōko-san to Takemoto Suzume-san." *Bungei Asahi* 4, no. 7 (July 1965): 82–89.

Asakusa Rokku kōgyōshi. Tokyo: Taitōku Kyōikuinkai, 1983.

Bungei Geijutsu. (Special: Golden Era of Silent Film Issue). March 1975.

Dai-Nippon Katsudō Shashin Kyōkai, ed. *Saikin jūkkanenkan no Nippon eiga kai shōshi*. Tokyo: Dai-Nippon Katsudō Shashin Kyōkai, 1934.

Dazai Osamu. *Kirigirisu*. Shinchō Bunko, 1974.

Deguchi Kisō. *Eiga kyakuhon no kakikata*. Tokyo: Masakōsha, 1922.

Eiga Dōkōkai, ed. *Ōbei tokusaku eiga setsumeishū*. Osaka: Yugawa Matsujirō, 1927.

"Eiga jiji zatsudan no yūbe." In *Eiga kagaku kenkyū kōza*, vol. 2, edited by Murata Minoru and Ushihara Kiyohiko (Tokyo: n.p. [ca. 1928]): 158–76.

Eisha Dōji. "Katsudō benshi no gensō: Ueda Hoteiken." *Shin'engei* 1, no. 3 (May 1916): 149–53.

Fujikawa Chisui. *Kumamoto shinema kōdan*. Kumamoto: Kumamoto Insatsu Sentā, 1978.

Fujimura Rokurō. *Eiga hyakunen: kao no nai senshitachi*. Tokyo: Kioi Shobō, 1988.

Funabashi Kazuo. *Katsuben monogatari* (Screenplay for the film, *The Tale of the Benshi*). Tokyo: Shochiku, 1957.

Furukawa Roppa. "Benshi toiu mono ga atta." *Esuesu* 4, no. 11 (November 1939): 218–22.

Furuta Tamotsu. *Waga Katsudō daishashin*. Tokyo: Seiwadō Shobō, 1972.

Furuya Tsunamasa. *Watashi dake no eigashi*. Tokyo: Kurashi no Techōsha, 1978.

Gonda Yasunosuke. *Eiga setsumei no shinka to setsumei geijutsu no tanjō.* Tokyo: Ōshima Hideo, 1923.

———. *Gorakugyōsha no mure.* Tokyo: Jōgyō no Hihonsha, 1923.

Haniya Yutaka and Maruyama Masao. "Taidan: Bungaku to gakumon." *Eureka* 10, no. 3 (March 1978): 72–90.

Hashikura Shingōrō, ed. *Shin rekōdo monkushū.* Tokyo: Rekōdo no Yūsha, 1918.

Hiyama Shigeo. "Tōkī hasshō gojū nen: sono hattatsu." *Tama geijutsu gakuen kiyō* 13 (1987): 1–25; 14 (1988): 1–27.

Ichikawa Miyabi. "Tōtaru shiatā toshite no katsuben musei eiga." *Supesu dezain* 83 (August 1971): 117–119.

Iguchi Seiha. *Pin kara kiri made.* Tokyo: Hiroba Shobō, 1956.

Iijima Tadashi. *Nihon Eigashi*, vol. 1. Tokyo: Hakusuisha, 1955.

———. "Tokyo no katsudō daishashin." *Kokubungaku kaishaku to kanshō* 28, no. 2 (January 1963): 145–50.

Ike Toshiyuji, ed. *Katsudō shashin meiserifu shū.* Tokyo: Mei Shobō, 1985.

Imano Kenzō. "Setsumeisha jidai monogatari." *Engeki eiga* 1, no. 6 (June 1926): 85–89; 1, no. 7 (July 1926): 64–67; 1, no. 8 (August 1926): 48–52.

Inagaki Hiroshi. *Hige to chommage: ikiteiru eigashi.* Tokyo: Chūō Kōronsha, 1981.

Inoue Kentrō. *Gendai eiga setsumeishū.* Osaka: n.p., 1931.

Ishii Bunsaku, ed. *Nippon eiga jigyō soran: 1926–nen han.* Tokyo: Kokusai Eiga Tsūshinsha, 1926.

Ishikawa Sai, ed. *Nippon eiga jigyō soran: 1928/29–nen han.* Tokyo: Kokusai eiga Tsūshinsha, 1928.

Itō Naoki. *Nipponohon onpumonku zenshu.* Tokyo: Ekisei Kankatsu Banbu, 1917.

Itō Shiei. *Shinema yoruhiru: kaikō Nagoya eigashi.* Nagoya: Itō Shiei, 1984.

264

Iwamoto Kenji. "Hikaku gentōshi kangae." *Nihon no bigaku*, no. 20 (1993): 178–91; no. 21 (1994): 164–77; no. 22 (1994): 190–204; no. 23 (1995): 187–204; no. 24 (1996): 170–95.

———. "Katsudō benshi to Nihon eiga no montāju." *Nihon engeki gakkai kiyō* no. 14, (March 1974): 15–18.

Iwamoto Kenji and Makino Mamoru, eds. *Eiga nenkan, 1941.* Tokyo: Nihon Tosho Sentā, 1994.

Jōhei Nakio. "Eiga gekijō o mawaru seiteki kōsatsu." *Hentai shiryō* 3, no. 4 (April, 1928): 84–96.

K no ji. "Katsudō shashin no torai." *Anona* 18 (June 11, 1925): 20.

Kaeriyama Norimasa. *Katsudō shashin no sōsaku to satsueihō.* Tokyo: Hikōsha, 1917.

Kata Kōji. "Taishū geijūtsu no nagare." In *Nihon no taishū geijutsu*, edited by Tsurumi Shunsuke and Kata Kōji. Tokyo: Shakai Shisōsha, 1962.

Katagiri Dōji. "Aa katsudō daishashin." *Nihon oyobi Nihonjin*, no. 1544 (November 1971): 122–29.

Katō Aki. *Eigakan no kenchiku keikaku.* Tokyo: Kyōyōsha, 1932.

Katō Hidetoshi. *Misemono kara terebi e.* Tokyo: Iwanami Shoten, 1965.

Katsudō shashin setsumeishō. n.p., c.1897 or 1898.

Keisatsu Kōshūjo Gakuyūkai. *Jikyoku kōenshū.* 2 vols. Tokyo: Keisatsu Kōshūjo gakuyūkai, 1919.

Kinema Junpō Bunkabū, ed. *Eiga hyakunen: eiga wa kōshite hajimatta.* Tokyo: Kinema Junpōsha, 1997.

Kinugasa Teinosuke. *Waga eiga no seishun.* Tokyo: Chūō Kōronsha, 1977.

Kinryūdō, eds. *Saikin ryūkō eiga setsumei zenshū.* Tokyo: Kinryūdō Shoten, 1929.

Kishi Matsuo. "Katsuben hanayaka narishi koro." In *Nihon eiga shinario koten*, vol. 1, 12–13. Tokyo: Kinema Jumpōsha, 1965.

Kiyose Eijirō. "Tōkī jidaigeki no daiarogu." *Eiga kagaku kenkyū* 9 (September 1931): 95–104.

Kobayashi Gentarō. *Utsushie.* Tokyo: Chūō Daigaku Shuppanbu, 1987.

Kobayashi Isamu. *Eiga no tōei.* Tokyo: Itō Shobō, 1933.

Kodama Kazuo. *Katsudōkyo jidai.* Tokyo: San'ichi Shobō, 1967.

Kokushō Kankōkai, ed. *Koya to meisaku no fūkei.* Tokyo: Satō Konchōfū, 1989.

Komatsu Hiroshi. "Tennenshoku kara jun-eiga e: Nippon eigashi ni okeru Tenkatsu no igi." *Geijutsugaku kenkyū* 5 (1995): 25–37.

Kunii Shikō. *Dadakko jinsei.* Tokyo: Myōgi Shuppan, 1956.

Makino Mamoru. "Katsudō shashinban: Ametsuchi no majiwarishi koro." In *Nihon eiga shoki shiryō shūsei 1: Katsudō shashin zasshi,* vol. 1, 1–15. Tokyo: San'ichi Shobō, 1990.

Matsuda Kan'ichi. *Okayama no eiga.* Okayama: Nihonbunkyō Shuppan, 1983.

Matsuda Shunsui. "*Mabuta no haha.*" *Daisatsujin* (November 8, 1976): 56–58.

———. "Shijō katsuben shinemakan." *Bungei shunshū derakkusu* (May 1976): 117–23.

———. "Tanoshikikana katsuben." *Shinario* 27, no. 5 (1971): 54–59.

Matsui Suisei. *Suisei on Parade.* Tokyo: Ōraisha, 1931.

Matsuki Kyōrō, Izumi Sōichirō, Ōtani Katei, and Satomi Yoshirō. *Setsumeisha ni naru chikamichi.* Osaka: Setsumeisha Dōjinkai, 1926.

Mifune Kiyoshi. "Musei eiga jidai no eigakan." In *Musei eiga no kansei,* edited by Imamura Shōhei, Satō Tadao, et al. *Kōza Nihon eiga,* vol. 2, p. 193–95. Tokyo: Iwanami Shoten, 1985.

Mikuni Ichirō. "Katsuben no wagei." In *Musei eiga no tanjō,* edited by Imamura Shōhei, et al. *Kōza Nihon eiga,* vol. 1, 298–308. Tokyo: Iwanami Shōten, 1985.

———. *Tokugawa Musei no sekai.* Tokyo: Seiabo, 1979.

Misono Kyōhei. *Aa, katsudō daishashin.* Tokyo: Katsudō Shiryō Kenkyūkai, 1966.

———. *Katsuben jidai.* Tokyo: Iwanami Shoten, 1990.

———. "Mukashi katsuben ga atta." In *Kōsa Nihon eiga ni geppō,* vol. 2, 3–8. Tokyo: Iwanami Shoten, 1986.

266

Mizuno Eizaburo. *Nagoya katsuben ichidai: shomin ga mita mōhitotsu no gendaishi.* Nagoya: Fūbasha, 1995.

Monbushō Futsū Gakumukyoku. *Zenkoku ni okeru katsudō shashin jōkyō chōsa.* Tokyo: Monbushō, 1921.

Monbushō Shakai Kyōikukyoku Shomuka. *Eiga setsumei daihon, 1923–35.* 6 vols. Tokyo: Monbūshō Shakai Kyōikukyoku Shomuka, 1923–1935.

Muromachi Kyōji. *Katsudō haiyū mi no ue banashi.* Tokyo: Sankōsha, 1920.

Musō Byōe. *Eiga setsumei no kenkyū.* Tokyo: Chōyōsha, 1922.

Nagai Kafū. *Kafū zenshū.* Tokyo: Chūō Kōron, 1949.

Naimushō. *Katsudō shashin (fuirumu) ken'etsu nempō, 1930–1936.* Tokyo: Naimushō keihōkyoku, 1931–37.

NHK "Documentary Shōwa" Research Group, eds. *Dokyumento Shōwa*, vol. 4, *Tōkī wa sekai o mezasu.* Tokyo: Kadokawa Shoten, 1986.

Nihon Eiga Terebi Purodūsa Kyōkai, eds. *Natsukashi no fukkokuban puroguramu eigashi: Taishō kara Senchū made.* Tokyo: Nihon Hōsō Shuppan Kyōkai, 1978.

Nihon Hōsō Kyōkai Hōsō Shi Henshūshitsu. *Nihon Hōsō Shi.* 3 vols. Tokyo: Nihon Hōsō Shuppan Kyōkai, 1965.

Nikkatsu yonjūnenshi. Tokyo: Nikkatsu Kabushiki Gaisha, 1952.

Nishimura Korakuten. *"Waga seishun no katsuben jidai."* *Geijutsu seikatsu* 307 (March 1975): 111.

———. *Watashi wa Shōwa no katari shokunin.* Tokyo: April Music, 1978.

Nojigiku Bunko, ed. *Kōbe shinkaichi monogatari.* Kōbe: Nojigiku Bunko, 1973.

Ogi Masahiro. *Shashin eiga hyakunen.* Tokyo: Bideo Shuppan, 1968.

Ōi Hirosuke. *Chambara geijutsu shi.* Tokyo: Jitsugyō no Nihonsha, 1959.

Okabe Ryū, ed. *Nihon eigashi sokō, 8: Kaeriyama Norimasa to Tōmas Kurihara no gyōseki.* Tokyo: Film Library Kyōgikai, 1973.

———. *Nihon eigashi sokō, 9: Takamatsu Toyojirō to Osagawara Meiho no gyōseki.* Tokyo: Film Library Kyōgikai, 1974.

Okada Susumu. *Nihon eiga no rekishi.* Tokyo: Daviddosha, 1967.

Okamura Shihō. *Katsudō shashin meikan.* Tokyo: Katsudō Shinbunsha, 1923.

Ōkura Mitsugi. *Waga gei to kane to koi.* Tokyo: Tokyo Shobō, 1959.

Ōnoda Tadashi, ed. *Jūmonji Daigen den.* Tokyo: Jūmonji Daigen Hakuki Hensankai, 1926.

Ōta Toshiho. *Musei eiga jidaigeki no seishun.* Tokyo: Yamato Shobō, 1978.

Raidai Kamezo. "Shishimatogurapu o miru," *Shōnen kurabu* 1, no. 6 (May 1897).

Sakai Hiroshi. "Watashi no shūhen ni tenkaishita eiga gijutsushi." *Eiga terebi gijutsu,* no. 213 (May 1970): 59–65; no. 214 (June 1970): 51–54; no. 215 (July 1970): 51–57.

Satō Seiichirō. *Akita-ken kōgyōshi: Eigagai, engekigai.* Akita: Mishima Shobō, 1976.

Satō Tadao. *"Benshi no gei, Matsuda Shunsui to Sawato Midori."* *Yokohama bunka jōhōshi,* no. 52 (June 1996): 2–8.

———. *Nihon eigashi.* 4 vols. Tokyo: Iwanami Shōten, 1995.

Satomi Ton. *"Katsuben to omowareru."* *Kaizō* 4, no. 2 (April 1920): 255–66.

Shibata Katsuo. *Jitsuen to eiga: Rensageki no kiroku.* Tokyo: n.p., 1982.

Shinba Akihiko. *Eigakyō jidai.* Shizuoka: Shinba Akihiko, 1978.

———. *Zoku zoku eigakyō jidai.* Shizuoka: Shinba Akihiko, 1983.

Shūhō. "Katsudō shashin no benshi." *Bungei kurabu* 16, no. 8 (August 1910): 203–208.

Shūkan Asahi, ed. *Nedan no fūzokushi: Meiji, Taishō, Shōwa.* 3 vols. Tokyo: Shūkan Asahisha, 1982.

Somei Saburō. Unpublished notebook. c. 1931–34.

Tachibana Takahiro. *Kage-e no kuni: kinema zuihitsushū.* Tokyo: Shuhōkaku, 1925.

———. *Kyōiku eiga gairon.* Tokyo: Fujiwara Sōtarō, 1928.

———. *Minshū goraku no kenkyū.* Tokyo: Keigansha, 1920.

Tachibana Takashirō. *Eigadō mandan.* Tokyo: Mumei Shuppan, 1926.

———. *Katsudōkyo no techō.* Tokyo: Kōbunsha, 1924.

268

"Taidan: Kankoku eiga-shi o kangaeru." *Film Network* 6 (Summer 1996): 2–5.

Takanashi Kōji, ed. *Inabata Katsutarō kun den*. Osaka: Inabata Katsutarō Okina Kijukinen Denkihenshūkai, 1938.

Takaoka Kurume, ed. *Dai ikkai setsumeisha kōshūkai koshūroku*. Tokyo: Dai Nippon Setsumeisha Kyōkai, 1921.

Takeda Akira. *Eiga jūni-kō*. Tokyo: Shirōtosha, 1925.

Tanaka Jun'ichirō. *Nihon eiga hattatsushi*. 5 vols. Tokyo: Chūō Kōronsha, 1957–1976.

Tanizaki Jun'ichirō. *"Katsudō shashin no genzai to shōrai."* *Shin-shōsetsu* 22, no. 9 (September 1917): 35–41.

Terakawa Makoto. *Eiga oyobi eigageki*. Osaka: Osaka Mainichi Shinbunsha, 1925.

Tokugawa Musei. *Anata mo sake ga yamerareru*. Tokyo: Bungei Shunjū Shinsha, 1959.

———. "Eiga setsumeishi." *Kinema kōza* 2 (Tokyo: Shigensha, 1927): 1–16.

———. *"Han tākī sutoraiki."* *Bungei shunju* 33, no. 16 (August 1955): 116–21.

———. *Kuragari nijūnen*. Tokyo: Aoi Shobōban, 1934.

———. *Musei Jiden*. 3 vols. Tokyo: Kodansha Bunko, 1978.

———. *Musei Mandan*. Tokyo: Shueikaku, 1927.

———. *Oya baka jūnen*. Tokyo: Sōgensha, 1950.

———. *Wajutsu*. 3rd ed. Tokyo: Hakuyōsha, 1961.

Tsukada Yoshinobu. *Eiga zasshi sōkangō mokuroku*. Tokyo: Tsukada Yoshinobu, 1965.

———. *Nihon eigashi no kenkyū: katsudō shashin torai zengo no jijō*. Tokyo: Gendai Shokan, 1980.

Waka Kōji. *Katsudō daishashin shimatsu ki*. Tokyo: Sairyūsha, 1998.

———. *Katsudō shashin kamifūsen*. Nagoya: Nihon Shuzai Sentā, 1988.

Watanabe Tsunao. *Nagoya no eiga*. Nagoya: Sakkasha, 1961.

Yamamoto Keiichi. *Edo no kage-e asobi*. Tokyo: Sōshisha, 1988.

Yamano Ichirō. *Ninjō eiga baka*. Tokyo: Nippon Shūhōsha, 1960.

Yoshida Chieo. "Katsuben no rekishi." *Eigashi kenkyū*, nos. 1–10; 12–14 (1973–78).

——. *Mōhitotsu no eigashi: katsuben no jidai.* Tokyo: Jiji Tsūshinsha, 1978.

Yoshida Yoshishige, Masao Yamaguchi, and Naoyuki Kinoshita, eds. *Eiga denrai: Shinematogurafu to Meiji no Nihon.* Tokyo: Iwanami Shoten, 1995.

Yoshiyama Kyokukō. *Nippon eiga-kai jibutsu kigen.* Tokyo: Shinema to Engeisha, 1933.

——. *Nippon eiga-shi nenpyō.* Tokyo: Eiga Hōkokusha, 1940.

Unpublished *Benshi* Scripts from the Following Films

(All were written between 1919 and 1921)

Adventures of Tarzan, The	*Band of Lovers*
Branding Iron, The	*Bring Him In*
Burning Daylight	*Close to Nature*
Dangerous Business	*Dangerous to Men*
Earthbound	*Edgar's Hamlet*
Fair and Warmer	*Further Exploits of Index, The*
Girls from Porcupine, The	*Godless Men*
Greater Claim, The	*Heart of a Child, The*
Isabel	*It's a Great Life*
It isn't Being Done this Season	*Kid, The*
Love Honor and Behave	*Man Who Dared, The*
Midlanders, The	*Modern Salome, A*
North Wind's Malice	*Pinto*
Plaything of Destiny	*Puppets of Fate*
School Days	*Shore Acres*
Should a Woman Tell	*Sister to Salome, A*
Song of Wallington, The	*Street Called Straight, The*
Tale of Two Worlds, A	*Three Sevens*

Vengeance of Durand, The   *What's Your Reputation Worth*

World and It's Women, The   *Yes or No*

Benshi Phonograph Recordings

Asahi Rakuten. *Ai no tobira.* Eigageki. Tōa-record, Toa Phone, 153 & 154.

Daitō Atsushi. *Jōshu mushukujin.* Eiga setsumei. Teichiku Gramophone, 5106 (699 & 700).

Daitō Kōrō. *Umon torimonochō.* Eiga setsumei. Taihei Gramaphone, 3236.

Fujioka Ginpa and Shizuta Kinpa. *O-Botchan.* Eiga setsumei. Hikōki Record, The Gōdō Phonograph, 7418 & 7419.

Gōtō Kōrō. *Bakumatsu sōdōin.* Eiga setsumei. Regal, Columbia 65864 (81013 & 81014).

———. *Gozonji kenka Yasubei.* Eiga setsumei. Regal, Columbia 65829 (81009 & 81010) & 65830 (81011 & 81012).

———. *Hiren shinjū ga oka.* Eiga setsumei. Nitto Record, Nitto Chikuonki, 2193.

———. *Kenka Yasubei.* Setsumeigeki. Orient Record, Nipponophone, 4601 (9549 & 9550).

———. *Konomura Daikichi.* Eiga setsumei. Orient Record 60043 (60318 & 60319) & 6044 (60320 & 60321).

———. *Matsudaira Choshichirō.* Eiga setsumei. Orient Record 60262 (61189 & 61190).

———. *Oro Chimaru.* Eiga setsumei. Orient Record 60493 (62121 & 62122).

———. *Ōsakajō.* Eiga setsumei. Orient Record, Columbia Chikuonki, 60711 (62685 & 62827).

———. *Shinsengumi.* Eiga setsumei. Regal, Columbia, Nipponophone, 66779 (175162 & 275163).

———. *Tsukigata Hanpeida.* Eiga setsumei. Regal, Columbia 65441 (63223 & 63224) & 65442 (63225 & 63226).

Gotō Kōrō and Izumi Shirō. *Yukinojō hengei*. Eiga setsumei. Regal, Columbia, Nipponophone, 67043 (181428 & 281429)

Gotō Kōrō & Matsuki Kyōrō. *Jūsei*. Eiga setsumei. Nitto Record, Nitto Chikuonki, 1487 & 1488.

Hamaguchi Ryutarō. *Ā, gunshin koga rentaichō*. Eiga setsumei. Taihei Gramaphone, 3248.

———. *Manmo sensen shisatsu*. Jikyoku eiga setsumei. Tsuru Record, Asahi Chikuonki, 6142.

Hanai Sanshō. *Shima no onna*. Eiga setsumei. Nitto Record, Nitto Chikuonki, 592.

———. *Yamato damashii*. Eiga setsumei. Nitto Record, Nitto Chikuonki, 1264 & 1265.

Hanaishi Kōjirō. *Hototogisu*. Eiga setsumei. Tsuru Record, Asahi Chikuonki, 6504 & 6505.

Higashi Tōsui. *Matatabi shigure*. Nikkatsu eiga setsumei. Parlophone E-1481 (121199 & 121200) & E-1482 (121201 & 121202).

Ishii Harunami. *Suihei no haha*. Setsumei-geki. Tokyo Record, Tokyo Chikuonki, 3234 & 3235.

Izawa Jun, Shimizu Akira, and Takizawa Hajime, eds. *Natsukashi no musei eiga: On niyoru Nihon eigashi*. Tokyo: Toshiba Records.

Izumi Shirō. *Aizen katsura*. Eiga monogatari. Columbia, Nippon Columbia, A 184 (182049 & 282050), A 185 (182051 & 282052), A 186 (182054 & 282054), A 187 (182055 & 282056).

———. *Haha*. Eiga setsumei. Regal, Columbia 65146 (60758 & 60759) & 65417 (60760 & 60761).

———. *Hatsukoi nikki*. Eiga setsumei. Regal, Columbia, Nipponophone, 67743 (176214 & 276215) & 67744 (176216 & 276217).

———. *Hebi-hime sama*. Eiga monogatari. Regal, Columbia, Nipponophone, 150052 (182233 & 282234), 150053 (182235 & 282236), 150054 (182237 & 282238).

272

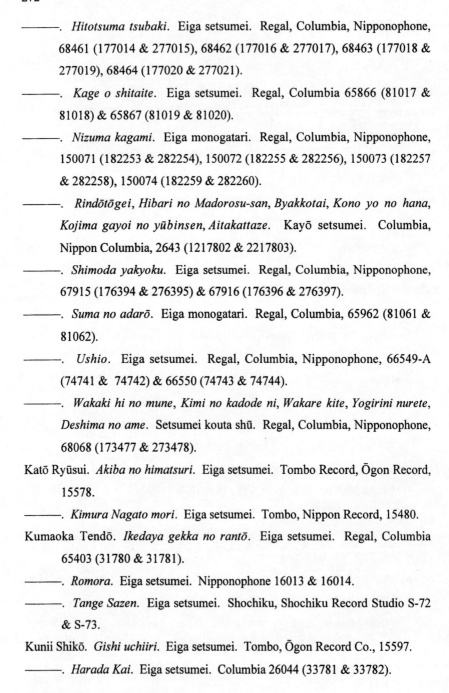

———. *Hitotsuma tsubaki.* Eiga setsumei. Regal, Columbia, Nipponophone, 68461 (177014 & 277015), 68462 (177016 & 277017), 68463 (177018 & 277019), 68464 (177020 & 277021).

———. *Kage o shitaite.* Eiga setsumei. Regal, Columbia 65866 (81017 & 81018) & 65867 (81019 & 81020).

———. *Nizuma kagami.* Eiga monogatari. Regal, Columbia, Nipponophone, 150071 (182253 & 282254), 150072 (182255 & 282256), 150073 (182257 & 282258), 150074 (182259 & 282260).

———. *Rindōtōgei, Hibari no Madorosu-san, Byakkotai, Kono yo no hana, Kojima gayoi no yūbinsen, Aitakattaze.* Kayō setsumei. Columbia, Nippon Columbia, 2643 (1217802 & 2217803).

———. *Shimoda yakyoku.* Eiga setsumei. Regal, Columbia, Nipponophone, 67915 (176394 & 276395) & 67916 (176396 & 276397).

———. *Suma no adarō.* Eiga monogatari. Regal, Columbia, 65962 (81061 & 81062).

———. *Ushio.* Eiga setsumei. Regal, Columbia, Nipponophone, 66549-A (74741 & 74742) & 66550 (74743 & 74744).

———. *Wakaki hi no mune, Kimi no kadode ni, Wakare kite, Yogirini nurete, Deshima no ame.* Setsumei kouta shū. Regal, Columbia, Nipponophone, 68068 (173477 & 273478).

Katō Ryūsui. *Akiba no himatsuri.* Eiga setsumei. Tombo Record, Ōgon Record, 15578.

———. *Kimura Nagato mori.* Eiga setsumei. Tombo, Nippon Record, 15480.

Kumaoka Tendō. *Ikedaya gekka no rantō.* Eiga setsumei. Regal, Columbia 65403 (31780 & 31781).

———. *Romora.* Eiga setsumei. Nipponophone 16013 & 16014.

———. *Tange Sazen.* Eiga setsumei. Shochiku, Shochiku Record Studio S-72 & S-73.

Kunii Shikō. *Gishi uchiiri.* Eiga setsumei. Tombo, Ōgon Record Co., 15597.

———. *Harada Kai.* Eiga setsumei. Columbia 26044 (33781 & 33782).

———. *Jirokichi tabinikki.* Eiga monogatari. Taiyō Chikuonki Co., 2011 (163 & 164).

———. *Kōjinyama.* Eiga setsumei. Nipponophone 16657 & 16658.

———. *Marubashi Chūya.* Eiga setsumei. Victor Talking Machine, 50922.

———. *Tange Sazen.* Eiga setsumei. Taiyō Chikuonki, 2491.

Makino Actors. *Rōka.* Makino eigageki. The Naigai Gramaphone, 3231 & 3232.

Minami Kenji. *Sakamoto Ryōma.* Eiga setsumei. Victor Talking Machine, 50417 & 59418.

Mitsuoka Issei. *Marubashi Chūya.* Eiga setsumei. Tombo, Tokyo Ōgon Record, 15661.

———. *Tange Sazen.* Eiga setsumei. Teichiku Taishuban 276 (3076 & 3077).

Miyashita Seiha. *Suigo no uta.* Gendai eiga setsumei. Hikōki, Imperial Phonograph, 1150.

Miyashita Tenshū. *Aikoku bidan.* Eiga setsumei. Futami Record, F 202 & F 203.

Nishimura Korakuten, Nakamura Seiha, Suzuki Bairyū, and Ishii Mitsumi. *Kawachiyama sōshun.* Setsumeigeki. Victor Talking Machine, 50749 (251 & 252) & 50750 (253 & 254).

Oo katudo daishashin. King Record, K25H-829.

Satomi Yoshirō. *Tsubaki hime.* Eiga setsumei. Nitto Chikuonki, 5173 & 5174.

———. *Tsubaki hime.* Eiga setsumei. Tombo Record, Ōgon Record, 15516.

———. *Tsubaki hime.* Eiga setsumei. Orient Record, Nipponophone, 3430 & 3431.

Shimazu Kenji. *Kondō Isami.* Eiga setsumei. Nitto Chikuonki, 4272 & 4273.

———. *Kunisada Chūji.* Eiga setsumei. Nitto Chikuonki, 3494.

———. *Sōba Taisaku.* Eiga setsumei. Nitto Chikuonki, 3592.

Shizuta Kinpa. *Sansō no musume.* Eiga setsumei. Taihei Gramaphone, 4336.

Somei Saburō. *Antonī to Kureopatora* & *Hito no tsuma.* Katsudō higeki. Tokyo Record, Tokyo Chikuonki, 107 & 108.

Susukida Hangyō. *Akatsuki no teisatsu.* Eiga setsumei. Yachiyo, 3028 & 3029.

————. *Hanzuiin Chōbei.* Eiga setsumei. Tsuruin, Asahi Chikuonki, 5845 & 5846.

————. *Kawachiyama Sōshun.* Eiga setsumei. Kirin, Taihei Gramaphone, K-956 & K-957.

————. *Kōjinyama no chikemuri.* Eiga setsumei. Sun-day, The Asahi Gramaphone, 5.

————. *Kondō Isami.* Eiga setsumei. Teichiku Gramophone, 5291 & 5292.

Suzuki Mitsutarō. *Chikumuri Takadanobaba.* Eiga setsumei. Nippon Polydor Chikuonki Co., 869.

————. *Kira no yukue.* Eiga setsumei. Nippon Polydor Chikuonki, 4190.

————. *Shirai Gonpachi.* Eiga setsumei. Nippon Polydor Chikuonki, 270.

————. *Shirai Gonpachi.* Eiga setsumei. Nippon Polydor Chikuonki, 4020.

Tani Tenrō. *Chimatsuri Kōjinyama.* Eiga setsumei. Hikōki 70043 (70087 & 70088).

————. *Chūshingura.* Eiga setsumei. Hikōki, The Gōdō Phonograph, 8309.

————. *Kunisada Chūji.* Eiga setsumei. Nipponophone, 16792 & 16793.

————. *Kutsukake Tokijirō.* Eiga setsumei. Hikōki, 70017 (70069 & 70070) & 70018 (70072 & 70071).

————. *Suihei no haha.* Record Drama. Regal, Columbia, 65908 (71717 & 71718) & 65909 (71719 & 71720).

Tanizaki Kinrō. *Akiba no himatsuri.* Eiga setsumei. Yachiyo, 3031.

Tsukioka Shūsui. *Rantō no chimata.* Eiga setsumei. Nipponophone, 16478.

————. *Shimizu no Jirōchō.* Eiga setsumei. Nipponophone, 16421.

Yamamoto Yōhō. *Merīgōraundo.* Eiga setsumei. Nipponophone, 15271.

Yamazaki Kinjō. *Ma no mori.* Katsudō shashin. Nitto Chikuonki, 345.

————. *Tasogare no koro.* Eiga setsumei. Orient Factory, Nipponophone, 2856.

Western Language Newspapers and Periodicals

The Japan Advertiser Annual Review of Finance, Industry and Commerce
(1930–37)

Japan Today & Tomorrow (1927–133)

Moving Picture World (1908–12)

Present Day Japan/Present Day Nippon) (1925–35)

Western Language Books and Articles

Abel, Richard, ed. *Silent Film*. New Brunswick, NJ: Rutgers University Press, 1996.

Adachi Kinnosuke. "Censorship Under the Cherry Blossoms." *Motion Picture Magazine* 22, no. 8 (September 1921): 40–41, 90, 92.

Anderson, Joseph L. "Spoken Silents in the Japanese Cinema; or, Talking to Pictures: Essaying the *Katsuben*, Contextualizing the Texts." In *Reframing Japanese Cinema: Authorship, Genre, History*, edited by Arthur Nolletti Jr. and David Desser. Bloomington: Indiana University Press, 1992.

Anderson, Joseph L., and Donald Richie. *The Japanese Film*. Expanded edition. Princeton: Princeton University Press, 1982.

Armour, Robert A. "Effects of Censorship Pressure on the New York Nickelodeon Market, 1907–1909." *Film History* 4 (1990): 113–21.

Barrett, Gregory. *Archetypes in Japanese Film: The Sociopolitical and Religious Significance of the Principal Heroes and Heroines*. London: Associated University Press, 1989.

Barthes, Roland. *Empire of Signs*. Translated by Richard Howard. New York: Hill and Wang, 1982.

Berg, Charles M. "The Human Voice and the Silent Cinema." *Journal of Popular Film* 4, no. 2 (1975): 165–79.

276

Bernardi, Joanne R. "The Early Development of the Gendaigeki Screenplay: An Introduction, 1908–1917." *Ibaragi daigaku kyōyōbu kiyō* 21 (1989): 113–26.

———. "The Early Development of the Gendaigeki Screenplay: Kaeriyama Norimasa, Kurihara Tōmas, Tanizaki Jun'ichirō and the Pure Film Movement." Ph.D. diss. Columbia University, 1992.

———. *Writing in Light: The Silent Scenario and the Japanese Pure Film Movement.* Detroit: Wayne State University Press, 2001.

Bordwell, David. "Mizoguchi and the Evolution of Film Language." In *Cinema and Language*, edited by Stephen Heath and Patricia Mellencamp. Los Angeles: The American Film Institute, 1983.

———. *Narration in the Fiction Film.* Madison: University of Wisconsin Press, 1985.

———. "Our Dream Cinema: Western Historiography and the Japanese Film." *Film Reader* 4 (1979): 45–62.

———. *Ozu and the Poetics of Cinema.* Princeton: University of Princeton Press, 1988.

Bowser, Eileen. *History of the American Cinema*, vol. 2, *The Transformation of Cinema, 1907–1915.* Berkeley: University of California Press, 1990.

Burch, Noël. "Approaching Japanese Film." In *Cinema and Language*, edited by Stephen Heath and Patricia Mellencamp. Los Angeles: American Film Institute, 1983.

———. *To the Distant Observer: Form and Meaning in the Japanese Cinema.* Berkeley: University of California Press, 1979.

Bush, Lewis. "The Japanese Cinema." *Eastern Horizon* 2, no. 14 (December 1963): 19–25.

Chaplin, Charles. *Charles Chaplin: My Autobiography.* Bodley Head, 1964. Reprint. New York: Plume/Penguin Books, 1992.

Cohen, Robert. "Toward a Theory of Japanese Narrative," *Quarterly Review of Film Studies* 6, no. 2 (Spring 1981): 181–200.

Coox, Alvin D. *Nomohan: Japan Against Russia, 1939.* 2 vols. Stanford: Stanford University Press, 1985.

Davis, Darrell William. *Picturing Japaneseness: Monumental Style, National Identity, Japanese Film.* New York: Columbia University Press, 1996.

Dennis, Jonathan. *Sublime Silents: The Art of Silent Cinema.* Canberra: The Museum of Contemporary Art and National Film and Sound Archive, 1995.

Ehrlich, Linda C. "Talking About Pictures: The Art of the Benshi." *Cinemaya* 27 (1995): 34–40.

Ernst, Earle. *The Kabuki Theater.* Oxford: Oxford University Press, 1956. Reprint. Honolulu: University of Hawaii Press, 1974.

Fell, John L., ed. *Film Before Griffith.* Berkeley: University of California Press, 1983.

"The Filmdom of Japan." *Japan Magazine* 19 (October 1928): 22–24.

Freiberg, Freda. "The Transition to Sound in Japan." In *History on/and/in Film,* edited by T. O'Regan and B. Shoesmith. Perth: History and Film Association of Australia, 1987.

Friends of the Silent Films Association, eds. *The Benshi: Japanese Silent Film Narrators.* Urban Connections, 2002.

Gerow, Aaron A. "The Benshi's New Face: Defining Cinema in Taishō Japan," *Iconics* 3 (1994): 69–86.

———. "Writing a Pure Cinema: Articulations of Early Japanese Film." Ph.D. diss. University of Iowa, 1996.

Giuglaris, Shinobu, and Max. *Le Cinéma Japonais: 1896–1955.* Paris: Editions du Cerf, 1956.

Gomery, Douglas. "The Coming of Sound: Technological Change in the American Film Industry." In *The American Film Industry,* edited by Tino Balio. Madison: The University of Wisconsin Press, 1985.

———. "Economic Struggle and Hollywood Imperialism: Europe Converts to Sound." *Yale French Review* 60 (1980): 80–93.

278

Goodwin, James. *Akira Kurosawa and Intertextual Cinema.* Baltimore: Johns Hopkins University Press, 1994.

Gunning, Tom. "The Cinema of Attractions: Early Film, Its Spectator and the Avant-Garde." In *Early Cinema: Space, Frame, Narrative,* edited by Thomas Elsaesser and Adam Barker. London: British Film Institute, 1990.

————. *D. W. Griffith and the Origins of American Narrative Film: The Early Years at Biograph.* Urbana: University of Illinois Press, 1994.

Hall, Mordaunt. "The Screen: A Japanese Production." *New York Times,* March 12, 1929, p. 26.

Hansen, Miriam. *Babel & Babylon: Spectatorship in American Silent Film.* Cambridge: Harvard University Press, 1994.

High, Peter. "The *Ancien Régime* of Japanese Film and the Revolt of the Fans: 1911–1918." *Gengo bunka ronshū* 10, no. 2 (1989): 121–48.

————. "The Dawn of Cinema in Japan." *Journal of Contemporary History* 19 (1984): 23–57.

————. "Japanese Film and the Great Kanto Earthquake." *Chūbū University: Kokusai kankei gakubū kiyō* 1, no. 3 (1985): 71–84.

Hirano Kyoko. *Mr. Smith Goes to Tokyo: Japanese Cinema under the American Occupation, 1945–1952.* Washington: Smithsonian Institution Press, 1992.

Hoff, Frank. "Killing the Self: How the Narrator Acts." *Asian Theatre Journal* 2, no. 1 (Spring 1985): 1–27.

International Motion Picture Almanac. New York: Quigley Publishing Company, 1930–97.

Iris 22 (Autumn 1996). (Special issue containing 13 articles devoted entirely to the lecturer in silent cinema).

Ishizaki Kenji, ed. *Japan Foundation Asia Center Asian Classical Cinema Series No. 2: Korean Silent Film and 'Benshi' Performer.* Tokyo: The Japan Foundation Asian Center, 1996.

Iwamoto Kenji. "Sound in the Early Japanese Talkies." Translated by Lisa Spalding. In *Reframing Japanese Cinema: Authorship, Genre, History*, edited by Arthur Nolletti Jr. and David Desser. Bloomington: Indiana University Press, 1992.

Jacobs, Lewis. *The Rise of the American Film: A Critical History*. New York: Harcourt, Brace, 1939. Reprint. New York: Teachers College Press, 1968.

Kasza, Gregory J. *The State and the Mass Media in Japan, 1918–1945*. Berkeley: University of California Press, 1988.

"Katsuben." *Japan Today and Tomorrow*, no. 2 (December, 1928): 93.

Katsumura T. "Japan's Talking Films." *The Japan Magazine* 20 (January 1930): 189–90.

Kirihara, Donald. "A Reconsideration of the Institution of Benshi." *Film Reader* 6 (1985): 41–53.

———. "Kabuki, Cinema and Mizoguchi Kenji." In *Cinema and Language*, edited by Stephen Heath and Patricia Mellencamp. Los Angeles: American Film Institute, 1983.

Kobayashi, Victor N. "Benshi in Hawaii." In *When Strangers Meet—Cross-Cultural Perspectives from the Humanities: Viewers Guide*, 82–83. Honolulu: Hawaii International Film Festival, 1984.

Koch, Carl. "Japanese Cinema." *Close up* 8 (December 1933): 296–99.

Kokusai Bunka Shinkokai, ed. *Cinema Yearbook of Japan, 1939*. Tokyo: Kokusai Bunka Shinkokai, 1939.

Komatsu Hiroshi. "The Fundamental Change: Japanese Cinema Before and After the Earthquake of 1923." *Griffithiana* 38/39 (1990): 186–96.

———. "Some Characteristics of Japanese Cinema Before World War I." Translated by Linda C. Ehrlich and Yuko Okutsu. In *Reframing Japanese Cinema: Authorship, Genre, History*, edited by Arthur Nolletti Jr. and David Desser. Bloomington: Indiana University Press, 1992.

Komatsu, Hiroshi, and France Loden. "Mastering the Mute Image: The Role of the Benshi in Japanese Cinema," *Iris* 22 (Autumn 1996): 33–52.

Komatsu, Hiroshi, and Charles Musser. "Benshi Search." *Wide Angle* 9 (1987): 71–90.

Koszarski, Richard. *History of the American Cinema*, vol 3, *An Evening's Entertainment: The Age of the Silent Feature Picture, 1915–1928*. Berkeley: University of California Press, 1990.

Kraft, James P. *Stage to Studio: Musicians and the Sound Revolution, 1890–1950*. Baltimore: Johns Hopkins University Press, 1996.

Kurosawa, Akira. *Something Like an Autobiography*. Translated by Audie E. Brock. New York: Vintage Books, 1982.

Layton, Edwin T., with Roger Pineau and John Costello. *"And I was There": Pearl Harbor and Midway—Breaking the Secrets*. New York: William Morrow, 1985.

Leyda, Jay. *Kino: A History of Russia and Soviet Film*. London: George Allen & Unwin, 1960.

Lindstrom, Siegfried F. "The Cinema in Cinema-Minded Japan." *Asia* 31, no. 12 (1931): 768–775, 806–8.

Low, Rachael. *The History of the British Film, 1896–1918*. 3 vols. London: George Allen & Unwin, 1949.

Malcomson, Scott L. "The Pure Land Beyond the Seas: Barthes, Burch and the Uses of Japan." *Screen* 26, no. 3–4 (May–August 1985): 23–33.

Malm, William P. *Nagauta: The Heart of Kabuki Music*. Rutland, VT: Charles E. Tuttle, 1963. Reprint. Westport, CN: Greenwood Press, 1976.

———. "Music in the Kabuki Theater." In *Studies in Kabuki: Its Acting, Music, and Historical Context*, edited by James R. Brandon, William P. Malm, and Donald H. Shively. Honolulu: University of Hawaii Press, 1978.

Marks, Martin Miller. *Music and the Silent Film: Context and Case Studies, 1895–1924*. Oxford: Oxford University Press, 1997.

Martin, Harris I. "Popular Music and Social Change in Prewar Japan." *The Japan Interpreter* 7, no. 3–4 (Summer–Autumn, 1972): 332–52.

Mellen, Joan. *The Waves at Genji's Door.* New York: Pantheon Books, 1976.

———. *Voices from the Japanese Cinema.* New York: Liveright, 1975.

McDonald, Keiko I. *Cinema East: A Critical Study of Major Japanese Films.* London: Associated University Press, 1983.

Miyagawa Kazuo. "Miyagawa Kazuo: My Life as a Cameraman Yesterday, Today, Tomorrow." Translated by Linda Ehrlich and Shibagaki Akiko. *Post Script* 11, no. 1 (Fall, 1991): 5–19.

Mizuno Yoshiyuki. "Educational Films." *Japan Today and Tomorrow*, no. 2 (December, 1928): 106–7.

Morioka, Heinz, and Miyoko Sasaki. "The Blue-Eyed Storyteller: Henry Black and His *Rakugo* Career." *Monumenta Nipponica* 38, no. 2 (1983): 133–162.

———. *Rakugo, the Popular Narrative Art of Japan.* Cambridge: Harvard University Press, 1990.

Munsterberg, Hugo. *The Photoplay: A Psychological Study.* New York: D. Appleton, 1916.

Musser, Charles. "Archaeology of the Cinema: 8." *Framework* 22/23 (Autumn 1983): 4–11.

Musser, Charles, and Carol Nelson. *High-Class Moving Pictures: Lyman H. Howe and the Forgotten Era of Traveling Exhibition 1880–1920.* Princeton: Princeton University Press, 1991.

Nagai Kafū. *A Strange Tale from East of the River and Other Stories.* Translated by Edward Seidensticker. Rutland, VT: Charles E. Tuttle, 1972.

Nolletti, Arthur, Jr. and David Desser, eds. *Reframing Japanese Cinema: Authorship, Genre, History.* Bloomington: Indiana University Press, 1992.

Novogard, Paul. "Rakugo: The Storyteller's Art." *Japan Quarterly* 21 (April–June 1974): 188–96.

Ogihara Junko. "The Exhibition of Films for Japanese Americans in Los Angeles During the Silent Film Era." *Film History* 4 (1990): 81–87.

"Our Movies Remaking Japan." *Literary Digest* (May 6, 1922): 53–55.

Richie, Donald. *Japanese Cinema: An Introduction.* Hong Kong: Oxford University Press, 1990.

———. *Japanese Movies.* Tokyo: Japanese Travel Bureau, 1961.

———. "Viewing Japanese Film: Some Considerations." *East-West Film Journal* 1, no. 1 (December 1986): 23–35.

Ross, Steven J. *Working-Class Hollywood: Silent Film and the Shaping of Class in America.* Princeton: Princeton University Press, 1998.

Ruch, Barbara. "Medieval Jongleurs and the Making of a National Literature." In *Japan in the Muromachi Age*, edited by John Whitney Hall and Toyoda Takeshi. Berkeley: University of California Press, 1977.

Sato Tadao. *Currents in Japanese Cinema.* Translated by Gregory Barrett. Tokyo: Kōdansha International, 1982.

———. "The Japanese Tradition of Accompanying Silent Films." Translated by Larry Greenberg. In *Retrospective of the Japanese Short Film 1955–1991*, edited by Angela Haardt, Machiguchi Yumi, Nikola Mirza, Reinhard Wolf, and Catherine Allinson. Oberhausen, Germany, 1994.

Seidensticker, Edward. *Low City, High City.* Rutland, VT: Charles E. Tuttle, 1983.

Silverberg, Miriam. "Constructing the Japanese Ethnography of Modernity." *Journal of Asian Studies* 51, no. 1 (February 1992): 30–54.

Sklar, Robert. *Movie-Made America: A Cultural History of American Movies.* 1974. Revised and Updated. New York: Vintage Books, 1994.

Sudzuky, J. Shige. "Cinema in Japan." *Close up* 4 (February 1929): 16–24.

Tachibana Takashiro. "The Cinema in Japan." *Contemporary Japan* 1, no. 1 (June 1932): 117–24.

Tadasi Iizima, Akira Iwasaki, and Kisao Uchida, eds. *Cinema Year Book of Japan, 1936–1937.* Tokyo: Sanseido, 1937.

Tessier, Max. *Images du Cinéma Japonais*. Paris: Henri Veyrier, 1981.

United States Bureau of Foreign and Domestic Commerce. "Motion Pictures in Japan, Philippine Islands, Netherland East Indies, Siam, British Malaya, and French Indo-China." *Trade Information Bulletin*, no. 634 (Washington, DC: Government Printing Office, 1929): 2–14.

Wade, James. "The Cinema in Korea." In *Korean Dance, Theater and Cinema*, edited by the Korean National Commission for UNESCO. Arch Cape, OR: Pace International Research, 1983.

———. "Korea's Film World." In *Korean Dance, Theater and Cinema*, edited by the Korean National Commission for UNESCO. Arch Cape, OR: Pace International Research, 1983.

Yoshiyama, Tats. "The Benshi." *Film Comment* 2, no. 2 (Spring 1964): 34–35.

Yūda Yoshio. "The Formation of Early Modern *Jōruri*." *Acta Asiatica* 28 (1975): 20–41.

INDEX

286

hidden dialogue. *See kagezerifu*
High Breakwater Waves, 33
High, Peter B., 79
Hiromeya Advertising Company, 25, 33
Hirota Kiichi. *See* Minamikaijin
History of the Last Days of Louis XVI: The French Revolution, 49
Hongōza, 176
Hototogisu, 165
human talkies, 205
Humanovo, 5

I

I am a Cat, 182
Ibsen, Henrik, 85
ichiga ichigi. See one film–one meaning theory
Ichikawa Danjūrō IX, 64
Ichikawa Mugō, 102
Iguchi Shizunami, 182
Ii Naosuke, 178, 179
Iioka Umeko, 88
Ikeru Shikabana, 156
Ikoma Raiyū, 50, 55, 78, 93–96, 177, 188, 190, 192, 216, 229
Inabata Katsutarō, 22–28, 32
Inagaki Hiroshi, 197
Ince, Thomas H., 57, 165
Inoue Masao, 169
Inoue Yōichi, 222
Inspection of the Manchurian–Mongolian Border, 207
intertitles, 2, 9, 44, 59, 73, 87, 106–8, 111, 136, 143–44, 148–61, 166, 168, 185, 196, 200
Intolerance, 38, 141
introductory remarks. *See maesetsu*
Inukai Tsuyoshi, 204, 209, 214
Ishikawa Goemon, 137
Ishikawa Mitsumaru, 90, 171
Itō Daisuke, 178
Itō Hirobumi, 48

Iwatō Shinsaburō. See Iwatō Shisetsu
Iwatō Shisetsu, 79–80, 87, 106, 127, 155
Izawa Ranja, 100
Izumi Kōfu, 182
Izumi Sōichirō, 81

J

Japan Motion Picture Company. *See* Nikkatsu
Japanese Samurai, The, 178
Jazz Singer, The, 194–95, 197
Jenkins, C. Francis, 23
jidai geki. See period drama
jinta bands, 25, 33
Jiyūtō, 29
jokyū, 51
Jolsen, Al, 194
jōruri, 10, 11, 184, 226
Judgments of Magistrate Ōoka, 220
Jūmonji Daigen, 31, 33, 35
Jūmonji Import Company, 24, 31
Jūmonji Shinsuke, 31
jun'eigageki undō. See Pure Film Movement

K

kabuki, 10, 27, 53, 55, 57, 64, 65, 84, 89, 138, 143, 145, 175, 180, 184
Kaeriyama Norimasa, 142, 146–49, 153–56, 161
kagezerifu, 65, 154–55, 167
Kairakutei. See Black, Henry James
kaisetsusha (commentator), 3
kakegoe, 55
kamishibai, 216
Kankan joshi, 88
Kansen Tetsudō, 39
Kataoka Nizaemon, 27
Katayama Sen, 47
katsuben (motion picture orator), 3
Katsuben monogatari, 137

T

Tachibana Kōyō, 157
Tachibana Takahirō, 133
Taii no musumei, 169
Taishō emperor, 25, 30, 174
Taiwan, 8, 48
Takahashi Senkichi, 27, 31
Takahashi Shinji, 21, 25, 28, 31
Takamatsu Toyojirō, 46, 47, 48, 79, 88
Takeda Akira, 149
Takeda Kōkatsu, 144, 150
Takemoto Shōko, 98, 189
Takemoto Take. See Mitake Suzume
Takemoto Tsutao, 28
Taki no shiraito, 223
Tale of the Benshi, The, 137
talkies, 1, 18, 57, 117, 174, 195–206, 210, 212, 215–16
Tamaki Kōsui, 83
Tamura Yoshihiko, 201
Tanaka Eizō, 147, 156
Tanaka Jun'ichirō, 16, 72
Tange Sazen, 220
Taniuchi Matsunosuke, 88
Tanizaki Jun'ichirō, 38
tehiki. See ushers
Teikokugekijō, 204
Teikokukan, 38, 58, 93, 165
Ten Commandments, The, 115
Tengoku to jigoku, 58
Tenkatsu, 155, 156
The Last Scoundrel. See Akkan no saigo
Tōgō Raishū, 76
tokiwazu, 64, 70
Tokugawa Musei, 55, 100–2, 151, 157, 160, 166, 169–71, 181–83, 187–190, 197–99, 202, 215–16, 221–24, 229
Tsubaki hime, 112
Tsuchihashi sound-on-film technology, 204

Tsuchiya Michinosuke. See Tsuchiya Shōtō
Tsuchiya Shōtō, 67, 68, 69, 76, 78, 126, 156, 157, 165, 170, 229
Tsuda Kintarō. See Tsuda Shūsui
Tsuda Shūsui, 91, 103
Tsukada Kiyū, 105
Tsunoda Shōtō, 43

U

Uchida Inosuke. See Uchida Tsukibito
Uchida Tsukibito, 66
Ueda Hoteiken, 28–29, 31, 35, 49
Uki shizumi, 170
Umeya Shōkichi, 78, 79, 80
Urakawa Naruo. See Somei Saburō
ushers, 14, 51, 212
Ushigomekan, 58, 125

V

Valentino, Rudolph, 91, 173, 174, 186
visual narrator system, 6, 7
Vitascope, 22–26, 28, 31, 33, 35, 37, 88, 152
vocal additives, 63–67, 70–74, 226

W

Wagahai wa neko de aru, 182
wajutsu, 226
Waka Kōji, 19, 222
Wakamizu Midori, 165
Warner Brothers, 194
wayō gassō, 57
Where Is My Mother?, 160
White Threads of the Cascades, 223
World and Its Women, The, 109
World's Columbian Exposition, 21, 31

JAPANESE STUDIES

1. Ira L. Plotkin, **Anarchism in Japan: A Study of the Great Treason Affair 1910-1911**

2. John Adlard, **A Biography of Arthur Diósy, Founder of the Japan Society: Home to Japan**

3. **An Anthology of Kanshi (Chinese Verse) by Japanese Poets of the Edo Period (1603-1868): Translations of Selected Poems with an Introduction and Commentaries,** Timothy R. Bradstock and Judith N. Rabinovitch

4. Jon LaCure, **Rhetorical Devices of the Kokinshû: A Structural Analysis of Japanese *Waka* Poetry**

5. Douglas Kenning, **The Romanticism of 17th Century Japanese Poetry**

6. Masako Nakagawa Graham, **The Yang Kuei–Fei Legend in Japanese Literature**

7. Terayama Shuji, **Gogatsu no shi/Poems of May: A Collection of Miscellaneous Poems,** translated from the Japanese by David A. Schmidt and Fusae Ekida

8. John Mock, **Culture, Community and Change in a Sapporo Neighborhood, 1925-1988: Hanayama**

9. Douglas Slaymaker (ed.), **A Century of Popular Culture in Japan**

10. David Andrew Schmidt, **Ianfu–The Comfort Women of the Japanese Imperial Army of the Pacific War: Broken Silence**

11. Daniel A. Metraux, **Aum Shinrikyo's Impact on Japanese Society**

12. W. Puck Brecher, **An Investigation of Japan's Relationship to Nature and Environment**

13. Jeffrey Johnson (ed.), **Bakhtinian Theory in Japanese Studies**

14. Louis G. Perez, **Mutsu Munemitsu and Identity Formation of the Individual and the State in Modern Japan**

15. John R. Bentley, **Historiographical Trends in Early Japan**

16. Noriko T. Reider, **Tales of the Supernatural in Early Japan: *Kaidan*,** Akinari, *Ugetsu Monogatari*

17. Kent H. Morris, **The Historical Development and Contemporary Perspective of the Japanese Urasenke Way of Tea as Practiced in California**

18. Gladys Emiko Nakahara, **A Translation of *Ryôjinhishô*, a Compendium of Japanese Folk Songs (Imayô) from the Heian Period (794-1185)**

19. Jeffrey A. Dym, ***Benshi*, Japanese Silent Film Narrators, and Their Forgotten Narrative Art of *Setsumei*: A History of Japanese Silent Film Narration**